Iranian History

*An Enthralling Guide to Ancient
Persia and Iran's Past*

Free limited time bonus

Stop for a moment. We have a free bonus set up for you. The problem is this: we forget 90% of everything that we read after 7 days. Crazy fact, right? Here's the solution: we've created a printable, 1-page pdf summary for this book that you're reading now. All you have to do to get your free pdf summary is to go to the following website:

https://livetolearn.lpages.co/enthrallinghistory/

Once you do, it will be intuitive. Enjoy, and thank you!

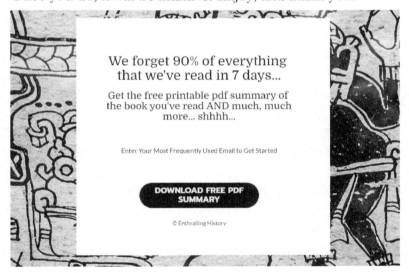

We forget 90% of everything that we've read in 7 days...

Get the free printable pdf summary of the book you've read AND much, much more... shhhh...

Enter Your Most Frequently Used Email to Get Started

DOWNLOAD FREE PDF SUMMARY

© Enthralling History

Table of Contents

Part 1: Ancient Persia

An Enthralling Overview of the Achaemenid Persian Empire

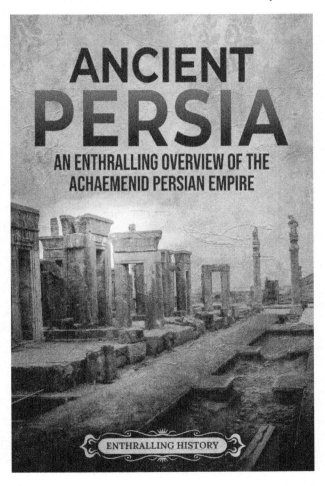

Introduction

The two Persian princesses, Alexander the Great's wives, clung to each other. Parysatis was the daughter of King Artaxerxes III, who was poisoned by his vizier Bagoas, who wiped out most of Persia's royal males. Stateira was the daughter of Darius III, the Achaemenid dynasty's last monarch, who was murdered by his men after Alexander conquered the Persian Empire. Shortly after marrying both princesses on the same day, Alexander suddenly died, leaving the women as widows and the Persian Empire in an uproar.

"Stateira! What will happen to us?"

Roxana swept into the room, smugly rubbing her swollen belly, followed by General Perdiccas, the supreme commander of the imperial army. Roxana was Alexander's first wife, the daughter of a Bactrian chieftain.

"Nothing to worry about, my dears. Perdiccas wanted to inform you of the council's decision regarding our husband's successors."

General Perdiccas cleared his throat, "The generals decided that Alexander's brother Arrhidaeus and Roxana's son will serve as joint kings."

Stateira frowned. "But Arrhidaeus hasn't the intellect to rule! And how do we know Roxana will have a son?"

Perdiccas smiled. "The council appointed me regent to Roxana's son and Arrhidaeus. If the baby is a girl, the council will reconvene."

Roxana had been pouring wine into goblets. "Now, let us toast our dear departed husband and the empire's future."

Stateira and Parysatis looked at each other. The wine must be safe if Roxana and Perdiccas were drinking from the same bottle. Minutes later, they realized their fatal mistake. Roxana smirked and strode out of the room with Perdiccas as the Persian women gasped their last breaths.

Thus ended the Persian Achaemenid Empire. But how did it begin? And how did it get to this point?

The Achaemenid Empire was the world's first mega-empire, spanning three continents and over two million square miles at its zenith. It triggered terror in their great rivals, the Greeks, yet they couldn't help but be mesmerized by the Persians' enthralling culture. Stretching from Southeast Asia to eastern Europe to North Africa, the Persian Empire's legacy impacted three separate continents for two millennia.

Why is it called the Achaemenid Empire? It's named after Achaemenes, about whom we know nothing except that he was a 7th or 8th-century Persian tribal leader and supposedly the ancestor of Cyrus the Great and Darius I. His real name was Hakamanish ("a friendly mind"), which was Achaemenes in Greek. Because the empire's kings were Persian, it's also often referred to as the Persian Empire. However, the name Achaemenid Empire describes a specific timeframe of Persian rule, setting it apart from the Seleucid, Parthian, and Sassanian dynasties that followed.

Persia exploded into an empire in 550 BCE under Cyrus the Great; it grew to rule over 44 percent of the global population under Darius the Great. The world had never seen an empire of this size before. A conglomerate of nations and ethnicities, the empire's core was the land of Persia (Parsa or Persis), roughly equivalent to today's Fars Province in southwestern Iran on the eastern side of the Persian Gulf.

How is this book different from others on ancient Persia? Many excellent books are available on the Achaemenid Empire; however, most are overly academic for a general audience or only cover certain aspects of the civilization. This history is broad in scope, giving an in-depth understanding of how the Persians changed the world. Meticulously researched yet easy to read, it brings the extraordinary Persians to life.

Researching the Achaemenid Empire is complicated. Few Persian records survived the chaos following the empire's fall, and recurring upheavals in the Middle East have disrupted archaeological explorations. Museums worldwide have storage areas filled with Persian documents and artifacts yet to be analyzed. We depend primarily on what the Greek historians wrote about the Persians, but the Greeks and Persians were often warring against each other. It's difficult enough for any historian to be objective, but when writing about one's nemesis, that challenge is almost insurmountable.

The Jews deported to Babylon supplied rosier accounts of their new Persian rulers and emancipators. Cyrus allowed them to return to their homeland and financed the rebuilding of Jerusalem's temple. They recorded their interactions with the Persian kings in the Tanakh (Old Testament) and Flavius Josephus's history. This book strives to find a middle ground, providing Greek, Jewish, and other sources with the reminder that accounts are usually slanted and that some historians wrote centuries after events occurred.

What are the benefits of learning history? The ancient stories are often riveting, and the Persians certainly had few dull moments. Their luxurious lifestyle, palace intrigues, and astounding conquests will keep you turning pages! But history is all about transformation. We learn about catalysts for transformation as we unpack how other civilizations evolved and grew. Additionally, the factors leading to a civilization's collapse provide a cautionary tale of what not to do.

Exploring the Persian Empire's unprecedented rise and catastrophic fall is an examination of change. What factors led to Cyrus conquering the entire Middle East? What propelled his successors to spread the empire into Africa and Europe? How did the tables suddenly turn after keeping a chokehold over the Greeks for over a century? Understanding Persia's metamorphosis aids us in recognizing how cultural, economic, and political transformations can happen in our own milieu. Let's step back in time to learn how the Persians impacted world history and the lessons we can glean from their stunning empire.

SECTION ONE:
BUILDING AN EMPIRE

Chapter 1: Origins of the Persians

Before the astounding Achaemenid Empire erupted on the world scene, Persian clans settled in southern Iran on the craggy foothills leading up to the snowy peaks of the Zagros Mountains. The virtually uninhabitable Kavir and Lut Salt Deserts lay to the northeast and east. Life was challenging on the rugged Iranian Plateau, but as Cyrus the Great once said, "Soft land breeds soft people." Where did the Persians come from before they settled in Iran? What brought them to their new homeland?

In the Bronze Age (3300–1200 BCE), people speaking variants of the Proto-Indo-Iranian language lived primarily in what is now Turkmenistan, Afghanistan, and Uzbekistan. Some Indo-Iranian tribes extended as far east as China's Xinjiang Province and as far south as the Indian subcontinent. These people called themselves Aryan, meaning "noble" or "free." The name Iran (ایران) means "the land of Aryans."

A mass movement of these Iranian tribes called the Aryan migration split into three groups in the late 2nd millennium BCE. One group remained in the core Aryan region or migrated slightly south, following the Oxus River (Amu Darya). They formed the Bactrian and Sogdian tribes north of the Hindu Kush mountains in today's Tajikistan, Uzbekistan, Afghanistan, Kazakhstan, and Kyrgyzstan. The second group, the Areians (Arians), Drangians, and Arachosians, headed south to the strip of plains lying between the mountains of Iran and Afghanistan.

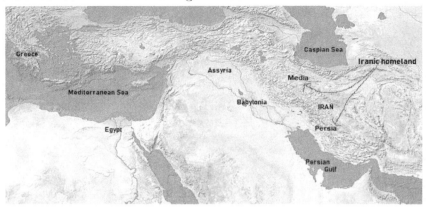

The Indo-Iranian tribes migrated from Central Asia to today's Iran.
Photo modified: zoomed-in, labels added. Credit: Natural Earth, CC BY-SA 4.0
<https://creativecommons.org/licenses/by-sa/4.0>, via Wikimedia Commons;
https://commons.wikimedia.org/wiki/File:Colorful_shaded_map_of_Middle_East.jpg

The third wave of Indo-Iranian-speaking people swept into the Iranian Plateau in two movements. The first to arrive, around 1100 BCE, migrated into northern Iran, eventually forming the Median kingdom. Slightly later, the ancestors of the Persians, who spoke a language known as Old Persian, settled in southwestern Iran. What triggered this migration from the northeast?

Why they left Central Asia is unknown, but it was likely due to overgrazing or being pushed out by more powerful tribes. The early Persians and Medes grew in ascendency during the power vacuum caused by a decline in the Elamite, Assyrian, and Babylonian kingdoms. Who was in Iran before the Medes and Persians? And what happened when the Persians moved in? Iran's Bronze Age population included the Gutians, Hurrians, and more, but the ancient Elamites dominated. The Elamites developed a sophisticated culture with cuneiform writing and the wheel by the 3rd millennium BCE, centered in what is now Khuzestan and Fars provinces in southwestern Iran. They controlled this homeland for the next two millennia, although they sometimes served as vassals to the Akkadians, Assyrians, and Babylonians and were often in conflict with these civilizations.

The Persians began migrating into southern Iran around 1000 BCE and, within two hundred years, peacefully carved out territory in today's Fars Province (known then as Parsua, Parsa, or Persis). They lived among the Elamites under Assyrian rule. The Persians had no written language, so they adopted the Elamite script for writing and even spoke Elamite for administrative affairs. As they intermingled and intermarried, the Persians acquired other Elamite customs, including their clothing styles and artwork.

The Persians lived side by side with the Elamites for four centuries without reports of antagonism between the two ethnicities. The one exception is Assyrian writings mentioning Persian raids on the Elamites in the mid-7th century BCE. This would have been when most Persians abandoned their nomadic ways and settled in villages and towns. The lifestyle change precipitated more internal friction within the Persian clans and more conflict with their neighbors.

The first written mention of the Persians in Iran was an inscription on the Black Obelisk. Assyrian King Shalmaneser III spoke of receiving tribute from twenty-seven Persian "kings" (likely clan chieftains) in 836 BCE:

"In my twenty-fourth regnal year, I [Shalmaneser III] crossed the Lower Zab River, crossed Mount Hashimur, and went down to the land Namri. Ianzu, king of the land Namri, took fright in the face of my mighty weapons and ran away to save his life. I captured his fortified cities. I massacred them, plundered them, razed, destroyed, and burned these cities. The survivors fled up a mountain. I laid siege to the mountain peak, captured it, slaughtered them, plundered them, and brought their property down. Moving from the land Namri, I received the tribute of twenty-seven kings of the land of Parsua. I went down to the lands Messu, Media, Araziash, and Harhar and captured the cities."[1]

[1] A. K. Grayson, *Assyrian Rulers of the Early First Millennium BC II (858-745 BC) (Royal Inscriptions of Mesopotamia. Assyrian Periods. Volume 3)* (Toronto: University of Toronto Press, 1996), 67-8.

The Black Obelisk shows people bringing tribute to Shalmaneser III.

Note that the Assyrians also captured Median cities in this campaign. Several decades later, an inscription by the Assyrian king Adad-Nirari III showed the Persians were still paying tribute to the Assyrians. The land of Namri in this inscription is probably Kassite territory; the Kassites ruled Babylon for four centuries but then fell to the Aramaeans, Chaldeans, and Assyrians.[2]

The Assyrian heartland was to the north, on the western side of the Zagros Mountains. However, the Assyrians coveted the Persians' horses and the iron and other metals mined from the mountains. The Khorasan Road passed through the region, a key trade route from the west to Central Asia. The Akkadians, Assyrians, and Babylonians had repeatedly invaded Iran, dominating the trade routes and demanding tribute of horses, camels, sheep, bronze, copper, gold, silver, linen, wool, wine, and minerals.

Sometimes, the tables turned, and the Elamites, Kassites, Gutians, and other tribes crossed the Zagros Mountains and raided the fertile "land between the rivers." They raided Sumer, Akkad, Babylonia, and Assyria for the grain Mesopotamia produced and the great wealth that the western empire-builders had accumulated from other lands. On rare occasions, as with the Kassites in

---

[2] J. E. Reade, "Kassites and Assyrians in Iran," *Iran* 16 (1978): 137.
https://www.jstor.org/stable/4299653?origin=crossref

Babylon, they settled down and ruled.

The Neo-Assyrians' newly developed siege warfare technology included metal-headed battering rams and fire-throwing machines. Previously, when the Assyrians invaded Iran, it was to raid, plunder, and collect tribute. Tiglath-Pileser III (r. 745–727 BCE) took a different approach: population relocation. Any troublesome territories that didn't regularly pay tribute or, worse yet, tried to fight against the Assyrians had their populations deported.

The exiled population would be enslaved or relocated to another region far away. Tiglath-Pileser relocated sixty-five thousand Medes from northwestern Iran to Phoenicia and Syria on the Mediterranean coast and brought the Phoenicians and Syrians to live in Iran. Cities that did not resist became tribute-paying provinces of the Assyrian Empire. Tiglath-Pileser didn't deport the Persians, but he did cut off the men's right thumbs. They couldn't throw a javelin or wield their scimitars (curved swords), but they could still work and pay tribute to Assyria.

An ancient Iranian myth reflects the atrocities and oppression of this period. It recalls a blissful time in distant history, where the animals and people coexisted peacefully, of when humans developed music, dancing, painting, and poetry. Sickness and death were unknown, and Yima (Jamshid) the Radiant ruled over them. However, Yima grew prideful, forgetting his blessings came from their creator god, Ahura-Mazda. Although he repented, it enabled Azhi Dahaka, the serpent, to overthrow and kill Yima. Dahaka then gained control of the world, ushering in chaos, drought, sickness, and death. To the Iranians, the Assyrians were the personification of Azhi Dahaka.

Iranians portrayed Dahaka (Zahhak) with serpents emerging from his shoulders.
https://en.wikipedia.org/wiki/Zahhak#/media/File:Mir_Musavvir_002_(Zahhak).jpg

One of the Medes the Assyrians deported to Hamath in Syria was called Daiukku in Assyrian, Dahyuka in Old Persian, and Deioces in Greek. The Greek historian Herodotus identified him as the founder of the Median kingdom from whom Cyrus the Great's mother descended. Herodotus's Histories supplies valuable information on the Achaemenid Empire, albeit sometimes slanted or dubious.

Herodotus grew up in the coastal Greek colony of Halicarnassus in today's western Turkey, which fell under Persian control, making Herodotus and his family reluctantly part of the Achaemenid Empire. His family joined rebels who unsuccessfully tried to overthrow their Persian overlordship. We will review his version of events throughout this book, but remember that the Persians, or "barbarians" as he called them, were his enemies.

In 691 BCE, the Assyrian king Sennacherib recorded that tens of thousands of Persians joined a coalition army with the

Aramaeans, Babylonians, Chaldeans, and Elamites, led by the Elamite king Humbanumena. This alliance may have been the only time the Persians warred against the Assyrians; these Persian warriors were the sons of the men whose thumbs had been cut off. Despite their massive numbers, the coalition could not prevail against the fierce Assyrians in the concluding battle on the banks of the Tigris River. According to Sennacherib's account, the terrified Persians and their cohorts lost control of their bowels and fled.

Decades later, the Assyrians led by King Ashurbanipal shattered the ancient Elamite capital of Susa, putting the Persian king Kurash into a panic, lest the same happen to his kingdom. Kurash was the Assyrian name for Cyrus; he was likely Cyrus I, the grandfather of Cyrus the Great. Kurash quickly sued for peace with Assyria, even sending his oldest son as a hostage, as the Assyrian king recorded.

"After the victorious weapons of Assur overcame and destroyed all of Elam, fear came upon the nations round about. The fear of my majesty overwhelmed them, and they sent their messengers to win friendship and peace with costly presents. They inquired after the wellbeing of my majesty; they kissed my feet and sought my lordship. When Kurash, Parsumash's king, heard of the mighty victory I had inflicted on Elam with the help of the great gods Ashur, Bel, and Nabu, and that I had overwhelmed all of Elam like a flood, he sent Arukku, his eldest son, together with his tribute, as a hostage to Nineveh, my lordly city, and implored my lordship."[3]

In ancient Greece, Macedonia, and the Middle East, dominant kings often held royal children of their vassal kingdoms as hostages. Most vassal kings wouldn't dare skip tribute payments or defy their overlords, as they feared harm would come to their child. By giving his crown prince to Ashurbanipal, Kurash signaled his enduring submission. Children held as hostages usually grew up in the dominant king's palace or a nobleman's home, learning the language and developing friendships with the royal family. In their late teens or early adulthood, they would return to their homeland to become the next king or assume eminent positions.

---

[3] Amélie Kuhrt, *The Persian Empire: A Corpus of Sources from the Achaemenid Period* (London: Routledge, 2007), 53-4.

Occasionally, this custom backfired on the kingdom that held the royal sons as captives. Growing up in the rival kingdom's palace or with a key nobleman, a prince would acquire valuable inside information that he might use against them when he returned to his homeland. This is precisely what happened in Macedonia, and a series of events ultimately led to the Persian Empire's fall. Philip II, the father of Alexander the Great, was taken as a hostage to Thebes at the age of thirteen. At that time, Thebes was Greece's strongest power and held Macedonia under its boot. Thebes' top general, Pelopidas, made Philp his eromenos (younger sexual partner), and his intimate friend Epaminondas trained Philip in Thebes' indomitable military arts.

Philip later used his astute knowledge of Theban tactics, especially the innovative Theban phalanx formation, when he ascended the throne of the struggling Macedonian kingdom. His training in the world's unrivaled military enabled him to defeat his kingdom's threats and ultimately conquer Thebes and the rest of Greece. He trained his son Alexander in these military tactics, which enabled Alexander the Great to conquer Persia.

In the 7th century BCE, the continued animosity between Assyria and Elam proved deadly for the Elamites. The Assyrians didn't just conquer cities; they obliterated them, massacred large population segments, and implemented shocking torture methods to terrorize kingdoms into submission. Their macabre inscriptions celebrated the horrific human agony they inflicted. They bragged of flaying the skin off of warriors, impaling others, and leaving pyramids of their victims' heads. They enslaved able-bodied adults and built pyres to burn their children. In 646 BCE, Ashurbanipal marched on Elam and demolished Susa and twenty-eight other Elamite cities, decimating the population.

Ashurbanipal humiliated the Elamite king, forcing him to serve him food.
Carole Raddato from FRANKFURT, Germany, CC BY-SA 2.0
<https://creativecommons.org/licenses/by-sa/2.0>, via Wikimedia Commons;
https://commons.wikimedia.org/wiki/File:Humiliation_of_the_Elamite_King_at_the_cour
t_of_Ashurbanipal.jpg

Meanwhile, Elam's Persian neighbors were careful to keep peace with Assyria and didn't suffer the same fate. When the Assyrians crossed the mountains and headed for Persian territory, the Persians typically offered horses and sometimes their royal children to appease the invaders. Other times, they abandoned their cities, carrying what valuables they could, and holed up in the Zagros Mountains until the danger passed. While the Assyrians inflicted massive casualties on the Elamites, the Persians' pragmatic refusal to engage in battle enabled them to survive and even thrive. Gradually, the Persians grew in numbers and strength, moving into the abandoned cities and regions once inhabited by the Elamites.

According to the Indian Rig Veda and Zoroastrian oral traditions, the earliest Persians were exceptional horsemen and cattle herders. They highly prized horses for several purposes; for instance, the Persians were known for their skills on horseback and fearsome war chariots. But they also considered their horses to be the ultimate sacrificial animal. The Persians sacrificed them not only to their gods but also to the ancestors of their great chieftains.

Priest-chieftains led the early Persians, governing administrative affairs and leading the community in worship. When the Persians originally arrived in Iran, they settled in the peripheries of Elamite communities. The Persians were a relatively peaceful group that usually lived amicably with their Elamite neighbors. However, they could fight fiercely if the need arose. They realized that war often brought more problems than it solved; thus, they preferred to negotiate peace rather than rush into combat with the Assyrians and other major powers.

Peaceful negotiations became increasingly impractical as competition grew for the Iranian grasslands surrounding the oases and streams. Hence, a warrior class appeared that also assumed an administrative role. Initially, their armed forces served as mercenaries to their Kassite and Elamite neighbors, but they eventually formed their own trained military. The Persians and other Iranians were master charioteers, developing the spoke-wheeled chariot around 2000 BCE, which radically increased a chariot's speed compared to the older, solid-wood wheels. Development of the bronze bit led to their unparalleled horsemanship skills and the organization of a formidable cavalry. They fought with bronze weapons and later with iron swords, lances, and armor once the technology for smelting iron developed.

The priests remained an influential force in Persian society. Even before migrating to Iran, the Persians worshiped the sun, moon, and sky; as tent dwellers in their early days, they perceived the sky as a vast celestial tent. They also worshiped the Vedic god Mithra (Hindu god Mitra), god of the covenant and light and guardian of cattle. Influenced by the Persians, the Romans later adopted the worship of Mithra in their mystery religion Mithraism. The Vedic religion, an ancestor of Hinduism, heavily influenced the Persians. Later, some of the Vedic deities became yazatas or lesser deities in the Zoroastrian religion.

The Vedic Mithra was an important god of the early Persians.
*https://commons.wikimedia.org/wiki/File:Figure_of_Persian_god_Mithras,_National_Aca
demy_of_Sciences,_Washington,_D.C_LCCN2011631968.tif*

As the nomadic Persian herders settled down, some turned to agriculture, abandoning their tents for reed or baked-clay brick houses. Unlike Egypt and southern Mesopotamia, which depended on irrigation from their great river systems to sustain farming, Persia usually had enough rain for growing crops. The increasingly sedentary lifestyle and growth of villages, towns, and cities led to more organized tribal administrations. City-states formed, with powerful clan chieftains and eventually kings ruling over broad swathes of territory. Other Persians continued as nomadic herdsmen. There are over one million nomadic herdsmen today in Iran, such as the Bakhtiari and the Qashqai tribes. The nomads created a mutually beneficial relationship with their sedentary kinsmen, trading cattle, horses, and cheese for grain, fruit, and pottery.

The shift from a nomadic lifestyle to town-dwellers led to clashes and power-plays as the city-states vied for agricultural land and dominion over surrounding towns. Although the Persians shared a common ethnicity, language, and culture, they never united as one kingdom until much later, when Cyrus the Great rose to power. Instead, Persia suffered through an era of chaos as the chieftains fought their rivals for the divine right to rule, which they believed came from the Indo-Iranian war god Verethragna. Verethragna is still worshiped today in Hinduism as the Vedic god Indra and in Zoroastrianism as Bahram, an Amesha Spenta, one of the seven deities under their chief god Ahura Mazda.

While the Persians grew in strength and numbers in southern Iran, their distant relatives, the Medes in the north, were also thriving, especially once the Assyrian Empire unraveled. Although the Persians and Medes shared the Vedic religion and the Indo-Iranian language group, they had little interaction in their first few centuries in Iran. But as each grew in power, a clash was inevitable. Which of the two would gain ascendency over the other?

Chapter 2: Persians and Medes

A tear trickled down Kyno's cheek as she milked the cows. Her own breasts were full and aching, but her infant had been born dead. Would she ever hold a baby to her breast? Just then, she heard a baby's whimper and swung around. There was her husband Mithradates, carrying a swaddled baby! She swept the child out of his arms and put him to her breast, where he suckled ravenously.

"Who is he? Where did he come from?" Kyno asked as she stroked the child's face.

"I can't tell you that. But he is yours now," Mithradates answered. "Just don't tell anyone our own baby died, and make sure everyone thinks this child is our real son."

And thus, according to Herodotus, the Persian king's son grew up as the son of a cowherd in the shadow of the Median king's palace. One day, this child would rule over three continents as Cyrus the Great, king of the Achaemenid Empire.

Our information on the Medes comes from multiple sources. In their inscriptions, the Assyrians frequently mentioned the Medes, who lived on their eastern border. The 4th-century Babylonian historian Berossus wrote of the Medes, who were one-time allies with Babylon and later Babylon's conquerors in alliance with the Persians. Ctesias, the 5th-century Greek physician and historian who lived in the Achaemenid Empire, wrote Persica: his history of Babylonia, Assyria, Media, and Persia.

The 4th-century Xenophon was a Greek who fought as a mercenary for the Persians. He wrote about his adventures fighting with the Persians and a biography of Cyrus the Great, portraying the Persians in a much more positive light than Herodotus. Yet Xenophon's description of the Medes as decadently wealthy and despotic is contradicted by the Hebrew Tanakh, which said the Medes "have no regard for silver and no desire for gold."[4]

This bas-relief from Persepolis shows the Persians in ankle-length gowns and sandals alternating with the Medes wearing short tunics and knee-high boots.
Aneta Ribarska, CC BY-SA 3.0 <https://creativecommons.org/licenses/by-sa/3.0>, via Wikimedia Commons https://commons.wikimedia.org/wiki/File:Persepolis_carvings.JPG

Beginning with the Assyrian king Tiglath-Pileser (r. 745–727 BCE), the western Median lands bordering Assyria were under Assyrian control, but the eastern Medes were fiercely independent. Tiglath-Pileser annexed Persia in 744 BCE and received tributes of mules, horses, Bactrian camels, sheep, and cattle from the Medes and Persians. In 737 BCE, Tiglath-Pileser recorded obtaining over 1,700 horses from the Median cities.

Herodotus said that Deioces (Dahyuka) was the Medes' first shah (king) and priest. Originally a modest village judge, his wise and impartial reputation drew other Medes to consult him until he

---

[4] Isaiah 13:17, Tanakh: Navi: Book of Yeshayahu, Jewish Virtual Library: A Project of AICE. 1997. https://www.jewishvirtuallibrary.org/the-tanakh-full-text.

eventually served as judge over the entire Median population. He united the Medes under one government and built its capital of Ecbatana (believed to be the Hagmatāna archaeological site). Herodotus said the Medes did not have direct access to their king but had to communicate with him via messengers. The Assyrian king Sargon II (r. 722-705 BCE) felt threatened by Deioces's actions of unifying the Medes and the northern Urartian-Armenian tribes, so he seized Deioces and exiled him to Syria.

Meanwhile, Persia's clans came together under the leadership of one king, Teispes (Caispis), Cyrus the Great's great-grandfather. Darius the Great said Teispes was Achaemenes's son (from whom we get the name Achaemenid). Darius claimed he also descended from Teispes but from a different family branch. These early Persian kings ruled from the ancient city of Anshan, which Teispes appropriated from the Elamites, whose own kingdom had become weak and fragmented after ongoing conflicts with Assyria.

KINGS OF PERSIA.
(Only those whose names are in capitals were rulers of the Persian Empire.)

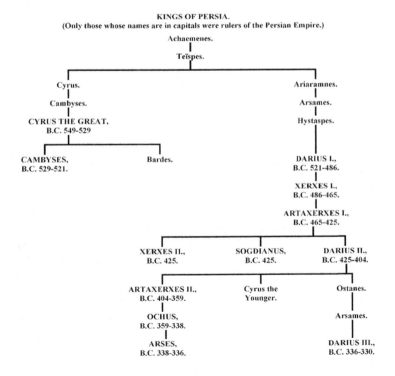

Author: Sir Charles William Chadwick Oman, 1860-1946
https://commons.wikimedia.org/wiki/File:Kings_of_the_Achaemenid_Empire.jpg

In 676 BCE, the Assyrian king Esarhaddon received ambassadors of the "distant Medes" in his capital of Nineveh. These Medes lived to the far east, alongside the Great Salt Desert, and desired the Assyrian king's assistance against other tribes harassing them. The Medes kissed Esarhaddon's feet and brought blocks of semi-precious lapis lazuli stone and choice warhorses. Esarhaddon trampled the Medes' enemies, marching farther east than the Assyrians had ever ventured. He deported their population to Assyria and amassed booty of camels, cattle, and horses.

Herodotus said Deioces's son Phraortes warred against the Persians and brought them under his control. Phraortes systematically began to conquer other tribal groups until he made the mistake of attacking the Assyrians, who killed him. His son, Cyaxares the Great (r. 625–585 BCE), organized the Median army into regiments of cavalry, archers, and spearmen. After fighting and subduing the Lydians in Asia Minor, it was time to avenge his father's death.

While Cyaxares was successfully laying siege to the Assyrian capital of Nineveh, the Scythian king Madyes suddenly attacked his rear, seemingly out of nowhere! The Scythians were also Aryan nomads, mostly from today's Ukraine, north of the Black Sea. The Scythians spoke a variant of the Iranian language and followed the Vedic religion. Pushed out of their homeland by their Saka relatives, the Scythians seized the Cimmerian territory, forcing them out of the steppes north of the Caspian and Black Seas.

The Cimmerian nobility, also Indo-Iranian, could not bear to leave their homeland, so they killed each other in a mass suicide pact. The Cimmerian commoners buried their royals, then migrated into Southwest Asia, still pursued by the relentless Scythians. They attempted to cross into Assyria in 705 BCE but were thwarted by Sargon II (although he died in the battle). They eventually settled in Anatolia (Turkey). During Cyaxares's father's reign, the Scythian king Madyes subdued the Medes and held overlordship for a violent, chaotic twenty-eight years. Scythians married into the Median aristocracy and influenced their culture, such as introducing pants. Artwork on the Persian palace walls and Greek vases showed the Medes wearing long-sleeved jackets over close-fitting pants and a hood with flaps covering the chin. The

Persian men wore pants for battle but long gowns at other times.5

The Medes adopted clothing similar to this Saka warrior chieftain.
Credit: Derzsi Elekes Andor, CC BY-SA 3.0 <https://creativecommons.org/licenses/by-sa/3.0>, via Wikimedia Commons;
https://commons.wikimedia.org/wiki/File:The_Golden_Warrior_from_the_Issyk_kurgan.jpg

Within two decades, the Scythians and Cimmerians temporarily allied against their common enemy, the Assyrians. This did not go well, as the Assyrian king Esarhaddon killed the Scythian king. The next Scythian king took a novel and audacious approach: he asked Esarhaddon for his daughter's hand in marriage and allied with the Assyrians. When Cyaxares the Mede was besieging Nineveh around 625 BCE, the Scythians came to the Ninevites' aid, fighting their vassals and conquering Cyaxares and his Median army at the bottom of Nineveh's walls.

After nearly three decades of Scythian tyranny, Cyaxares concocted a scheme to break free. Later in 625 BCE, Cyaxares invited the Scythian lords to a magnificent banquet. The Medes drank diluted wine but served full-strength wine to the Scythians. Once the Scythians were drunk and sliding under the table, the Medes massacred the entire Scythian nobility. The bloodbath left

---

[5]Reza Zarghamee, *Discovering Cyrus: The Persian Conqueror Astride the Ancient World* (Washington, DC: Mage Publishers, 2018), 77.

---

only the Scythian commoners, who joined up with the Medes, and the joint forces successfully took Nineveh. Gaining ascendency over the Scythians brought Cyaxares dominance over the powerful Scythian and Saka tribes scattered over northern Iran and Central Asia.

Meanwhile, King Nabopolassar of Babylon attacked southern Mesopotamia's Assyrian garrisons, evicting the Assyrians and gaining control of all of Babylonia. He next prevailed in invading Assyrian territory along the Euphrates in Syria, despite the Egyptian pharaoh coming to the Assyrians' aid. Step three in Nabopolassar's strategy of obliterating Assyria was to ally with King Cyaxares of Media, who brought the Persians and Scythians with him. Nabopolassar arranged a marriage between his son, Crown Prince Nebuchadnezzar II, to Princess Amytis, Cyaxares's daughter. Nebuchadnezzar allegedly later constructed Babylon's famed hanging gardens to please his bride, who missed the mountains and greenery of Media.

The Medes had been on the receiving end of the Assyrians' brutality for over a century; now, they turned the tables. King Cyaxares brutally attacked Assyria's sacred city of Assur in 615 BCE. Nabopolassar and his Babylonian forces arrived late, after the Medes and Scythians had taken the city. He found them massacring most of the civilians and destroying the breathtaking temples. Although delighted that his allies had conquered the ancient city, Nabopolassar was appalled by their ravaging of the holy places. He left his hair disheveled and slept on the ground to signal to the gods his mourning for the desecration.

The grisly defeat was the beginning of the Assyrians' ultimate fall. According to Ctesias, the Chaldean priest Belesys, an expert in divination, persuaded the Medes to form a massive coalition force of Medes, Persians, Babylonians, Scythians, and Cimmerians. His divinations promised success in completely obliterating the Assyrian Empire. Cyrus I, the grandfather of Cyrus the Great, probably led the Persian troops.

The flabbergasting alliance of 400,000 warriors descended on Assyria in 612 BCE. Despite their staggering numbers, the battle-hardened Assyrians marched out to meet them on the banks of the Euphrates and trounced the coalition forces. When all hope seemed lost, the Bactrians from eastern Iran defected to the Babylonian-Iranian alliance. The Assyrians were unaware of this development, as they were celebrating their victory. When they were staggering drunk, the coalition launched a surprise attack. So many Assyrians were killed in the battle that the Euphrates ran red with blood.

The surviving Assyrians withdrew to Nineveh, the world's largest city at that time. Its thick and impregnable walls had twenty feet of stone topped by thirty-three feet of brick. The coalition forces surrounded the city, yet they lacked the Assyrians' siege technology and were unable to penetrate the walls. But then, it happened! A prolonged, torrential rainfall caused the Tigris River to flood Nineveh, washing out the foundation and destroying a wall section.

"The river gates are thrown open, and the palace collapses."[6]

The united forces surged into the city, plundering the palace and the temples of unimaginable treasures. The Assyrian king committed suicide as Nineveh went up in smoke. In the eyes of the Medes and Persians, the evil snake Azhi Dahaka was no more.

"Shields flash red in the sunlight!

See the scarlet uniforms of the valiant troops!

Watch as their glittering chariots move into position,

with a forest of spears waving above them.

The chariots race recklessly along the streets

and rush wildly through the squares.

They flash like firelight

and move as swiftly as lightning...

Loot the silver! Plunder the gold!

There's no end to Nineveh's treasures—

its vast, uncounted wealth.

Soon the city is plundered, empty, and ruined.

Hearts melt, and knees shake.

---

[6] Nahum 2:6, Tanakh: Navi: Book of Nahum.

The people stand aghast,

their faces pale and trembling.

Where now is that great Nineveh,

that den filled with young lions?"[7]

The Medes' surge in power led to their expansion and ascendency over all of Iran, including the Persians. Babylonia claimed most of the former Assyrian heartland except for the northernmost region, which the Medes took. The Medes spread their power north to Turkey's Halys River into the Kingdom of Armenia and west toward the Black Sea, conquering Cappadocia. They also formed strong alliances to the east into Central Asia. The Medes and Persians renewed their treaty several decades later, sealing it with a royal marriage. King Cyrus I's son, Cambyses of Persia, married Mandane, the Median king Astyages's daughter and Cyaxares's granddaughter. Media remained the dominant kingdom, with Persia as its vassal.

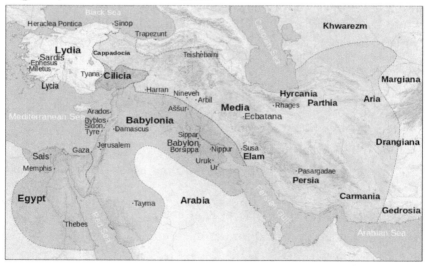

The Medes ruled from Ecbatana over an empire stretching from Cappadocia on the Black Sea to Carmania on the Arabian Sea.

---

[7] Nahum 2:3-4, 9-11, Tanakh: Navi: Book of Nahum.

Around 600 BCE, Cambyses and Mandane gave birth to Cyrus II (Cyrus the Great). When Herodotus wrote about Cyrus II's childhood, he said he chose one of several stories. In the tale Herodotus recorded, King Astyages dreamed that his grandson Cyrus (named Agradates at birth) would topple him. His astrologers advised him that the only way to keep that from happening was to kill the infant. Astyages summoned his daughter Mandane back from Persia to Ecbatana, ordering his general Harpagus to steal the baby when Mandane was distracted and kill him.

Harpagus stole the baby but couldn't bring himself to harm the innocent infant, so he handed him over to the cowherd Mithradates, telling him to abandon the child in the wilderness. Instead, Mithradates gave the baby to his wife and wrapped his stillborn son in the royal baby's swaddling cloth. He gave the dead infant to Harpagus several days later to prove he had abandoned the infant to his death.

When Cyrus was ten, Astyages discovered his identity. In Herodotus's tale, to punish Harpagus for not following his orders, Astyages killed Harpagus's son, cut him into pieces, cooked him, and served his body to Harpagus at a feast. His astrologers reported that Cyrus was no longer a threat, so Astyages returned his grandson Cyrus to his true parents, the king and queen of Persia.

Xenophon said when young Cyrus visited his Median grandfather Astyages at court, he thought it peculiar that Astyages wore kohl around his eyes, rouge, a wig, a purple robe, and bracelets. They ate at a table covered with multiple dishes of assorted delicacies. The Persians dressed plainly, ate simply, and lived a relatively austere lifestyle. But Cyrus happily let his grandfather adorn him with bracelets, necklaces, and an elegant robe and give him a horse with a gold-studded bridle to ride.

When he returned to Persia, Cyrus distributed his treasures among his friends. Later, Astyages rebuked him for giving the gifts away, but the egalitarian Cyrus replied it was the only way he could hold his head high. When Cyrus reached his teen years, he learned the art of war under Astyages's tutelage. The 4th-century Greek historian Dinon and the Greek poet Ibycus (a contemporary of

Cyrus) said that Cyrus served as a general of his Median grandfather's military.

Cyrus ascended the Persian throne in 559 BCE with the title "King of Anshan" when his father died, taking the throne name Cyrus II to honor his paternal grandfather. Persian stories described Cyrus as handsome, generous, respectful, idealistic, courteous, eager to learn new things, and accepting of correction. He also had unbridled ambition, was willful, and would seek revenge if betrayed. Plutarch said he was "hawk-nosed," which the Persians considered attractive, and Herodotus reported he had an unnerving and piercing gaze.

Cyrus married his beloved relative Cassandane, also from the Persian Achaemenid family. They were happily married with at least four children together; their daughter Atossa would marry Darius the Great. Cassandane died in 538 BCE, just as Cyrus was besieging Babylonia, saying leaving Cyrus's side was more bitter than leaving the earth. The Nabonidus Chronicle recorded that the heartbroken Cyrus ordered six days of mourning for his cherished wife throughout the empire.[8]

According to the Nabonidus Chronicle (which was mostly a history of the last Babylonian king), conflict broke out between Cyrus and his grandfather Astyages, who was still ruling over the Median kingdom. Although the Persians acknowledged Median overlordship, they had always enjoyed local autonomy. They only needed to pay tribute and supply men to serve in the military, who could enrich themselves with the spoils of war. Now, Astyages's spies were everywhere. He set up checkpoints between Media and Persia and appropriated Persia's farmers to work his fields.

Even the Medes were dismayed by Astyages's increasingly despotic reforms, and they conspired with Cyrus and his offended chieftains. Herodotus wrote that Astyages's general Harpagus, in revenge for his son's murder, wrote to Cyrus, reminding him of how he had spared his life as an infant. "To me, you owe your

---

[8] *The Chronicle Concerning the Reign of Nabonidus (ABC 7),* Livius, 2020. https://www.livius.org/sources/content/mesopotamian-chronicles-content/abc-7-nabonidus-chronicle/.

deliverance. Do as I advise, and Astyages's kingdom will be yours. Convince the Persians to rebel and march against the Medes. We will desert Astyages and come over to your side."

When Cyrus rebelled against his grandfather, King Astyages mustered his army and marched against Cyrus to conquer Anshan, Persia's capital. Astyages's army revolted, to his surprise, taking him prisoner and handing him over to Cyrus. Cyrus then marched to Ecbatana, the Medes' royal city, plundered its silver, gold, and other valuable goods, and carried them back as booty to his capital of Anshan. Astyages's dream, or rather nightmare, had come true: his grandson Cyrus toppled his kingdom. Nevertheless, Cyrus treated his grandfather kindly; Herodotus said Astyages lived with Cyrus in his palace, and Ctesias said Cyrus appointed Astyages as Parthia's governor.

A golden rhyton or drinking vessel like this one from Ecbatana in the shape of a ram's head may have been among Cyrus's plunder.

National Museum of Iran, CC BY-SA 3.0 <http://creativecommons.org/licenses/by-sa/3.0/>, via Wikimedia Commons; https://commons.wikimedia.org/wiki/File:Rython_boz.jpg

After Cyrus deposed his grandfather, sources disagree on whether Cyrus became king of the Medes immediately or later. Herodotus said Cyrus ruled over both the Medes and Persians after conquering Ecbatana. Xenophon said that Cyaxares II, Astyages's son, led the Medes in an alliance with his nephew Cyrus until the fall of Babylon. At that point, Cyaxares II gave his daughter in marriage to Cyrus, with the Median kingdom as her dowry, and Cyrus gave his uncle a palace in Babylon[9] (and apparently kingship over Babylonia).[10] The Greek tragedy writer Aeschylus and inscriptions on the Harran Stele and Persepolis reliefs support Xenophon's account. Cyaxares II may have been the throne name of Darius the Mede. The historian Josephus called him Darius, identifying him as Cyrus's cousin and the sixty-two-year-old son of Astyages.[11]

After Ecbatana's fall, Cyrus likely held Median overlordship, with Cyaxares II/Darius serving as the Median king, just as Media had previously dominated Persia. The Persians now ruled over all of Iraq and today's Tajikistan, Uzbekistan, Armenia, and northern Mesopotamia. Cyrus the Great's new empire was budding.

---

[9] Xenophon, *Cyropaedia: The Education of Cyrus*, (8.5.19) trans. Henry Graham Dakyns (Project Gutenberg eBook). https://www.gutenberg.org/files/2085/2085-h/2085-h.htm.

[10] Daniel 5:31, 6:1-2, Tanakh: Ketuvim: Book of Daniel.

[11] Flavius Josephus, *Antiquities of the Jews*, trans. William Whiston (Project Gutenberg). https://www.gutenberg.org/files/2848/2848-h/2848-h.htm.

Chapter 3: Cyrus the Great

King Nabonidus of Babylonia couldn't seem to break out of his inertia. He'd supported the coup d'état led by his son Belshazzar against King Labashi-Marduk, but it had gone horribly wrong. Somehow, his fellow conspirators had thrust him onto the throne. After a series of coups, there didn't seem to be anyone else who was royal enough, and he was the grandson of Assyria's last king. But he had been trained as a priest; what did he know about ruling an empire? He couldn't even fulfill his dream of modifying Babylon's worship system. Babylon's priests and even his son Belshazzar had staunchly opposed his religious reforms.

Nabonidus left for a military campaign in Arabia and remained in the desert for ten years. Possibly mentally ill, Nabonidus handed the running of the Babylonian Empire over to his son and regent, Belshazzar.[12] The elderly king seemed oblivious to the ominous threat posed by Cyrus the Great's growing Achaemenid Empire, which would soon swallow up the Middle East and eclipse Babylonia. While Nabonidus was brooding in Arabia, Cyrus was conquering the lands surrounding Babylonia before he came for Babylon. One empire would fall, and another would rise.

---

[12] Paul-Alain Beaulieu, "Nabonidus the Mad King," in *Representations of Political Power*, ed. Marlies Heinz and Marian H. Feldman (Winona Lake: Eisenbrauns, 2007), 137-167.

Meanwhile, King Croesus of Lydia, from whom we get the term "rich as Croesus," was indeed wealthy but also wily. His ancestors had ruled all of western Anatolia (western Turkey) two centuries earlier, from the ruins of ancient Troy in the northwest to the Taurus Mountains in the east. But the Greeks, Scythians, and Cimmerians began grabbing territories on Lydia's coastal lands. Then, after crushing Assyria with their allies, the Medes surged west, conquering Cappadocia.

However, the Median army had betrayed their king, Astyages, to the Persians. Croesus stroked his beard and nodded to himself. The time was ripe for taking back Anatolia! With the right allies, he could take Cappadocia. But which allies? He sent his ambassador to the Oracle of Delphi in Greece. The priestess sat on her stool over a fissure as fumes from the decaying body of the mythical Python wafted up, sending her into a trance. She prophesied that if Croesus warred against the Persians, he would shatter a great empire. She also recommended allying with the Greek state of Sparta, which Croesus did, having already formed alliances with Egypt and Babylonia.

Croesus led his Lydian forces into Cappadocia, capturing the Median city of Pteria and selling its citizens into slavery. But he didn't anticipate that Cyrus would consider Lydia's invasion of Median territory an affront to his Median kinsmen on his mother's side. It also gave Cyrus an excuse to expand his empire into Anatolia. His joint Median-Persian forces marched to Cappadocia.

The first stage of the war between Lydia and Persia was inconclusive. Finally, it was time for the troops to take their customary winter break. Croesus expected Cyrus to head home to Persia, so he withdrew to his hilltop citadel of Sardis, summoning his allies in Greece, Egypt, and Babylon to come to his aid in the spring. But Cyrus didn't withdraw! Hearing a commotion, Croesus stood on the ramparts, horrified to see Cyrus's army approaching. They had marched with lightning speed from Cappadocia to his capital! None of his allies had arrived yet. Croesus quickly mustered his Lydian forces and marched out to meet Cyrus with 420,000 men compared to Cyrus's 196,000 soldiers.

The Persians' dromedaries panicked Lydia's cavalry.
https://commons.wikimedia.org/wiki/File:Defeat_of_Croesus_546_BCE.jpg

Then Cyrus's Median general Harpagus recommended the coup de grâce: put their three hundred dromedary camels on the front line! These weren't war camels; they were pack animals, but the Lydian horses had never seen such enormous creatures. Terrified by the camels' pungent odor, the horses charged off the field. The Lydians retreated into the city, but Cyrus had a half-dozen mobile siege towers. Each held twenty men, lifting them high enough to send missiles over Sardis's walls. Within two weeks, Sardis fell.

Cyrus called for a giant bonfire to execute Croesus. Yet, as the smoke began rising, the Lydian king's dignity moved Cyrus. He ordered the fire put out, but the flames were climbing too high by then. Suddenly, the heavens opened. An opportune rainstorm quenched the fire, and Croesus was saved. His first words to Cyrus were, "You should stop your soldiers from burning and looting Sardis!"

"Why?"

"Because you have defeated me. The city belongs to you! Why let your men destroy it?"

Cyrus laughed and decided to keep Croesus in his company as an advisor.

This Greek Attica vase depicts Croesus's execution, from which he escaped.
https://commons.wikimedia.org/wiki/File:Kroisos_stake_Louvre_G197.jpg

Lydia was the buffer zone for Ionia's twelve Greek colonies on the Aegean Sea. In those days, over 40 percent of Greeks lived outside today's Greece in the five hundred Greek colonies around the Mediterranean and the Black Sea. They stayed intricately connected to the motherland through trade and culture but had independent governments. General Harpagus swiftly conquered the Ionian Greek states, stunning the Greek world. However, the Ionians maintained a measure of local autonomy as long as they paid tribute and sent men to fight in the Persian military.

While Harpagus overpowered Ionia, Cyrus headed east to conquer the Sogdian nomads of today's Uzbekistan; for the next 150 years, they paid Persia a tribute of semi-precious stones. His next target was Phoenicia on the Mediterranean coast. The ancient cities of Byblos, Sidon, Tripoli, and Tyre pragmatically surrendered rather than fought. Their gamble paid off: all they had to do was pay their share of 350 talents a year, as did Israel, Cyprus, and Syria. The Phoenicians' shipbuilding expertise and naval strategies brought tremendous strength to the Achaemenid

Empire in the upcoming naval wars against Egypt and Greece.

Cyrus's conquest of Phoenicia stirred Babylonia's King Nabonidus out of his inertia. He had shrugged when Cyrus conquered other lands, but Tyre was his! Several decades earlier, Babylonia's great king Nebuchadnezzar II had conquered Tyre after a thirteen-year siege. Ending his ten-year hiatus, Nabonidus returned to Babylon, which meant his citizens could celebrate their festivals again; that hadn't happened under the regent Belshazzar.

Cyrus's next move was to conquer the Elamite capital of Susa, one of the world's oldest cities. Radiocarbon dating indicates a Neolithic culture founded Susa around 4395 BCE, predating the Elamites by over a millennium. In the Early Bronze Age, the Sumerians ruled Susa, and then the Akkadians took over. The Elamites took Susa in 2004 BCE, making it their capital city for almost 1,500 years. Cyrus the Great captured Susa in 539 BCE, establishing it as the capital of the Persian-Achaemenid Empire.

From Susa, Cyrus and his army descended on northern Babylonia. King Nabonidus headed north to defend the cities of Sippar on the Euphrates and Opis on the Tigris. The cities guarded each end of the Median Wall that Nebuchadnezzar II had built to keep the Medes from attacking Babylonia from the north. The two rivers provided a natural barrier to the east and west of Babylonia, as did the Persian Gulf to the south.

Cyrus marched toward Babylonia with his astute general Gubaru, whose novel tactics swung the victory over to the Median-Persian forces. In September of 539 BCE, Cyrus reached the Tigris River when it was at its lowest level. His forces overran Opis, killing the citizens and amassing great treasures. Meanwhile, Cyrus's engineers were busy diverting the Tigris into irrigation canals, dropping the water level low enough for his men to wade across on the southern side of the wall.

When Opis fell, no one was left to guard the wall or the river. The Persians were in Babylonia! At this point, Cyrus split his army into two forces. He led half of his men west to attack Sippar and directed General Gubaru south to attack Babylon. The people of Sippar surrendered without a fight, and King Nabonidus fled.

Meanwhile, in Babylon, the citizens were happily celebrating their festival to the moon god, which they hadn't been able to do for a decade.[13] Word had not reached them that Cyrus had taken Opis and forded the Tigris. They had no idea that half of Cyrus's army was headed their way! The co-regent Belshazzar was celebrating a grand feast with a thousand of his nobles. But then he looked up to see the horrifying sight of a ghostly hand inscribing something on the wall!

None of his astrologers could read the writing, but the queen mother strode in when she heard the commotion. She told Belshazzar to call for the seer Belteshazzar (Daniel), who had been an advisor to Nebuchadnezzar. The aged Daniel entered the banquet hall, read the writing on the wall, and interpreted it. "Your days are numbered. You have been weighed in the balance and found wanting. Your kingdom is divided and given to the Medes and Persians."[14]

As Daniel was speaking, the Medes and Persians were assembling on the far side of the Euphrates. The Babylonians were reveling in the streets, celebrating the Festival of Sin (the moon god), oblivious to their presence. Once again, General Gubaru's engineers diverted the river into nearby canals, lowering it enough to wade across. The drunken shouts of the partying Babylonians obscured the noise of Gubaru's forces breaking down the Enlil Gate.

Once inside Babylon, the Persians killed anyone who attempted to confront them. Some people sounded the alarm, but the Persians made loud drunken-sounding shouts, drowning out the warning cries. Most citizens had no idea their city was under attack. The Persians hurried down the Processional Way, the most direct path to the city's center, where the palace was located.

Outside the closed palace gates, the guards were relaxing and drinking around a blazing fire. The Persians struck them down, attracting attention within. Belshazzar, the regent, sent several men to see what was happening outside the palace gates. As soon as they opened the gates, the Persians forced their way in and rushed into the banquet hall to see Belshazzar holding his scimitar, surrounded

---

[13] *The Reign of Nabonidus (ABC 7)*.

[14] Daniel 5, Tanakh: Ketuvim: Book of Daniel.

by his nobles. The Babylonians were too drunk to defend themselves well. On top of this, they were vastly outnumbered. The Persian forces cut down Belshazzar and all the Babylonian nobles.[15]

Two weeks later, Cyrus made his grand entrance into Babylon. The city gates were thrown open by Babylon's citizens, who were relieved that Cyrus's military had already shown reverence to the city's shrines. Assuming the title "King of Babylon, Sumer, and Akkad, King of the Four Corners of the Earth," Cyrus dutifully marched to Marduk's temple to worship the city's patron god. His reverence of Marduk won the hearts of the Babylonians. They resented their king, Nabonidus, who had tried to supplant Marduk with Sin as the chief of gods.

Cyrus II grew his modest kingdom into a mega-empire.
DiegoColle, CC BY-SA 4.0 <https://creativecommons.org/licenses/by-sa/4.0>, via Wikimedia Commons; https://commons.wikimedia.org/wiki/File:Cyrus_the_Great_of_Persia.jpg

---

[15] Xenophon, *Cyropaedia: The Education of Cyrus,* trans. Henry Graham Dakyns. (Project Gutenberg E-book). https://www.gutenberg.org/files/2085/2085-h/2085-h.htm.

The Persians killed Belshazzar, but what about his father, King Nabonidus? The Nabonidus Chronicle said the Persians captured Nabonidus, but Cyrus extended grace, sending him to govern Iran's province of Carmania. According to the Book of Daniel, Darius the Mede (probably Cyaxares II) ruled briefly as king of Babylonia, appointing satraps or governors over Babylonia's 120 provinces.[16] The Babylonian historian Berossus and the Roman lexicographer Valerius Harpocration mention a Darius ruling in this period.

In the first year of Cyrus's reign, he permitted the Medes, Syrians, Jews, and other populations that had been relocated by previous Babylonian and Assyrian rulers to return to their homelands. Many exiles were now in high-ranking positions, which they retained under Cyrus, and remained in Babylon. Among them was Daniel the seer, who may have shown Cyrus the prophecies of Isaiah, which were written before Cyrus was born:

"This is what the LORD says to Cyrus His anointed, whose right hand I have grasped to subdue nations before him, disarm kings, and open the doors before him so that the gates will not be shut. 'I will go before you and level the mountains; I will break down the gates of bronze and cut through the bars of iron. I will give you the treasures of darkness and the riches hidden in secret places so that you may know that I am the LORD, the God of Israel, who calls you by name.'"[17]

"Accordingly," wrote Josephus, "when Cyrus read this and admired the divine power, an earnest desire and an ambition seized upon him to fulfill what was written."[18]

Cyrus gave this proclamation, as recorded by Ezra the Scribe:

"Concerning the house of God at Jerusalem, let the temple, where sacrifices are offered, be rebuilt. Let its foundations be retained, its height being sixty cubits and its width sixty cubits, with three layers of huge stones and one layer of timbers. And let the cost be paid from the royal treasury. Also, let the gold and silver

---

[16] Daniel 5:30 – 6:3, Tanakh: Ketuvim: Book of Daniel.

[17] Isaiah 45, Tanakh, Nevi'im, Yeshayahu.

[18] Flavius Josephus, *Antiquities of the Jews*, Book XI, Chapter 1.

---

utensils of the house of God, which Nebuchadnezzar took from the temple in Jerusalem and brought to Babylon, be returned and brought to their places in the temple in Jerusalem; you shall put them in the house of God."[19]

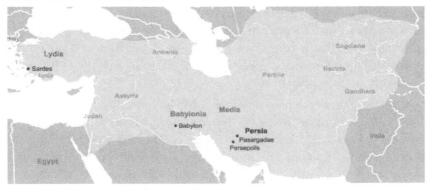

Cyrus's empire reached from the Aegean Sea to the Indian subcontinent.
SG at the English-language Wikipedia, CC BY-SA 3.0
<http://creativecommons.org/licenses/by-sa/3.0/>, via Wikimedia Commons;
https://commons.wikimedia.org/wiki/File:Persia-Cyrus2-World3.png

When Cyrus was seventy years old, his massive Achaemenid Empire stretched from the Mediterranean to Afghanistan. Indefatigable, he focused on the expansive steppes of Central Asia. Appointing his son, Cambyses II, as his co-regent and the king of Babylonia, Cyrus retained rulership over the rest of the empire before heading northeast to take on the Scythians and Massagetae.

The Scythians were distant relatives of the Medes and Persians, speaking a variant of the Indo-Iranian language. They had once exercised dominion over the Medes until the great Median king Cyaxares had massacred their leadership and subjugated them. The Scythians had allied with the Medes, Persians, and Babylonians as they ruthlessly accomplished Assyria's cataclysmic downfall. However, these untamed nomadic raiding parties threatened the Achaemenid Empire's cities and farming communities.

The Massagetae were a branch of the Scythians. Herodotus said these skilled horsemen and roaming nomads lived north of the

---

[19] Ezra 6. Tanakh: Ketuvim, Book of Ezra.

Araxes River, which flowed from Mount Ararat into the Caspian Sea. They would throw hemp seed on their campfires, and the smoke would make them "drunk," jumping up to dance and sing. Gold and brass were abundant in their lands, which they used for their weapons and armor. When the Massagetae grew old, their families sacrificed them with some cattle in what they considered an honorable death. In their minds, human sacrifice was preferable to natural death for the elderly, as feeble or sick people would hinder their nomadic lifestyle.

Queen Tomyris ruled over the Massagetae after her husband died. Cyrus thought his best chance of conquering the Massagetae would be to marry their queen, so he attempted to court her. But Tomyris saw through his subterfuge and rejected his advances. Cyrus then took the direct approach of amassing his forces, marching to the Araxes River, and building boats to carry his siege towers across.

Queen Tomyris sent her herald to him, who relayed her message to him. "King of the Medes, how can this be of any true advantage to you? Be content to rule your own kingdom in peace, and let me govern my country. If not, then back off from the riverbank by three days' march, and my soldiers will meet you there."

Cyrus discussed her offer with his war council, and the Persian chiefs voted in favor of Queen Tomyris meeting them on the Persian side. But Croesus, the former king of Lydia and now Cyrus's advisor, strongly protested:

"My king! I can't agree! If we lose this battle, the Massagetae will push into your empire! And if you win, you still have to cross the river before following through on your victory. And, by backing off three days' march, you're yielding ground to a woman! I suggest we cross the river, then prepare a great banquet with roasted lamb and lots of wine. The Massagetae aren't used to drinking wine. We'll abandon our camp except for our weakest troops, allowing the Massagetae to capture it, eat the food, and drink the wine. When they're drunk, we'll attack!"

Cyrus followed Croesus's advice, and the Persians slaughtered the drunken Massagetae and captured Spargapises, Tomyris's son. The bereft Tomyris messaged Cyrus, "You bloodthirsty Cyrus!

Your poison grape juice ensnared my child. It wasn't a fair fight! Give me back my son and leave my land. Otherwise, you'll die in a bloodbath."

However, as soon as the Persians united Spargapises, he committed suicide. The wrathful Queen Tomyris led her forces in the "fiercest of all battles" against the Persians. After a drawn-out battle, the vengeful Massagetae prevailed, destroying most of the Persian army and killing Cyrus. Tomyris dipped Cyrus's severed head in a bag of human blood, saying, "I promised you would die in a bloodbath." [20]

Cyrus's grave is in Pasargadae in Iran's Fars Province, Persia's homeland.
Bockomet, CC BY-SA 4.0 <https://creativecommons.org/licenses/by-sa/4.0>, via Wikimedia Commons; https://commons.wikimedia.org/wiki/File:Cyrus_the_Great_Tomb.jpg

When Cyrus died in 530 BCE, he left behind a massive empire with an efficient central government and provinces ruled by satraps (governors). Under Persian rule, Babylon experienced a renaissance of mathematic and scientific advancements. Cyrus won the respect of his conquered civilizations by honoring their customs, giving them a high degree of autonomy, and promoting their prosperity. Cyrus was great, not only for his outstanding military accomplishments but also for his stellar leadership.

---

[20] Herodotus, *The Histories, Book One,* trans. George Rawlinson (New York: Dutton & Co, 1862). http://classics.mit.edu/Herodotus/history.1.i.html.

Chapter 4: Conquest of Egypt and Scythia

"Cats!" Phanes blurted out.

"Cats?" King Cambyses asked, bewildered.

"Yes, my lord! Cats will be our secret weapon! We'll also use dogs, sheep, and ibis."

Who would ever guess that cats would be the deciding factor in Persia's first victory in North Africa? We'll unpack that story and more as Cyrus's legacy continued with the conquests of his son Cambyses and his distant relative Darius I (the Great). Cambyses would conquer Egypt, most of North Africa, and Cyprus, while Darius would extend the empire into the Indus Valley and the Balkan Peninsula of Europe.

Cyrus's death by the Massagetae came as a shock, but he was already seventy years old and had been preparing his son Cambyses II to rule in his place. Cambyses had governed northern Babylonia as a co-ruler with his father. Cyrus's second son, Bardiya, ruled over Central Asia. After ascending the throne, Cambyses soon began planning to fulfill his father's goal of overpowering Egypt.

Amasis II had been Egypt's pharaoh for over forty years. He was allied with Polycrates, the ruler of Samos, a Greek colony in the Aegean Sea off Turkey's western coast. Polycrates controlled the Aegean Sea with the world's most powerful navy of the time, and Amasis controlled the southeastern Mediterranean. Together, they had taken the sizeable strategic island of Cyprus in the Mediterranean and were staging raids on Persian coastal territories. While Cambyses was plotting his attack on Egypt, Polycrates unexpectedly switched over to the Persian side, bringing his formidable navy with him.

Polycrates wasn't the only Greek defector to Cambyses. Phanes of Halicarnassus had served as a mercenary general under Amasis. Mercenaries were common in those days, pragmatically fighting for the pay they received rather than defending some political ideology. Since the mercenaries weren't patriotically motivated, they tended to switch to the side with the best expectations of winning.

Pharaoh Amasis of Egypt suspected Phanes of Halicarnassus of plotting against him, so he sent assassins after him. Phanes eluded the hitmen and defected to Cambyses, proving a great asset with his brilliant strategies and knowledge of the Egyptian military machine. Losing Phanes was a blow to Amasis, but losing Cyprus was worse, for the Mycenaean Greeks and Phoenicians of Cyprus switched their allegiance from Egypt to Persia.

Before launching a military campaign, Cambyses prudently attempted a peaceful negotiation with Egypt, requesting the hand of Pharaoh Amasis's daughter in marriage. Amasis couldn't bear to part with his daughter, so he sent the lovely Nitetis, daughter of Pharaoh Apries, from whom he'd usurped the throne. But when Nitetis arrived, she told Cambyses of Amasis's deception, giving Cambyses the pretext he needed to invade Egypt.

The Phoenicians built ships for Cambyses's navy, and the Ionian Greeks also provided a fleet. Following Phanes's advice, Cambyses formed a treaty with the Arabs who controlled the Sinai Peninsula between Israel and Egypt. As his men marched through the Sinai Desert, the Bedouin chieftains provided them with needed water. Cambyses's navy sailed along the coast from Phoenicia toward Egypt.

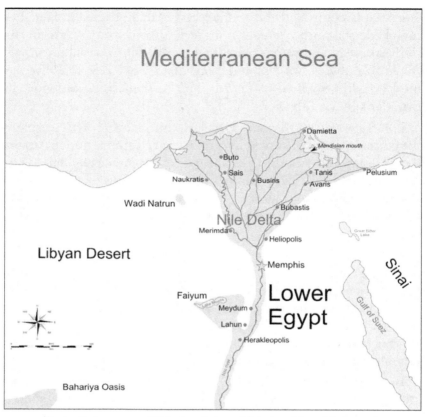

Darius first conquered Pelusium (upper right), then Memphis (center).
*Lower_Egypt-en.png: *Ancient_Egypt_map-en.svg: Jeff Dahlderivative work:
MinisterForBadTimes (talk)derivative work: MinisterForBadTimes, CC BY-SA 3.0
<https://creativecommons.org/licenses/by-sa/3.0>, via Wikimedia Commons;
https://commons.wikimedia.org/wiki/File:Lower_Egypt_460_BC.png*

As Cambyses advanced on Egypt, Pharaoh Amasis died, and his son, Psamtik III, became pharaoh. Psamtik sent his ships to confront Cambyses's Phoenician-Greek navy, but Psamtik's admiral Udjahorresnet defected, providing Cambyses with more vessels and naval expertise. In 525 BCE, the Persian navy sailed into the Nile Delta, where Psamtik awaited him at the fortress of Pelusium.

The Egyptians initially held off the Persians with their platoons of archers and chariot formations with unmatched speed and agility. Their catapults were their deadliest weapon, as they hurled small boulders and flaming projectiles at the Persians, killing thousands. This is where the cats came in! The 2nd-century CE Greek writer Polyaenus told the story in his book, the *Stratagems*.[21]

Egyptians were fond of their pet cats, and if one died, they would shave their eyebrows in a sign of mourning, mummify the cat, and bury it with jewels. Their warrior goddess Bastet, often depicted with a woman's body and a cat's head, was highly offended if someone killed a cat, which brought the death penalty. Egyptians also held their whippet-like dogs in high regard; their jackal-headed god Anubis protected the spirits of the dead. The Egyptians depicted their creator god Amun as a ram; unlike the Israelites, they did not sacrifice sheep but worshiped live rams. The Egyptians regarded the white ibis bird as an incarnation of their god Thoth, the maintainer of the universe; millions of mummified ibis have been uncovered in Egyptian catacombs.

This reverence for certain animals led to Phanes's ingenious tactic. Cambyses had the image of Bastet painted on his soldier's shields and then released sacred animals on his front lines. Cats, dogs, ibis, and rams all ran ahead. Panicked, the Egyptians couldn't fight their goddess nor harm the animals with their catapult missiles and arrows. They turned and ran with the Persians in hot pursuit; fifty thousand Egyptians died compared to seven thousand Persians. A century later, Herodotus visited the battle site and found skulls and bones still littering the sand.

The Egyptians fled one hundred miles south to their capital stronghold of Memphis. Cambyses sent a Greek Mytilene ship to Memphis to negotiate the terms of a peaceful surrender. However, the Egyptians attacked the vessel and dismembered the crew. After laying siege and defeating Memphis, Cambyses executed two thousand Egyptian princes in retaliation for the Mytilene massacre but spared Psamtik.

---

[21] Polyaenus, *Stratagems: Book Seven*, trans. R. Shepherd (1793). http://www.attalus.org/translate/polyaenus7.html.

This image from a 6ᵗʰ-century Persian seal shows Cambyses capturing Psamtik.
https://commons.wikimedia.org/wiki/File:Cambyses_II_capturing_Psamtik_III.png

While consolidating Egypt, Cambyses sent a fifty-thousand-man army to the Siwa Oasis to destroy the priests of the Temple of Amun who had refused to legitimize Cambyses as Egypt's pharaoh. Cambyses had crowned himself pharaoh, taking an Egyptian throne name and making sacrifices to Egyptian gods, but the Amun priests considered him an illegitimate interloper.

After a one-week journey, the Persian force reached the El-Kharga Oasis, where they rested before continuing their desert trek. A deadly south wind arose, stirring up a sandstorm that buried the troops. Since no one ever found a trace of the missing army, most scholars dismissed Herodotus's story. However, in 1996, an expedition discovered a mass grave of human bones, bronze weapons, and silver jewelry dating to the Achaemenid era.[22]

Libya soon formed a treaty with the Achaemenid Empire, as did the Greek colonies of Cyrene and Barca. Cambyses restored Memphis, making Egypt a satrap (province) of Persia, with the Persians forming Egypt's Twenty-seventh Dynasty. Cambyses's

---

[22] Rossella Lorenzi, "Vanished Persian Army Said Found in Desert," *NBC News: Science News*, November 9, 2009. https://www.nbcnews.com/id/wbna33791672.

victory over Egypt marked the end of Egyptian self-rule. The Persian monarchs ruled as pharaohs over Egypt throughout the Achaemenid Empire, which was followed by the Macedonian Ptolemy dynasty, then the Roman Empire.

Cambyses remained in Egypt for three years before an attempted coup back in Persia demanded his return. While hurrying home, he suffered an accidental self-injury to his thigh, piercing himself with his sword as he mounted his horse. Herodotus said Cambyses had the "sacred sickness" (epilepsy), so he possibly injured himself during a seizure. The wound became gangrenous, and within three weeks, Cambyses died of septic shock in 522 BCE.

Cambyses's lance bearer, Darius, was with him. In hushed whispers, some wondered if Darius somehow caused Cambyses's death, and soon, the whispers grew louder. Cambyses had no children, so his younger brother Bardiya (Smerdis in Greek) was next in line for the throne. However, Bardiya died mysteriously. Darius claimed that Cambyses killed his brother before leaving for Egypt to prevent him from usurping the throne in his absence.

Darius said a Magian (Iranian priest) named Gaumata, who resembled the young man, commandeered the throne, pretending to be Bardiya. This was what propelled Cambyses to leave Egypt for Persia. After Cambyses died en route, Darius returned to Persia and stormed Gaumata's stronghold in Media with six other co-conspirators and killed the pretender. Or did they actually kill Bardiya? Darius was the only one who reported Bardiya's death by Cambyses. Could Bardiya have usurped his brother's throne for a few months before his assassination? Did Darius manufacture the fake Bardiya story so he couldn't be accused of regicide?

At any rate, Cambyses and Bardiya were dead, leaving no male heirs to the Achaemenid dynasty. That is until Darius claimed to be a distant cousin of Cyrus and Cambyses and a direct descendent of Achaemenes. On the Behistun Inscription carved 330 feet high on a cliff in western Iran, Darius explained his lineage:

"I am Darius, the great king, the king of kings, the king in Persia, the king of countries...My father is Hystaspes. The father of Hystaspes was Arsames; the father of Arsames was Ariaramnes. The father of Ariaramnes was Teispes; the father of Teispes was

Achaemenes...We are called the Achaemenids; from antiquity, we have been noble; from antiquity, our dynasty has been royal."[23]

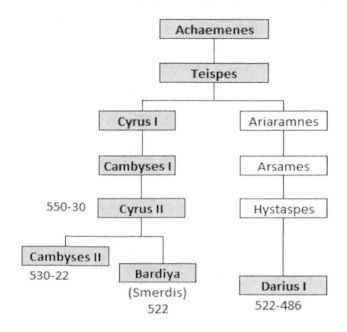

Darius I claimed to have descended from Achaemenes.
Ekvcpa, CC BY-SA 4.0 <https://creativecommons.org/licenses/by-sa/4.0>, via Wikimedia Commons; https://commons.wikimedia.org/wiki/File:Lineage_of_Darius_the_Great.jpg

Many satraps (governors) over the Achaemenid Empire rejected Darius's story about Bardiya, his family tree, and his right to rule. Multiple satraps almost simultaneously declared themselves independent of Persia, crowning themselves king of their countries or satrapies: Elam, Babylonia, Persis Media, Assyria, Egypt, Armenia, Parthia, Margiana (in Bactria), Scythia, and Sattagydia (in Pakistan). One by one, in nineteen battles in a single year, Darius reconquered the countries and captured the rebel kings and satraps.

Although Darius rose from relative obscurity with a questionable pedigree and may or may not have killed one or both

---

[23] Darius I, *The Behistun Inscription*, Livius.
https://www.livius.org/articles/place/behistun/behistun-3/.

of Cyrus's sons, Darius lifted the Achaemenid Empire to astounding new heights. He brought stability, developed intrinsic infrastructure, and expanded the empire to a size never before seen in the world. It covered three continents and included almost half of the world's population.

After squelching the multiple rebellions around the empire, Darius headed to Egypt to reconsolidate Cambyses's previous conquests. He then turned his focus eastward to the Indus Valley. Cyrus the Great had conquered the territory between Afghanistan and the Indus River (today's Pakistan), but the people had rebelled in the chaotic period following Cambyses's death.

By 518 BCE, Darius's troops scaled the Himalayas to retake the previous territory and expand into Punjab in northern India, forming three Indus provinces: Sattagydia, Gandhara, and the Indus Valley. These provinces were the Achaemenid Empire's most prosperous region, as they contained vast amounts of gold. They paid eight tons of gold dust in tribute annually: about one-third of the value of the empire's total tribute revenues from all twenty-three of its countries. The Indians also supplied teak, ivory, and war elephants.

In 513 BCE, Darius turned northwest to the Scythians of Europe, having already reined in the Central Asian Scythians. The Scythian territory stretched from the northern steppes of Central Asia to the Black Sea and into Thrace (today's Bulgaria, northeast of Greece). The Scythians' question, according to Herodotus, was, "Why? We don't have cities for you to conquer and no crops for you to destroy. We're in no rush to fight you!"

Why indeed? Herodotus suggested it was to settle old scores going back to early Persian history. More likely, Darius wanted to take land and lay the groundwork for a later invasion of Greece. Whatever his motive, the Scythians didn't make it easy for Darius. Without cities and agricultural fields, all they had to do when the Persians approached was pack up their wagons, in which they lived, and head somewhere else. The Scythians were fierce warriors who decorated their horse bridles with the scalps of their victims, but they preferred to choose their battles. Why waste energy fighting?

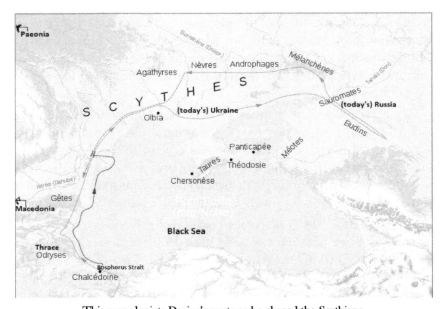

This map depicts Darius's route as he chased the Scythians.

Photo modified: English labels added. Credit: anton Gutsunaev, traduction GrandEscogriffe, CC BY-SA 4.0 <https://creativecommons.org/licenses/by-sa/4.0>, via Wikimedia Commons; https://commons.wikimedia.org/wiki/File:DariusScythes_fr.svg

Darius's men built a bridge across the Bosphorus Strait, then marched north through today's Bulgaria to the Danube in Romania. He urged the Scythian king Idanthyrsus to either fight or surrender, which he refused to do. Darius followed them all the way around the north end of the Black Sea to the Volga River in Russia. The Persian forces were exhausted and ill by this time, running out of water and food in the harsh steppes. They built eight forts to guard the frontier, but the bitter Russian winter was setting in, and they had no choice but to withdraw. Although Darius never engaged in a full-out battle with the Scythians, he had successfully driven them out of the Baltic Peninsula.

While Darius was chasing the Scythians, he left part of his army and his general Megabazus behind to finish conquering Thrace, a vital launching point for his later campaign in Greece. After Darius crossed over to Asia, he encountered a curious sight. A tall, beautiful woman in a lovely gown was leading a horse while balancing a pitcher on her head and spinning flax as she walked to the river to water the horse and fill her pitcher. The stunning and skilled multitasker piqued Darius's curiosity. He commanded the young woman be brought to him, and her brothers, who had been watching nearby, accompanied her.

"Where are you from, and why are you here?"

"We are Paeonians," they answered. "Our country lies on the Strymon River, and our people are originally from ancient Troy. We're here to put ourselves under your power."

"Do all the women in your country work so hard?" Darius inquired.

"Oh, yes! Our women are tireless in their work and unmatched in beauty."

It was a scam, of course. The young noblemen's scheme was to induce Darius to invade Paeonia (Northern Macedonia), then appoint them as his satraps to rule the country. But their plot didn't conclude as swimmingly as they'd hoped. Darius wanted these tall, beautiful, industrious people in his own country, so he messaged Megabazus in Thrace to conquer Paeonia and relocate the men, women, and children to Persia. This was the first time a population-relocation program ever happened under Persian rule.

Once General Megabazus had packed off all the Paeonians he could round up to Persia, he focused on Macedonia, which was south of Paeonia. He sent seven Persian ambassadors demanding that King Amyntas "give earth and water," recognizing Persian authority. King Amyntas agreed to submit and hosted a grand feast for the Persian nobles. The Persians commented that it was their custom to enjoy a banquet with their wives and concubines sitting with them. King Amyntas said the men feasted separately from the women in Macedonia. Still, he would honor the Persian custom and invite the women to join them. The royal ladies entered the room and sat next to their husbands, facing the Persians on the other side of the table.

Then, the Persians remarked, "Your women are so lovely that it is torture to look across the table at them! Send them over to our side."

Although unhappy, Amyntas remembered what had just happened to Paeonia and signaled the ladies to sit on the Persian side. The drunk Persians began inappropriately touching the women and trying to kiss them. Amyntas sat in stormy silence, but his son Alexander (an ancestor of Alexander the Great) had a plan.

"Father, I know you're tired. Go on to bed, and I'll take care of our guests and give them what is fitting."

After his father left the room, Alexander stood up and magnanimously said, "Dear visitors, consider all these ladies your own. Just let them slip out now and bathe while you enjoy your wine, and then they'll be back."

Alexander hustled the women off to the harem, then rounded up the same number of beardless, slender youths. He dressed them in the women's robes, armed them with daggers, then presented them to the drunk Persians. When the men began to grope, they were each stabbed by the "ladies." The Persians never discovered what happened to their lost ambassadors. Alexander bribed the search party, even giving his sister in marriage to the Persian Bubares, who spearheaded the investigation.[24]

This bas-relief carving depicts Darius I (the Great).
Frank-Haf, CC BY-SA 4.0 <https://creativecommons.org/licenses/by-sa/4.0>, via Wikimedia Commons; https://commons.wikimedia.org/wiki/File:Darius_the_Great.jpg

---

[24] Herodotus, *The Histories: Book Five.*

Despite losing the seven envoys and their entourage, the Persians now controlled Macedonia. Megabazus headed to Sardis to meet up with Darius, who was preparing to return home to Susa in Persia. Megabazus confided to Darius his concerns about Histiaeus, the ruler of the Greek island of Miletus off Turkey's coast. After Histiaeus had faithfully served Darius in the Scythian campaign, Darius permitted him to build a settlement in Paeonia.

"Sir! Histiaeus is Greek! And he's shrewd! Now he's ensconced in Paeonia and will gain control of Thrace's silver mines and forests of timber for shipbuilding. We need to keep him away from Greece!"

Darius called Histiaeus to Sardis and told him, "I need your wisdom and insight. Come back with me to Susa, live in my splendid palace, share all I have, and be my advisor."

Histiaeus found Darius's invitation flattering, although he may have wondered if he had a choice in the matter. Darius headed back to Persia with Megabazus and Histiaeus, leaving General Otanes as the commander of the troops on the seacoast. Otanes's father, Sisamnes, had served as a judge during King Cambyses's reign, and when Cambyses discovered he was taking bribes, he executed him and flayed his skin. He cut the skin into strips, formed a lattice-work cushion for his judge's chair, and appointed Otanes as the next judge.

No doubt, Otanes was relieved to escape from his gruesome throne to serve in the military, and he brought the rest of the Balkan tribes under Persian dominion. His conquests left Persia controlling all of the Balkan Peninsula, except for Greece. That would be Darius's next move, and he had set the stage for it.

SECTION TWO:
THE GRECO-PERSIAN WARS

Chapter 5: The Ionian Revolt

Histiaeus paced back and forth in Susa's exquisite palace, ornamented with gold, lapis lazuli, turquoise, ebony, and ivory. He felt like a bird in a gilded cage. Why did he ever agree to come to Persia with King Darius? In Ionia, he had ruled Miletus, the wealthiest Greek city-state. And with his new city in Paeonia, his control of the silver mines and forests of the northern Balkan Peninsula would have brought unimaginable riches.

But now he was stuck in Persia, powerless! He needed to get back to Ionia, and he had a plan. He would direct his son-in-law, who was now ruling Miletus, to stir up trouble against Persia. Then he'd ask Darius for permission to return home and set everything right. But how could he get a message past the Persians? He looked up to see his favorite servant approaching and smiled. Wrapping his arm around the man's shoulders, he said, "I'm sending you to Ionia. But first, you need to shave your head. And then keep your turban on for a while."

Where was Ionia? It was a group of Greek city-states located on the islands and coastal areas of today's western Turkey, across the Aegean Sea from Greece. As we mentioned earlier, almost half the world's Greek population lived in colonies around the Mediterranean, Aegean, and Black Seas. According to their traditions, the Ionians arrived in the eastern Aegean coastal region from Athens about 140 years after the Trojan War.

Ancient Troy was on Turkey's coast, north of what later became Ionia. The Dorian and Aeolian Greeks also established colonies in coastal Turkey, but the region was collectively called Ionia after its first Greek settlers. The Greeks never formed a central government in Ionia; each city-state was an autonomous power linked to others by religion and culture. Over time, these colonies became extraordinarily wealthy centers of art, philosophy, and scientific and mathematical advancements.

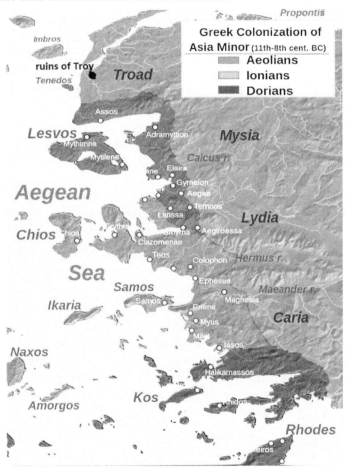

The Ionians colonized central Ionia, with the Aeolians to the north and the Dorians to the south.

Photo modified: location of Troy added. Credit: Alexikoua, CC BY-SA 3.0
<https://creativecommons.org/licenses/by-sa/3.0>, via Wikimedia Commons;
https://commons.wikimedia.org/wiki/File:Western_Asia_Minor_Greek_Colonization.svg

Cyrus the Great brought Ionia under Persian dominance, but each city-state continued with self-rule, although some rulers were tyrants. Today, the word tyrant conjures up images of a despotic and cruel dictator, but in Greek city-states, a tyrant was someone who became a ruler outside the usual channels. A tyrant usurped the throne and ruled with absolute power rather than being the previous king's son or part of the aristocratic ruling council.

Tyrants were often more benevolent rulers than monarchs or aristocratic councils because they needed the support of the people to maintain their rule. Thus, they tended to forgive debts, initiate reforms, and codify laws to protect ordinary people from injustice. Nevertheless, any totalitarian ruler can quickly descend into a draconian despot, so the Greeks considered a different political direction.

Polycrates, who helped Darius I conquer Egypt, was a tyrant ruler of Samos from 540 to 522 BCE. He took control of the island with only his two brothers and fifteen men. After killing one brother and exiling the other, he became Samos's sole and absolute ruler, with the ultimate (and unfulfilled) plan of consolidating all of Ionia under his rule. During his reign, the Samians built the four-thousand-foot Aqueduct of Eupalinos. Two teams on opposite ends bored through a mountain to meet in the middle, demonstrating an astounding grasp of geometry and engineering.

Another tyrant was Histiaeus, ruler of Miletus, who assisted Darius in his invasion of Thrace, but Darius took him back to Persia with him after General Megabazus expressed his distrust. Megabazus's instincts were right, as it turned out, according to Herodotus.[25] Although Histiaeus remained under Darius's watchful eye in Persia, he still manipulated events in Miletus, where his nephew and son-in-law Aristagoras now ruled.

Some aristocrats who had been kicked off Naxos Island in the Cyclades (islands between Greece and Ionia) came to Aristagoras for aid in retaking their country. Aristagoras told them, "I don't have enough power to help you, but King Darius's brother

---

[25] Herodotus, *The Histories: Book Five & Six*.

Artaphernes is my friend. Darius appointed him as ruler in Sardis with oversight over all Ionia. Let me talk to him and see what we can work out."

So, Aristagoras met up with Darius's brother Artaphernes in Sardis, tempting him to invade the Cyclades (which were independent of Persia) and reinstate the exiles. "Naxos is a large, rich, and fertile island with silver mines and marble quarries. We will supply your military expenses and a large gift in return for your trouble. One hundred ships are all you need. You will gain not only Naxos but the other surrounding islands, which will give you control of the mouth of the Aegean."

Artaphernes liked the plan, but he needed to check in with his brother, King Darius. He also wanted two hundred ships. Darius said yes, so the Persian-Ionian coalition amassed a fleet of two hundred triremes and a mammoth army led by the Persian admiral Megabates, Darius's nephew or cousin. They set sail to Naxos, but trouble broke out between the Persians and Greeks. While Megabates was making his inspection rounds, he discovered a Greek ship without anyone on watch. He punished its captain, Scylax, by tying him to a porthole, with his head sticking outside the boat. When Aristagoras heard this, he interceded with Megabates for his friend to no avail, so he set Scylax free himself. Megabates was infuriated, but Aristagoras loudly shouted, "Don't forget you are under *my* command!"

Humiliated and seething, Megabates decided to get back at the Ionian Greeks by secretly sending a boat to Naxos to warn its citizens of the impending danger. The Naxians knew the two hundred ships were sailing in their direction but had no clue their island was the target, as they assumed the ships were headed to Greece or the Mediterranean. As soon as they received Megabates's warning, they quickly harvested whatever crops were ready and stockpiled water and supplies within their city walls. The Naxians endured a four-month siege before the Persians finally gave up.

Financially ruined after underwriting the siege, Aristagoras could barely pay the troops and could not fulfill his promises to Artaphernes. He fretted over whether his campaign's failure and his clash with Megabates, Darius's relative, would cost him his rule over Miletus. He believed the only way out of his predicament was to unite his fellow Ionian Greeks and break free from Persia. Then, he could keep his kingdom. While mulling this over, he received a strange message from his father-in-law, Histiaeus, in Persia.

The message itself wasn't bizarre; it was the way he received it. Histiaeus was growing increasingly irritated in Persia, as he was unable to return to Ionia and unable to send any messages to Aristagoras that wouldn't be intercepted. He wanted to stir up a revolt among the Ionians, hoping that Darius would send him back home to quell them. So, he called his most trusted servant, shaved his servant's head, and tattooed the message "Revolt!" upon it.

After the hair grew back enough to cover the message, he sent the man to Miletus, telling him, "When you get to Miletus, ask Aristagoras to shave your head."

The message confirmed what Aristagoras had already decided to do. His only problem was that he was now penniless, with no way to fund a new military endeavor. One of his friends encouraged him to raid the temple at Branchdae, which had been enriched by King Croesus, but Aristagoras didn't want to anger the gods. Despite still lacking funds, Aristagoras proceeded with the rebellion. He encouraged his fellow Ionian rulers (mostly tyrants) to give up their thrones, as he had done, and form a democratic commonwealth with him in charge. He drove out any tyrant unwilling to revolt against Darius.

Aristagoras next sailed to Greece to ask the Spartans for assistance. King Cleomenes, who Herodotus said was "not quite right in the head," declined, unwilling to get involved in a venture so far from Sparta. Aristagoras then headed to Athens in the Attica Peninsula, the ancestral homeland of the Ionian Greeks. The Athenians had recently rid themselves of tyrant rule and were experimenting with democracy. They agreed to help but could only spare twenty ships. The city of Eretria, another mother city of the Ionian colonies, sent five vessels.

After returning to Miletus, Aristagoras sent a force led by his brother Charopinus on a surprise attack on Sardis. Its ruler, Artaphernes, retreated to the acropolis on the hill in the city center, but one of the temples caught fire, forcing the Persians down into the marketplace. Just as the Greeks were sacking Sardis, Persian reinforcements arrived, driving the Greeks to Ephesus on the coast.

The Ionian Greeks scattered to the four winds, and the Athenians decided it was time to head home. Surprisingly, the Greek colonists of Cyprus, a large island in the eastern Mediterranean, chose to jump into the revolt at this point. The Mycenaean Greeks had settled Cyprus over a thousand years earlier, but the Persians conquered the island in 545 BCE. The Cypriot king Onesilus led the revolt, and the Ionian Greeks sent ships to help. But Darius sent a Phoenician fleet to quell the rebellion, and a simultaneous land and sea battle took place. The Ionians won the sea battle, decimating the Persian navy. In the land battle, Onesilus killed the Persian commander Artybius, but a faction of Onesilus's own army treacherously killed him.

Darius sent his three sons-in-law and Persian reinforcements to launch a multi-pronged counterattack against Ionia. His brother Artaphernes and the former judge Otanes led the fourth army. The successful campaigns of these armies convinced Aristagoras to escape to Thrace, where he eventually died while attacking a Thracian town. Meanwhile, Histiaeus convinced Darius to allow him to return to Ionia, promising he could bring all the city-states back in line.

Histiaeus first had to report to Darius's brother, Artaphernes, in Sardis, who asked him, "Why did the Ionians rebel?"

"I can't imagine!" Histiaeus answered, pretending to know nothing. "I was dumbfounded when I heard, as I'm sure you were."

Artaphernes didn't fall for Histiaeus's duplicity, having already investigated the revolt's outbreak. "I'll tell you what I know," Artaphernes answered Histiaeus. "You stitched the shoe that Aristagoras put on."

Alarmed by this remark, Histiaeus fled Sardis that night, headed toward the coast, and crossed over to the island of Chios, one of Ionia's twelve Greek city-states. Since he'd just arrived from Persia's court, the Chios inhabitants tied him up, accusing him of supporting Darius against them. After he convinced them of their mistake, they set him free. However, they demanded to know why he had encouraged Aristagoras to revolt, which had thrown all their city-states into disarray.

Careful not to reveal what really happened, Histiaeus deceived the people of Chios, telling them that Darius was planning to implement a population-relocation program. He said Darius would remove the Phoenicians from the coast of Lebanon and resettle them in Ionia while removing the Greeks from Ionia and resettling them in Phoenicia. Of course, this was never Darius's plan, but recent events in Paeonia made them believe it was possible.

Histiaeus sent letters to some of the Persians in Sardis who had earlier discussed defecting from the empire. Unfortunately for Histiaeus, his courier took them straight to Artaphernes. Realizing a coup d'état was in the works, Artaphernes told the courier to take the letters to the intended recipients and then bring their replies to him. Once he had proof of their treachery, Artaphernes executed the traitors, causing great upheaval in Sardis.

When Histiaeus heard that his planned overthrow of Sardis had failed, he sailed back to Miletus, but his people were unwilling to receive him. They'd happily rid themselves of Aristagoras and were now enjoying a taste of democracy. Rejected, Histiaeus returned to Chios. He needed ships, but the people wouldn't help him, so he headed to Mytilene on the large Ionian island of Lesbos.

The Lesbians agreed to help, outfitting Histiaeus with eight triremes and sailing with him to the Hellespont (Dardanelles Strait). Ship traffic flowed from the Aegean Sea through the Hellespont into the Sea of Marmara and then through the Bosphorus Strait to the Black Sea. Anyone who controlled either of the straits controlled the prolific shipping trade. Stationed at the Hellespont, Histiaeus and the Lesbians seized all the vessels passing into the Aegean unless the crews joined their forces.

Meanwhile, the Persians were amassing an enormous navy of Phoenicians, Cyprians, Cilicians, and Egyptians. They were bearing down on Miletus, deciding that it was the rebellion's kingpin. If they could overwhelm Miletus, the revolt would fade away. The Ionian city-states joined their navies into one fleet of 353 triremes to confront the Persians' six hundred ships.

The Ionian coalition navy worried the Persians. Even though they vastly outnumbered the Greek ships, the Ionians had a keen knowledge of the seas in that region. What if they couldn't defeat the Ionians? Darius would skewer them! Maybe the Ionian tyrants who had been ejected from their thrones by Aristagoras and had defected to the Persian side could help. The Persians rallied the former tyrants.

"Men of Ionia! Now is the time to show your loyalty to our great king Darius! Go back to your city and convince your people to break away from the Ionian coalition. Promise them that if they submit to Persia, no harm will come to them. We will spare their homes and temples, and everything will be just like before the rebellion. But tell them that if they don't surrender, we will enslave them, make their boys eunuchs, send their girls to the Bactrian harems, and their state will fall under foreign rule."

The ex-tyrants took this message back to their states, but the Ionians refused to listen. Instead, Dionysius, one of the captains, spurred them on, "Our fate hangs on a razor's edge! Choose to be free or to be slaves. Choose to endure hardship, for now, to gain freedom. Or persist in disorder and laziness and suffer Darius's vengeance."

Under Dionysius's command, the Greek ships trained repeatedly in naval maneuvers as they awaited the Persians. But after seven days of grueling training under the hot sun, the crews were worn out. "We were fools to bring this punishment down on ourselves! Dionysius only provided three ships, but now he's acting like the fleet's admiral! If we keep going like this, we'll all be sick!"

So, on the eighth day, the crews went on strike and relaxed in the shade on the island, refusing to set foot on their ships for more training. This disorder caused the captains from Samos to accept the Persian offer of surrender. After all, even if they defeated this first Persian fleet, another would come behind it. The Persian resources were limitless, but theirs were not. They had better ensure the safety of their temples and lands.

Just then, the Persian fleet sailed in, and the Ionian crews boarded their ships and sailed out to meet them in the practiced formation. But the vessels from Samos abruptly changed course and sailed off over the horizon, back to Samos. When the Lesbians saw the Samians sail away, they did the same, and soon only a third of the fleet was left to face the six hundred ships of the Persian navy. At first, the Ionians fought resolutely, but eventually, they gave up and fled. Captain Dionysius sailed to Sicily, where he became a pirate, although he never plundered Greek ships.

After winning the naval battle, the Persians attacked Miletus, tunneling under the walls and collapsing them. They carried the entire population off to Persia, but Darius treated them kindly and gave them the city of Ampe on the Persian Gulf. The people of Samos, angry that their navy had abandoned the battle, preferred to emigrate rather than be under Persia's thumb. They accepted the invitation of the Greeks of Sicily to establish a new colony on their island.

Histiaeus was still at the Hellespont, intercepting ships and conscripting the crews. As soon as he heard the news of the naval debacle, Histiaeus sailed with the Lesbian ships to Chios and commandeered the island until he heard the Persian fleet was sailing that way. He escaped to the mainland only to be captured by the Persians there. Artaphernes executed him in Sardis and sent his head to Darius, who grieved his death, still oblivious to Histiaeus's treachery.

The following spring, in 492 BCE, furious with Athens and Eritrea for interfering in his war and joining in the sacking of Sardis, Darius sent his close relative General Mardonius to reap revenge. Passing through Ionia with his naval force and land army, Mardonius ejected all the remaining tyrants and set up democracies in the city-states. He reconsolidated the Persian rule over Thrace and Macedonia, then set sail for southern Greece to attack Athens and Eritrea.

But a violent storm shattered three hundred of his ships and killed over twenty thousand men. While Mardonius was marching with his land army, the Byrgi tribe of Thrace attacked. Mardonius succeeded in subduing the Byrgi, but his army was in bad shape. He limped in retreat to Persia; nevertheless, Darius now held Ionia, Thrace, and Macedonia in an even firmer grip. Not yet done with Greece, Darius would rebuild his fleet and sail back to Greece in two years.

Chapter 6: The First Campaign against Greece

King Darius strolled along the beach, watching the Phoenicians rebuilding his fleet of ships and enjoying the breeze from the Mediterranean. He'd ordered 600 new triremes plus enough transport ships to carry 10,000 horses and supplies for his 200,000 infantrymen. The Phoenicians told him it would take two years to build this many ships, and he was pleased to see that after a year, the project was running ahead of schedule.

In the meantime, Darius wanted to test the waters with Greece, needing to know where the strongest holdouts were. Like Ionia, Greece was not a unified country but a collection of independent city-states that constantly fought amongst each other. But now, Greece faced the greatest outside threat they'd ever encountered since they emerged from their Dark Ages three centuries earlier.

Darius had already sent his envoys to his seaport cities scattered around his empire, requiring them to provide more ships and horses. Now, he sent his emissaries all over Greece, visiting each prominent city-state and demanding "earth and water," which meant unconditional submission to Persia. As his emissaries returned, he was pleased to hear that all the Greek cities agreed to bow to Persia. All, that is, except Athens and Sparta.

Darius growled. Athens again! These Athenians needed to be punished. First, they and the Eretrians had interfered in the Ionian

Revolt, sending ships and men; they even joined in the sacking of Sardis. He would target those two cities first when he sailed to Greece. He would tear down their walls, burn the cities to the ground, and enslave the entire population! And what about Sparta? They also refused to bow to Persia, but at least they had refused to aid the Ionian Revolt. He would decide Sparta's fate later. They might be useful in destabilizing Athens.

Meanwhile, the Athenians stewed over the Greek cities that had capitulated to Darius. These traitors would do nothing to resist a Persian invasion. What's worse, they could potentially join the Persians to attack Athens. The Athenians were especially outraged by the Eginetans of Aegina, an island in the Saronic Gulf between Athens in the Attica Peninsula and the Peloponnese, where Sparta lay. The Persians could use that island as a launching pad for attacks on both cities!

Athens informed Sparta that Aegina had bowed to Persia. Typically, Athens and Sparta were fierce rivals, but in this instance, they cooperated against their mutual enemy. Cleomenes, who was still king of Sparta, traveled to Aegina to discipline the Eginetans, but they were sassy, demanding to know why the other king didn't accompany him. The "other king" was Demaratus; Sparta had a system of two kings ruling simultaneously, each descended from twins who co-ruled in ancient times.

King Demaratus had remained behind, stirring up an insurrection against Cleomenes in his absence. When Cleomenes returned, he retaliated by questioning Demaratus's legitimacy: was the previous king, Ariston, really Demaratus's biological father? Ariston had stolen his friend's wife, and Demaratus was born seven months later. Ariston suspected Demaratus must be his friend's child, not his own. Yet, he kept silent and raised Demaratus as his biological son because he had no other children.

King Cleomenes conspired with Leotychidas, a family member of Demaratus, to give testimony that Demaratus couldn't be Ariston's biological child. This resulted in Demaratus losing his throne and defecting to Darius the Great. Leotychidas became the next king, co-ruling with Cleomenes. With the kingship issue settled, the co-kings Cleomenes and Leotychidas traveled together to Aegina to deal with the island's insubordination.

Since the two kings arrived together, the Eginetans felt it best to comply this time. The Spartan kings chose their ten wealthiest noblemen to take to Athens as hostages to ensure they would not cooperate with the Persians in a naval attack. The kings returned to Sparta, but Cleomenes, who had struggled with mental illness for years, went completely psychotic, striking everyone within reach with his scepter. His family locked him up, but he managed to get a knife and began harming himself, slashing his legs and then his belly until he finally bled out and died.[26]

Meanwhile, Darius was preparing to launch his navy, appointing two new generals: a Mede named Datis and Artaphernes, his brother's son. The six hundred triremes and accompanying transport ships set sail from Cilicia and sailed to Ionia. Instead of hugging the mainland, they sailed straight across the Aegean Sea through the Cyclades in hopes of avoiding storms like the one that destroyed the last expedition.

Naxos had yet to be conquered, and most of the people fled to the mountains, but the Persians burned their city and enslaved anyone they could find. While Artaphernes was wrapping up affairs in Naxos, Datis sailed to the nearby island of Delos, the mythical birthplace of Apollo. The people fled, but Datis assured them he meant no harm to the holy island or the people and offered frankincense on the sacrificial altar.

Datis sailed through the Cyclades, conscripting men from the islands for his army. Some islanders refused, unwilling to fight against their fellow Greeks in Eretria and Athens, but Datis ravaged their fields until they complied. Leaving the Cyclades, they sailed into the South Euboean Gulf toward Eretria. Just after Datis left Delos, an earthquake struck the island for the only known time in known history. The Greeks considered it an omen of impending doom. Herodotus pointed out that in the reigns of Darius, his son Xerxes, and Xerxes's son Artaxerxes, the Greeks suffered more calamities than they had in the previous twenty generations.

As the Persian navy grew closer, the Eretrians desperately sent messages to Athens for help. The Athenians sent four thousand

---

[26] Herodotus, *The Histories: Book Six.*

farmers with some military training. The Eretrians fretted about their best course of action. Most planned to abandon the city and flee to the forbidding heights of Mount Olympus, but others plotted treason, hoping for a reward from the Persians. No one seemed inclined to hold their ground and defend the city. Aeschines, a city leader, sent the Athenians back home. "No one here plans to fight. Why should you die?"

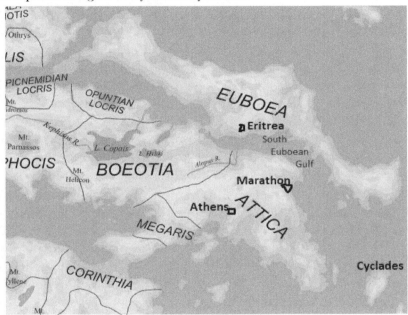

The Persians sailed from the Cyclades up the South Euboean Gulf to Eretria.
Photo modified: cropped and labels added. Credit: User: MinisterForBadTimes, CC BY-SA 2.5 <https://creativecommons.org/licenses/by-sa/2.5>, via Wikimedia Commons; https://commons.wikimedia.org/wiki/File:Ancient_Regions_Central_Greece.png

The Persians reached Eretria, brought their horses ashore, and prepared for battle. But the Eretrians remained ensconced within their city walls. After seven days of siege warfare, two Eretrians betrayed their city by opening a gate to the Persians. They poured in, plundering the city and burning the temples in retribution for the sacking and burning of Sardis's sacred sites. Following Darius's command, the Persians enslaved the population. Within a few days, the Persians sailed back down the South Euboean Gulf toward Athens, their next target, confident they would enjoy a similar victory.

With the Persians headed their way, the Athenians sent Philippides, a long-distance runner, to Sparta to tell them that Eritrea had fallen to the Persians. The Spartans agreed to the Athenian's plea for help, but they couldn't come immediately. They were celebrating the Carneia, a festival, and couldn't go to war until the moon was full. However, the people of Plataea, a city north of Athens, sent an army of one thousand to the Athenians. Even with these reinforcements, the Persians still vastly outnumbered the Greeks, but the Athenians had some tricks up their sleeve.

Choosing your battles is always a good idea, but choosing your battlefield may be equally critical. When the Athenians chose their battlefield, they had several variables in mind. They could have waited for the Persians to come to Athens. Instead, they marched twenty-five miles across the peninsula to meet the Persians in Marathon on the South Euboean Gulf. They knew some things about the layout of the land of which the Persians were unaware.

The Persians had anchored in Marathon, planning to ride their horses through the valley between the mountains to Athens and lay siege. This was the quickest route from Eretria to Athens, and they wouldn't have to put themselves at risk of storms by sailing out into the open sea and around the peninsula. They were a bit startled to be met by the Athenians but shrugged. A land battle would be quicker than laying siege to the city.

The Athenians took the battle to the marshy, mountainous terrain of Marathon.

The land around Marathon was swampy and dotted with mud pits that could swallow a man. Fingers of the mountains extended down to the shore. The Persians, who were expert horsemen, had planned to use their cavalry, but the horses couldn't maneuver well. They would either get bogged down in the swamp or have to clamber over ridges and through wooded patches. The Athenians did not use horses; they fought on foot.

The Greeks lined up in their famous phalanx formation. Rows of soldiers stood shoulder to shoulder, holding their shields so they slightly overlapped on either side with their long lances extending out. They would have at least three rows of men behind the front row, and the ones behind would push the ones in front with their shields. It was like a gigantic bulldozer with eight-foot spears extending out, crushing and impaling the enemy.

Since the Greeks knew the terrain, they set up their formation to give them the best advantage possible: a mile-long line of soldiers on a ridge away from the mud pits. This was the first time the Greeks had faced the Persians; previously, they had surrendered immediately or turned and ran. The Persians looked at the sparse Greek force and laughed. "These crazy Athenians! They have no horses and no archers, and they've only got a handful of men. They're insane!"

Usually, the men in a phalanx formation would use a measured march across the battlefield and break into a run within fifty feet of the enemy. But the Athenians ran full speed the entire mile down the ridge and across the small plain to crash into the Persians. The Persians were startled by their speed, and their archers barely managed to shoot a volley or two before the Greeks were upon them.

The center of the Greek line was thin, only four men deep, but they heavily manned their left and right flanks eight men deep. The Persian forces broke through the middle, but the Athenians closed the gap behind them, cutting off those Persians from the rest of their army. The Greeks on the sides outflanked the Persians and circled behind them. The Persians had never encountered phalanx maneuvers and were disoriented and panicked.

Finally, the Persian troops turned and ran pell-mell. In desperation, some ran into the swamps to be swallowed up in the mud pits. The Athenians followed but navigated around the quagmire, cutting down any who made it through the swamp to the beach. Most of the Persian army broke out in a frantic dash toward the beach, followed by the relentless Greeks who struck them down from behind.

The Athenians plunged into the sea behind the fleeing Persians and set some of the ships on fire, capturing seven vessels. The rest of the vessels pushed off with the Persians who had managed to climb aboard. The Greeks counted 6,400 Persian bodies on the battlefield that day, not including the unknown number who sank in the quagmire, never seen again. The Athenians only suffered 192 casualties, and the Plataeans lost 11.

The Tumulus of the Athenians is a burial mound for the 192 Athenians who perished at the Battle of Marathon.

The Persians had left the enslaved Eretrians on an island in the gulf. Their remaining ships sailed to the island to pick up the Eritreans, then headed south. The Athenians who were celebrating on the shore suddenly realized their plan. The Persians would sail around the Attica Peninsula and then up into the Saronic Gulf to Athens. Now it was the Greeks' turn to panic. What if the Persian navy got to Athens before they could travel the twenty-five miles by foot?

Although weary from the day's drawn-out battle, the Athenians raced back the twenty-five miles toward Athens, stumbling along in the dark after night fell. They made it back to their city the next day before the Persian ships reached it. The Greek army set up camp at the shrine of Heracles, and when the Persian fleet sailed into the Saronic Gulf, they could see campfires blazing at the top of the bluffs. The Persians weighed anchor off of Piraeus, Athens' harbor, and considered their options.

They really had none. The Spartans were likely to show up at any moment, making a siege impractical. After floating offshore, the Persians abruptly weighed anchor and sailed home. The next day, the Spartans finally marched in since it was now the full moon. They were too late to help fight but were ecstatic to hear about the great victory and wanted to see the battlefield and the Persian bodies. After that, they congratulated the Athenians for their outstanding win and headed back home.

Among the ten Greek generals that led the Athenian forces was Miltiades, the ingenious innovator of the strategies used at Marathon. Although pleased that the Athenian infantry had won the day, Miltiades realized it was critical for Athens to build up its navy; after all, the Persians would eventually be back. Another general, Themistocles, one of Athens' leading citizens, likewise promoted ramping up Athens' navy. Two hundred new triremes were constructed. Athens would be renowned for its nearly indomitable navy from this point on.

When the Persian generals Datis and Artaphernes reached Persia, they had to face King Darius's wrath. But at least they had the Eretrians they had enslaved. The army marched them overland, across the desert, to Darius's palace in Susa. Darius had been livid when Eretria and Athens attacked Sardis and supported the Ionian Revolt. But when he saw the men, women, and children of Eretria, worn and weary after their months-long journey, he felt only pity. He resettled them in his estate of Ardericca, in the fertile Cissian region, where they lived throughout the remainder of the Achaemenid Empire, retaining their Greek dialect and customs.

Darius was indeed infuriated by the catastrophic loss at Marathon and became even more intent on wiping Athens off the face of the earth. He immediately began preparations for a new invasion. He raised taxes, ordered new ships to be built, and gathered men, horses, and provisions. The Persian Empire was immersed in preparations for three years, but then the Egyptians revolted, leaving Darius with two fronts to march against.

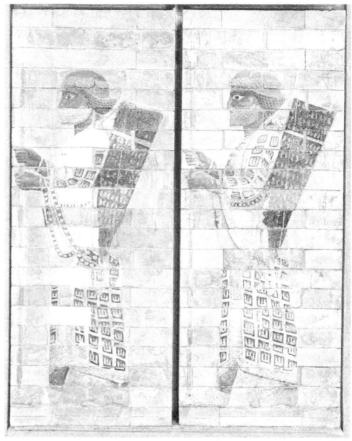

This frieze from Darius I's palace in Susa depicts elite Persian archers.
Carole Raddato from FRANKFURT, Germany, CC BY-SA 2.0
<https://creativecommons.org/licenses/by-sa/2.0>, via Wikimedia Commons;
https://commons.wikimedia.org/wiki/File:Frieze_of_Archers_from_the_Palace_of_Dariu
s_I_in_Susa, Achaemenid_Persian_Period, reign_of_Darius_I, c._510_BC, Louvre_M
useum_(12251246605).jpg

Darius planned to lead his armies himself this time, first to Egypt and then Greece. However, he had to settle the matter of succession. Which of his sons would succeed him if he died on the battlefield? He had three sons from his first wife and four sons from his second wife, Atossa, daughter of Cyrus the Great. Although his son Artabazanes was the oldest of all his sons, he appointed Xerxes, Atossa's oldest son, as his crown prince. He was the grandson of Cyrus the Great, the hero of the Persians; no one would challenge Xerxes's lineage as a descendant of the Achaemenid dynasty.

Before Darius could lead his armies to war, he died unexpectedly after reigning for thirty-six years. Xerxes wasn't especially keen on invading Greece, as he considered the Egyptian matter to be a greater priority. Why lose the rich and fertile Egyptian farmland that his uncle Cambyses had worked hard to conquer? But General Mardonius, Xerxes's cousin, slowly convinced him to follow through on his father's plans for Greece.

"We can't just let them get away with this travesty. We need to deal with Egypt first, but we must go after Athens to save face. If we grind that city into the dust, no other country will dare attack us! And think of all the wealth Greece will bring us. They have olive trees and fruit trees of all sorts. Only one as great as you are worthy of owning such a beautiful land!"

And so, Xerxes began to plot his own invasion of Greece, determined to succeed where his father had failed.

Chapter 7: Xerxes I's Campaign

King Xerxes had a problem with a ghost.

In the year following his father's death, he marched on Egypt and put down the revolt, then placed his brother Achaemenes as Egypt's satrap. Now it was time to fulfill his father's desire to obliterate Athens, so he called together his war council to discuss plans.[27]

"I intend to throw a bridge over the Dardanelles Strait, march into Greece, and reap vengeance against Athens for their diabolical actions against Persia and my father. I will not rest until Athens burns to the ground! We will then extend the Persian Empire into Europe as far as heaven reaches. We shall bring all mankind under our yoke and be the empire upon which the sun never sets!"

The Persians sat in stunned silence, afraid to say anything until Xerxes's uncle, Artabanus, dared to speak:

"I warned my brother Darius about fighting the Scythians, yet he did anyway and lost some of his most courageous warriors. The Scythians, fierce as they are, pale in comparison to the Greeks. And just getting to Greece presents all sorts of dangers. Don't forget the horrific storm that decimated Darius's fleet and the blood-thirsty tribes that attacked Mardonius's army. And now, the Athenians have built up their navy! They could defeat us at sea or

---

[27] Herodotus, *The Histories: Book Seven.*

destroy our bridge over the Hellespont. We narrowly escaped catastrophe before when your father bridged the Bosphorus."

Xerxes replied, "Artabanus, you're my father's brother, but you are a coward. We don't need you to fight the Greeks; you can stay here with the women. I tell you, if we don't strike first, the Greeks will invade *us!* There's no middle ground: we either invade or be invaded!"

Despite his bravado, Xerxes reconsidered his uncle's words on his bed that night. His uncle was right; it was foolhardy to invade Greece. But when he fell asleep, he saw a ghost, which asked him, "Did you really change your mind, Persian? You need to follow your original plan!"

Yet, the following day, Xerxes called his war council. "Men! I spoke rashly yesterday and did not give my uncle the respect he deserves. I've changed my mind about invading Greece."

That night, the ghost appeared again. "Know this! If you *don't* march on Greece, you will experience catastrophe!"

Terrified, Xerxes jumped out of bed and called his uncle Artabanus. "I am haunted by a ghost threatening me with harm if I don't march on Greece. Maybe it's just a dream from my own imagination. Let's test it. Lie down on my bed. If the word is from God, you will see the ghost also."

So, Artabanus went to sleep on his nephew's bed, and the ghost appeared, saying, "You! You pretend to care about Xerxes, warning him about attacking the Greeks. You will not escape judgment: not now and not in the afterworld."

As the ghost attempted to gouge out Artabanus's eyes with a red-hot poker, he screamed and ran to Xerxes. "I've changed my mind! The fates have ordained it. March on Greece!"

Xerxes was a meticulous planner and spent four years preparing for his assault on Greece. The nations throughout his empire provided what was needed: warships, transport ships, horses, one million men, and provisions. He ordered his engineers to accomplish two astounding feats. The first was building a bridge across the Hellespont (Dardanelles Strait), where Asia meets Europe, between the Aegean Sea and the Sea of Marmara.

The Hellespont is three-quarters of a mile across and three hundred feet deep at its narrowest point; building a traditional bridge with pilings over such deep water was impossible. Instead, his engineers strapped 674 ships together. They laid wooden planks over the ships' decks, forming two spans for Xerxes's army to march over. It took months, but they finished just as Xerxes reached them in 480 BCE with his million-man army from all the nations of the Achaemenid Empire.

Just then, a violent storm hit the region, churning the water and splintering the bridge. Xerxes went ballistic. He decapitated his engineers and even ordered his men to give the water three hundred lashes and brand it with red-hot irons! The setback forced the supersized army to winter in Sardis while rebuilding the bridge. Some of his officers must have wondered why they didn't just use the 674 ships to ferry the men; why did they have to *walk* across?

Finally, his Phoenician workers got the bridge back together, and Xerxes's one-million men army marched across; it took seven days and seven nights. Meanwhile, the fleet of 1,200 ships sailed along the coastline of the Aegean. Xerxes's second engineering wonder was a new passageway for the vessels. Years earlier, a horrific storm had devasted his father's fleet on his first attempted invasion of Greece as they sailed around the Athos Peninsula. Xerxes's way of solving that problem was sailing *through* the peninsula; his men had been toiling for three years, constructing a one-mile canal across the strip of land. Once again, some of his men must have been scratching their heads. Why waste three years building a channel? The ships would still have to sail across the Aegean Sea to reach Athens or Sparta. Weren't storms out there as well?

Xerxes led his colossal land army from the Hellespont to Thrace, then through Thessaly and into Greece. The Greek city-states offered no resistance to the Persian army until they reached the Rocks of Trachis, which were rugged and inaccessible mountains barring the way to Athens and Sparta in southern Greece. As far as the Persians knew, the only way through was the Thermopylae Pass, but about six thousand Greeks barred its entrance. Yet what could six thousand warriors do against a force of one million?

Once again, Sparta and Athens had allied to face their common enemy, and Thebes, Arcadia, Corinth, and other Greek cities joined them. Led by King Leonidas of Sparta, the Greeks blocked the narrow mountain pass guarding southern Greece. The coastal pass was narrow: only sixteen feet wide from the swampy shoreline of the Malian Gulf to the sheer cliffs of Mount Kallidromo, and it extended four miles. The crumbling ruins of an ancient defensive wall ran from the mountain to the sea, which the Greeks had quickly shored up as best they could before the Persians arrived.

King Xerxes marched into the valley, observed the tall mountains and the small Greek force, and sat down to wait. The Greeks would run away in horror once they grasped how many men lined up behind Xerxes. Four days passed, and the Spartans stood resolute. Xerxes called Demaratus, the former Spartan king who had defected to Persia after being dethroned because of his rumored illegitimacy.

"What are these crazy Spartans doing?" Xerxes asked.

"I already told you about them: they are Greece's greatest warriors. If you can win this battle, no other Greeks will stand against you."

So, Xerxes sent his envoys to the Greek coalition. They relayed his message: "This is your last chance to avoid bloodshed. Simply lay down your arms."

Leonidas snarled, "Come and get them!"

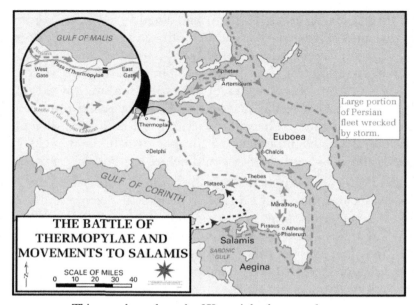

This map shows the path of Xerxes's land army and navy.

Normally, six thousand warriors against one million would be doomed. However, the constricted space and the existing wall permitted the Greeks to completely block the entrance to the pass using the phalanx formation. Standing shoulder to shoulder, with their shields overlapping slightly and thousands of comrades behind them, the rigidly disciplined Spartans held the line. If one man fell, another quickly stepped into his place.

The usual Persian battle tactic was shooting volleys of arrows, so many that it darkened the sky, followed by a cavalry charge. But the Greeks wore bronze helmets and armor and held heavy bronze shields. The men in the front row stood behind the old defensive wall and protected their faces and chests from the arrows with their shields. The men behind them formed a bronze roof with overlapping shields that the arrows couldn't penetrate. The long lances protruding from the first row of Greeks held off the Persian foot soldiers with their daggers and battle-axes, as they only had wicker shields to guard them. The crumbling wall extending to the sea prevented the Persians' horses from charging. The six thousand Greeks successfully held off the Persian army for two days, even the heavily-armed ten thousand elite Persian Immortals.

But on the third day, a Greek traitor revealed an alternate path used by shepherds. It was too narrow for a large division, but Xerxes sent a regiment up and over the mountain to attack the Greeks from the rear. Leonidas saw them coming and sent a platoon to hold them off, keeping another contingent to continue blocking the main pass. He then ordered the rest of the army to retreat to safety. They needed to stay alive to fight the next battle. King Leonidas and his 1,400 remaining men faced off against the Persian hordes, sacrificing themselves to the last man so the rest of the army could escape.

While the Greeks and Persians battled at Thermopylae, the Persian fleet of 1,200 ships was sailing toward Greece. Anticipating a naval attack, the Athenians' newly renovated navy of two hundred ships, combined with the vessels of their allies, sailed into the Aegean Sea to block the Persians. On the Persian side, Queen Artemisia of Halicarnassus (a Greek colony on the coast of western Turkey) commanded five triremes.

The map traces Xerxes's fleet along the coast of Greece.

Photo modified: labels added. Credit: Aegean_Sea_map_bathymetry-fr.svg: Eric Gaba (Sting - fr:Sting)derivative work: MinisterForBadTimes, CC BY-SA 3.0
<https://creativecommons.org/licenses/by-sa/3.0>, via Wikimedia Commons;
https://commons.wikimedia.org/wiki/File:Thermopylae_%26_Artemisium_campaign_map.png

The Persian fleet navigated Xerxes's newly built one-mile canal through the Athos Peninsula without incident, but they still had to sail into the Aegean Sea to reach Greece. And that's when a storm hit off the northern Greek coast of Magnesia, sinking one-third of their ships. The Athenian and part of the Corinthian navy were stationed at the Straits of Artemisium, preventing entrance into the Euboean Gulf. They laughed when they heard that a storm had pulverized the Persian fleet. They laughed even harder when it happened again off the coast of Euboea, shipwrecking another two hundred Persian ships. After three years of building a canal, Xerxes lost half his fleet anyway!

Themistocles commanded the Athenian navy, which battled the remaining half of the Persian fleet at the Straits of Artemisium. Despite the Persians losing half their ships, they still outnumbered the Athenian and Corinthian ships. But they didn't expect the Athenians' innovative naval tactics. The Greeks formed a circle with their boats, with their sterns close together and their bows facing out, impregnable to attack. Then, several Greek ships launched unexpected attacks on the Persian fleet, managing to capture thirty triremes. As night fell, the two sides retreated. The Persians were unsettled; this wasn't the easy victory they'd expected.

On the second day, the Greeks again prevailed. Still, by the third day, the Persians gained the upper hand when Egyptian sailors captured five Greek ships and damaged half of the Athenians' remaining vessels. Although both sides suffered losses, the Greeks' smaller navy couldn't afford to lose many ships. That's when they got word that the Persians had defeated the Spartan coalition at the Thermopylae Pass and were pouring into southern Greece.

The Greek fleet abruptly turned and sailed full speed to the island of Salamis in the Saronic Gulf, one mile from Athens' port of Piraeus. They needed to protect their city! The Athenians had already begun evacuating citizens to the island of Salamis, and the Athenian navy helped get the remaining citizens to safety on Salamis. The Corinthian and Spartan fleets also moored at Salamis. More ships sailed in from around Greece and Macedonia over the next few days.

Xerxes marched into Athens, finding it nearly empty. His forces plundered the ancient city, killing any Greeks who remained and burning the exquisite temples on the Acropolis. Most of Athens' citizens were out of reach on the island of Salamis, so Xerxes decided to march toward Sparta on the Peloponnese Peninsula. But to get to the Peloponnese, he had to cross the Isthmus of Corinth. The Spartans and other Peloponnesians had anticipated this move and constructed a heavily fortified, four-mile wall from the Saronic Gulf to the Gulf of Corinth. Exasperated, Xerxes set up camp, preparing to lay siege to the Corinthian wall.

The Spartan and Athenian coalition held a council of war on the island of Salamis. The Athenians were safe on the island, but Sparta and the rest of the Peloponnese were in great peril. How long could the Corinthians and Spartans hold the Isthmus of Corinth against Persia's million-man army? It was only a matter of time before the Persians broke through and ravaged all the Peloponnese city-states.

"We need to lure Xerxes away from the wall," the Spartans said. "But how?"

Themistocles, Athens' shrewd naval commander, leaned forward. "We'll bring him here! We'll entice him into a naval battle against Salamis."

The other Athenian military leaders protested. "But our women and children are here! We have no protective walls! His navy is bigger than ours. This is insane!"

Themistocles smiled. "Don't worry; I have a plan. The Persians will never set foot on this island. The Persian navy might be stronger in the open sea, but our ship captains are skilled navigators in narrow confines. We'll prepare an ambush for his navy."

The Spartans and Athenians were a little skeptical, but they trusted Themistocles's instincts. Now, Themistocles needed to set the bait for Xerxes. He sent his messenger to the Persians, who told them, "The admiral of the Athenian navy has sent me to you privately. The other Greeks don't know I'm here. Themistocles secretly supports the Persians and wants you to know that the Greeks are confused and panicked and planning to flee Salamis. No one can agree on what to do, and they are so shaken up they will not resist you. In fact, you may even find them fighting among themselves."

Xerxes smiled at the news and ordered his four hundred ships to sail to the Saronic Gulf. But Queen Artemisia cautioned him, "Wait! It's risky to fight in the straits of Salamis; the Greeks will have the advantage there."

Although Xerxes had profound respect for Queen Artemisia, he didn't heed her warning. He ordered his men to set up his white marble throne at the top of Mount Aigaleo overlooking the Saronic Gulf for a bird's eye view of the battle. He was so confident of victory over the "demoralized" Greeks that he even sent runners to Persia announcing a great triumph before the battle ensued.

Xerxes didn't know a sizeable naval force from all of Greece had gathered in the Saronic Gulf and were hidden behind the islands. As the Persian fleet sailed into the Saronic Gulf, all they saw were fifty Corinthian ships. As the Persians bore down on the small fleet, the Corinthians slipped through the strait between Salamis and the mainland into the Bay of Eleusis with the Persians in hot pursuit.

It was a trap! The rest of the Greek ships came out of hiding. They sailed toward Salamis, blocking the straits and hemming the Persian fleet in the Bay of Eleusis with no escape and no room for their usual maneuvers. When those at the front of the Persian fleet saw what was happening, they tried to swing around, only to be crashed into by their own ships behind them. As Xerxes watched in horror from his mountain-top throne, the Greeks repeatedly plowed into the Persian ships with their battering rams, breaking them into pieces. Xerxes's brother, General Ariabignes, died, as did many others in the Persian fleet who drowned when their ships sank. The sea was strewn with wrecked ships and floating corpses. Most of the seafaring Greeks were excellent swimmers, and even if their boats sank, they could swim to safety. The Greeks were especially eager to capture Queen Artemisia, as they were offended that a woman would fight against them, and a Greek woman at that! But Artemisia escaped. The great Salamis triumph was a watershed moment in the conflict between Persia and Greece. Greece had been on the defense, and now the tide had turned against Persia.

As Xerxes watched the debacle unfold beneath him, raging and blaming everyone, a sudden terrifying thought came to mind. What would keep the Greeks from sailing to the Hellespont and destroying his bridge? His million-man army would be stuck in Europe, and they had already run out of food. He had to get his army back to Asia. Meanwhile, his cousin Mardonius wondered if Xerxes would punish him for convincing him to invade Greece. Perhaps he could redeem himself.

"Noble king, I think it best for you to get back to Persia quickly. You've achieved your goal of sacking and burning Athens. You won! Now, leave 300,000 men with me, and I'll enslave the rest of Greece for you in the spring."

Xerxes beckoned Queen Artemisia, asking her opinion.

"I agree with Mardonius. If he wins Greece next year, the glory is yours. If he doesn't, the shame is his. Now is the time for you to march home in triumph after burning Athens, which was the chief purpose of this expedition."

Cyrus marched home, leading two-thirds of his land army, many of whom died on the way from starvation and dysentery. When they arrived at the Hellespont, a storm had broken up the bridge again, so they had to wait for their ships to come and ferry them. Mardonius and the 300,000 men wintered in Thessaly while he planned his assault on Greece in the spring. He wouldn't attempt a land attack on the Peloponnese because of the wall at the Isthmus of Corinth. But he received word that the Athenians had returned to their city.

Mardonius marched on Athens in the spring. The Athenians again fled to Salamis, but Mardonius flattened the city walls, homes, and temples left standing from the first attack. But then a massive coalition army of Spartans and other Greek allies came to Athens' defense. Mardonius quickly retreated with his army to Boeotia in central Greece, where he fought the Spartans in the brutal Battle of Plataea.

The Spartans had positioned themselves in the mountains around the plain where Mardonius and his men were, making it difficult for the Persian cavalry to reach them. Mardonius managed to cut off their supply lines, so they were without food and water, but then the Spartans pulled one of their old battle tricks. They pretended to flee the area. When the Persians charged after them, the Spartans suddenly swung around and formed their lethal phalanx formation. Once again, the Persians could not withstand the Spartan battlefield maneuvers and fled, with the rest of the Greek coalition pouring out of the hills to massacre 260,000 Persian soldiers. Only forty thousand survived to limp home to Persia. [28]

As Queen Artemis said, the glory of conquering Athens belonged to Xerxes, but the shame of Plateau's catastrophe belonged to Mardonius, who perished in the battle. And yet, another fiasco would unfold later on the same day.

---

[28] Herodotus, *The Histories: Book Eight.*

Chapter 8: The Aftermath and Peace of Callias

The Ionian Greeks were under the rule of the Persian Achaemenid Empire, but where did their true fealties lie? Were they loyal to King Xerxes or their ancestral homeland of Greece across the Aegean Sea? This question arose during the naval battle at Salamis when part of the Persian fleet included Ionian ships that had been captained and manned by Greeks. Some Phoenicians whose ships wrecked climbed the mountain to Xerxes's throne, accusing the Ionian Greeks of treason. But Xerxes observed the valor of the Ionian Greeks in the battle and ordered the Phoenicians beheaded for slander.

Nevertheless, while many Ionian Greeks fought heroically on the Persian side, others sided with their mainland Greek brothers, eager for an opportunity to throw off the Persian yoke. On the very day Mardonius was fighting the Greeks in the Battle of Plataea, the Greek fleet engaged in a struggle with Persia in Ionia. The Spartans had sailed to Delos in the Cyclades with 110 ships, and some Ionian Greeks from the island of Samos secretly met with them.

"If the rest of the Ionians knew you were here, they would immediately revolt from the Achaemenid Empire and drive off the Persians. In the name of the gods we both worship, we beg you to deliver us from slavery! Your ships are far superior to theirs, and their morale is low."

At this point, the Athenian fleet arrived to join the Spartans, and the Greeks sailed from Delos to Samos and anchored offshore, prepared for a sea battle. The remnant of the Persian fleet had wintered in Ionia, and most were in Samos at this time. Unwilling to engage the Greeks in a naval battle after the apocalypse in Salamis, the Persians sailed to the foot of Mount Mycale on the mainland. They met up with the sixty thousand Persian soldiers left by Xerxes under General Tigranes, the tallest man in Persia.

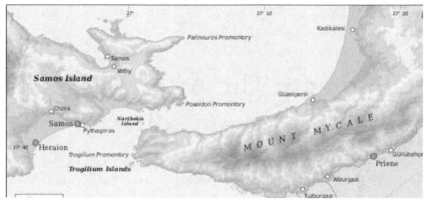

The Greeks and Persians fought the Battle of Mycale across from Samos Island.
Photo modified: zoomed in. Credit: Eric Gaba, Wikimedia Commons user Sting, CC BY-SA 3.0 <https://creativecommons.org/licenses/by-sa/3.0>, via Wikimedia Commons; https://commons.wikimedia.org/wiki/File:Miletus_Bay_silting_evolution_map-en.svg

The Persians pulled their ships ashore and built a stockade around them made of stone and tree trunks, with protective stakes sticking out. After debating their next move, the Greeks eventually headed to the mainland after the Persians. As they sailed past the Persian enclosure, they saw a large army positioned on the beach but were surprised that no ships came out to confront them. They called out to the Ionians among the Persian forces in the Greek language, "Men of Ionia! Remember your freedom! Pass this along to the other Greeks!"

The Spartan king, Leotychidas, hoped to sway the Ionian Greeks to his side or at least engender Persian mistrust of the Ionians. It certainly had the latter effect, as General Tigranes immediately relieved the Ionian Greeks of their weapons. The Spartans and Athenians beached their ships and leaped out to fight the overconfident Persians, who outnumbered the Greeks and didn't expect sailors to be trained for land battles.

They didn't know that all Spartan boys left home at age seven for the military barracks, where they would train in warfare and live with their fellow soldiers until the age of thirty. All male Spartans learned the lethal phalanx formation and practiced various maneuvers and strategies, even if they were later trained in the navy. The Athenian sailors, who were also trained in land combat, lined up in the middle of the beach, determined not to be outdone by the Spartans, who were on the flanks, circling around the camp.

Startled by the Greeks' fervor and fighting maneuvers, the Persians retreated behind their blockade. Most bolted for the hills when the Spartans came up on their rear guard. Unfortunately, the fleeing Persians encountered the Milesians, another Ionian-Greek group that had just defected from Persia. They slaughtered their one-time overlords mercilessly. Diodorus of Sicily recorded that forty thousand Persians died that day, but the Greeks also lost many men. The Greek victors burned the Persian ships, breaking Xerxes's naval power and leaving the coalition Greek navy in dominion over the seas.

After the decisive victory in Ionia, King Leotychidas of Sparta met with the Ionian Greeks. "Come back and live in the motherland. You will be safe from Persia's attacks in Greece, but here you are too vulnerable."

But the feisty Ionians rejected his proposal. "We've been here for six hundred years! We're not going anywhere!"

However, in 477 BCE, the Ionians formed the Delian League, a confederacy of Ionian Greek city-states and other coastal Greek cities around the Aegean Sea, Black Sea, and Adriatic Sea. The league helped each city-state keep its autonomy, and together they launched strikes on Persia. They named Athens as their head, and every city-state provided ships, supplies, or money to fight the Persians.

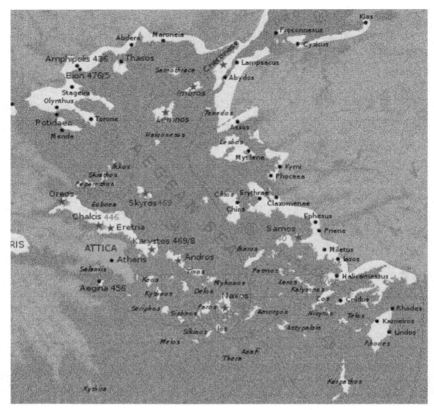

Most of the coastal city-states around the Aegean Sea that joined the Delian League.
Photo modified: zoomed in. Credit: Map_athenian_empire_431_BC-fr.svg:
Marsyasderivative work: Once in a Blue Moon, CC BY-SA 2.5
<https://creativecommons.org/licenses/by-sa/2.5>, via Wikimedia Commons;
https://commons.wikimedia.org/wiki/File:Map_athenian_empire_431_BC-en.svg

Cimon, who fought at the Battle of Salamis, was the league's principal commander; he took back one-time Greek territories from the Persians and rid the Aegean Sea of the Dolopian pirates who had been disrupting trade. Plutarch told how one conquest brought Cimon and his allies extraordinary spoils of war: great riches and Persian prisoners. Cimon told his allies to choose the loot or the prisoners, and they grabbed the gold and lavish robes, thinking the Persian nobility would make worthless slaves. However, Cimon ransomed the prisoners back to their families, making him fabulously wealthy. Herodotus said he used the money for the Delian League's fleet and to feed the poor.

The Athenian historian Thucydides, who lived during the reigns of Artaxerxes I and Darius II, reported that the Delian League's first campaign was against the remaining Persian garrisons in Thrace. It took place around 476 BCE. Cimon's siege of the city of Eion had the objective of ridding Europe of any remaining Persian presence. Due to Thrace's silver mines and massive forests providing timber, it was markedly strategic as the gateway from Asia to Europe.

Cimon led the campaign, defeating the Persians in a land battle and besieging the city of Eion, where the Strymon River empties into the Aegean Sea. The food in the city ran out, and Cimon offered the Persians safe passage out of Europe. But Eion's commander Boges refused, fearful that Xerxes would consider him cowardly. Instead, he threw the city's gold and silver stores into the Strymon, then killed his family and servants. He built a massive pyre upon which he cremated their bodies, then threw himself into the fire. Cimon enslaved what remained of the starving population.

One by one, the other Persian cities on Thrace's coast abandoned their strongholds and evacuated Thrace under the Delian League's pressure. Some of the native Thracians rebelled against the Greek rule and collaborated with the Persians in a resistance movement. Cimon put down the action by capturing thirteen Persian ships with only four triremes and driving out most of the Persians. The last holdout was the city of Doriscus, which the Greeks were unable to conquer. Around the time of Xerxes's death, Governor Mascames of Doriscus was recalled to Persia, ending the Achaemenid presence in Europe.

When Xerxes returned to Persia from Greece, it marked a transition within the empire from expansion to consolidation. The Achaemenid Empire had its challenges, with revolts, such as in Egypt and Ionia, and murders within the royal family, including multiple kings. And yet, the Persian Empire persevered through these crises. The Achaemenids now concentrated more on streamlining their administration than growing the empire's borders. After returning to Persia, Xerxes focused on completing several construction projects initiated by his father.

This era also marked a transition in the relationship between Persia and Greece. Persia had been the aggressor and Greece the defender up to this point. Now the tables were turned. The Greeks were more confident in their battle maneuvers on land and sea, and rather than simply defending themselves, they went on the offensive, winning decisive victories against the Persian Empire that led to the Peace of Callias.

For a decade after Xerxes's demoralizing losses in Greece and Ionia, he immersed himself in other matters within his empire. But he grew increasingly alarmed by the rise of the Delian League and the audacity of its leader, Cimon, who threatened the rest of the Anatolian Peninsula (western Turkey). He needed to rein Ionia back in and launch a third foray into Greece. Xerxes gathered a naval fleet of 340 triremes, commanded by his son Tithraustes, with 80 more ships expected from the Phoenicians. Xerxes planned to use his navy simultaneously with his land army, which assembled at the Eurymedon River in southwestern Turkey. His strategy was to work his way up through Ionia, reclaiming each of the rebel city-states and eventually launching an attack from Ionia on Thrace and Greece.

However, Cimon sailed a fleet of 250 ships from Athens to the Ionian city of Phaselis, which would have been Xerxes's first city to conquer in his campaign. Cimon convinced the people of Phaselis to join the Delian League. Tithraustes didn't want to engage the Greek navy until the Phoenician forces arrived, so he sailed into the Eurymedon River. But Cimon decided to launch a preemptive strike.

Tithraustes needed more room for his ships to maneuver, so he sailed back into the Mediterranean Sea, while Ariomandes, the Persian commander, ordered the land troops to move inland to protect their supplies. Both sides implemented brilliant tactics in the brutal naval battle, but the Persian fleet was no match for Cimon's ingenious naval maneuvers. The Greeks broke through the Persians' line of ships, swiftly turning to ram their unprotected sterns and sides, sinking many ships in the process.

According to Thucydides, after the Greeks captured over one hundred Persian ships along with their crews, the remaining Persian fleet retreated into the river. They banked their vessels and jumped ashore to join the land army. But Cimon deceived the Persians by putting his Greek warriors on the captured Persian ships, dressing them in Persian clothing, and sending them up the river after the Persians.

Cimon's ships reached the Persian camp just as night was falling, and the Persians recognized their ships and thought the disguised Greeks were Persians. The Persians let their guard down, and that's when Cimon and his men attacked. They killed Xerxes's nephew, General Pheredates, and killed and wounded many unsuspecting Persians. The Battle of Eurymedon was a decisive loss for Persia. It lost its territory in Europe, and more Ionian Greeks joined the Delian League, which would soon become the Athenian Empire.

In 465 BCE, palace intrigue led to the murders of King Xerxes and his oldest son, Crown Prince Darius, by the commander of the royal bodyguard. Xerxes's younger son, Artaxerxes, avenged the assassinations of his father and brother by killing the bodyguard and his sons. He then ascended the Achaemenid Empire's throne. It wouldn't be long before he would be tested in conflict with the long reach of the growing Athenian Empire. It would happen in Egypt of all places.

What was the Greeks' interest in Egypt? Diodorus Siculus, a 1st-century BCE Greek historian, claimed that Greeks built the Egyptian city of Heliopolis before the Great Flood. Archaeological discoveries indicate that Hellenes (Greeks) and Egyptians engaged in trade during the Bronze Age. Herodotus said the earliest Greeks to settle in Egypt were Ionian pirates who shipwrecked in Egypt. The Egyptian Pharaoh Psamtik I hired the pirates to fight for him so he could win back his throne from a usurper. Once he was king again, Psamtik granted the Greek pirates land along the Nile to settle, and eventually, their port city of Naucratis became a prominent Mediterranean trade center.

Cambyses had conquered Egypt during his short reign, but Egypt chafed under Persian rule. It rebelled against Darius the Great and again against Xerxes I. Persia put down both revolts, but in 460 BCE, Egypt revolted against Artaxerxes I's rule. This rebellion was led by two Egyptian princes: Inaros and Amyrtaeus. Inaros was Libya's king and the grandson of Egyptian Pharaoh Psamtik III, who had faced off with Persia's King Cambyses and lost.

This time, Egypt allied with Athens, which diverted two hundred ships commanded by Charitimides from Cyprus to Egypt. The Greeks readily agreed to get involved in Egypt's conflict with Persia; they needed Egypt's grain surplus and wanted to restore their thriving trade center in Egypt. The Athenian fleet sailed up the Nile River and attacked fifty Phoenician ships fighting for Persia. Charitimides sank thirty vessels and captured the other twenty.

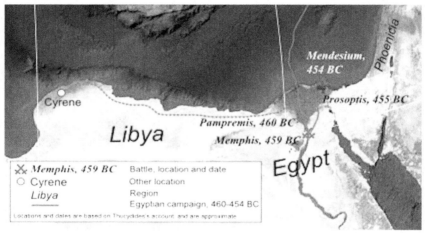

Athens allied with the Egyptian rebels against the Persian Empire.
https://commons.wikimedia.org/wiki/File:Wars_of_the_Delian_League_Egyptian_campaign.jpg

King Artaxerxes amassed a land army of 300,000 men to quell Egypt's rebellion; these soldiers were led by his brother Achaemenes. They encamped near the city of Papremis on the Nile, almost immediately engaging in battle with the Egyptian-Greek coalition. The massive Persian force prevailed initially, but the Greeks managed to outmaneuver them. They broke through the Persians' line and killed about one-quarter of the Persian forces, including Commander Achaemenes, whose body the Greeks sent to his brother, King Artaxerxes.

The Persians fled to their Egyptian capital of Memphis on the Nile, which was called "White Castle" because of the palace's white-washed bricks and the massive white walls surrounding the city. The Egyptian-Athenian coalition besieged Memphis for over four years. Artaxerxes tried to draw off the Athenians by sending General Megabazus to bribe the Spartans to attack Athens, but the Spartans refused.

Megabazus then put together a fleet of three hundred triremes manned by sailors from Cyprus, Cilicia, and Phoenicia, spending a year training them for war. He then sailed up the Nile and quickly defeated the Greek-Egyptian forces laying siege to Memphis. The Athenians fled to the island of Prosopitis in the western Nile Delta, but General Megabazus pulled an old Persian trick. He diverted the river, making the island accessible by foot from the mainland. Only a few Athenians survived, and the Egyptians surrendered to Persia.

The Persian victory caused Athens to panic. The Delian League had kept its treasury on the centrally-located, sacred island of Delos in the Cyclades, but they moved the treasury to Athens. Moving the treasury raised the suspicion of the Ionians and other members of the Delian League, as they believed Athens would use the money for its own ends, not for the good of the league. Meanwhile, flushed with victory, the Persians sent their fleet to retake the island of Cyprus.

Cimon, who had been ostracized and exiled from Athens by his political rivals, returned after a decade, just in time to lead a Greek counterattack against the Persian stronghold in Cyprus. In 451 BCE, his fleet of two hundred ships first attacked the city of Citium, but Cimon died in the battle. The Athenian leaders concealed his death from their forces, not wanting them to lose heart. Under what they thought was Cimon's command, the Greeks won a dual land and sea battle at the city of Salamis in Cyprus, driving the Persians out of the Aegean Sea for good.

The Greek victory in Cyprus ended the Greco-Persian Wars. The Athenian statesman Callias negotiated a thirty-year truce between the Achaemenid Empire and the Delian League in 449 BCE. The Athenians were fighting the Spartans, Thebans, and Corinthians in the First Peloponnesian War and didn't want to divert ships and troops to fight Persia. Artaxerxes likewise had other issues to deal with in his still-vast empire; he was ready to concede the Aegean Sea to the Greeks in exchange for the Black Sea.

In the Peace of Callias, Persia acknowledged the autonomy of the Ionian-Greek city-states and agreed not to send ships into the Aegean Sea and not to send Persian satraps within a three-day walking journey of the Aegean. The Greeks conceded Persian dominance of the Black Sea, Cyprus, Egypt, and Persia's remaining territories in western Turkey. Both Greece and Persia respected the terms of the Peace of Callias past the stipulated thirty years, with neither empire engaging in overt warfare with the other.

What happened to the Delian League? The main reason for forming the league was to fend off Persia's attacks and achieve independence for the Ionian-Greek city-states. But even though the Peace of Callias achieved those objectives, Athens did not release its allies from the league. Athens held control over the funds, and the Delian League morphed into the Athenian Empire. Athens forced the other city-states to continue supplying ships or funds. Instead of using the funds to benefit all the city-states, the Athenians used the league's money for a massive building project of temples and palaces in Athens.

While the Persians technically followed the Peace of Callias, they engaged in insidious intrigues with Athens and Sparta, fanning the flames of the heated rivalry between the cities. Their interference successfully culminated in the eruption of the Second Peloponnesian War in 431 BCE, with unremitting warfare for twenty-seven years weakening Greece. In 412 BCE, Persia assisted Sparta and its allies against Athens by supplying timber and funds for a fearsome fleet led by Lysander, which led to the crushing defeat of the Athenian Empire.

SECTION THREE:
FROM XERXES II TO DARIUS III

Chapter 9: Artaxerxes I and Darius II

"Your wine, Sire." The cupbearer Nehemiah handed the golden goblet to Artaxerxes I.

The king slowly sipped, gazing over the city from his hilltop palace until a servant interrupted his reverie. "King of kings, you have a visitor. Themistocles of Athens."

"Themistocles? How intriguing!" Artaxerxes wondered why his father's nemesis was in his court. Themistocles had been the Athenian naval commander who defeated his father Xerxes in the debacle at Salamis.

"I heard he fled Athens rather than stand trial for treason." Artaxerxes mused.

"He has many political enemies," Nehemiah answered. "Perhaps he is seeking asylum here."

"Well! Let's see what he has to offer." Artaxerxes strode into the audience hall, with its massive pillars and exquisite bas-reliefs.

Themistocles bowed low before Artaxerxes. "King of kings, as you know, I was once your father's enemy. But as you also know, circumstances can quickly change in the political world, especially in Athens. My evil adversaries have falsely accused me, and any defense is a hopeless task. Thus, I offer myself to you."

Artaxerxes frowned. "You would betray Athens?"

The Athenian general Themistocles sought refuge in Artaxerxes's court.
https://commons.wikimedia.org/wiki/File:He_stoods_silent_before_King.jpg

"Sadly, Athens isn't the noble city it once was. I offer myself, my knowledge of Athens, and my military and political skills. I will help you avenge the evil Athens has inflicted upon you, and Persia *will* conquer Greece! I only ask for one year to learn the language and customs of Persia. Then I will be your faithful servant."

Artaxerxes smiled. "Welcome! I value your service. After your year of study, I will appoint you as governor of Magnesia. And what about your family? Bring them here! We will make them comfortable. Now, I was just heading out to a hunt. Will you join me? We have lots to discuss."

Artaxerxes's reign ushered in the "Cultural Phase" of the Achaemenid Empire. In this era, West Asia's more widely spoken Aramaic language replaced the Elamite and Persian languages in court affairs. Something approaching monotheism arose with Zoroastrianism, the worship of the ancient Indo-Iranian god Ahura Mazda. Persia's overt warfare with Greece segued into covert dealings to disrupt the two powerhouses of Athens and Sparta.

Artaxerxes, the "long-handed" (Plutarch said his right hand was longer than his left), was known as a serene, mindful, and generous ruler. Immediately after Artaxerxes I ascended the throne, Bactria revolted. Following an indecisive first battle, Artaxerxes won the second battle when "the wind blew in their faces," apparently referring to a sandstorm.[29] Artaxerxes restored the palace in Susa after it burned and completed Persepolis's Hall of One Hundred Columns.

Artaxerxes successfully put down the Egyptian revolt, but his brother Achaemenes died in the conflict, which broke his mother's heart. The revolt's ringleader Inarus fled to the unassailable Egyptian fortress of Byblos, which General Megabyzus of Persia could not overcome. So, Megabyzus offered terms of surrender to Inarus and the six thousand Greek warriors with him. "King Artaxerxes will not harm you, and the Greeks are free to return home."

Persia began using coinage under Cyrus the Great. This coin shows Artaxerxes I.
Classical Numismatic Group, Inc. http://www.cngcoins.com, CC BY-SA 3.0
<http://creativecommons.org/licenses/by-sa/3.0/>, via Wikimedia Commons;
*https://commons.wikimedia.org/wiki/File:Coin_of_Ardashir_I_(also_spelled_Artaxerxes_*
I)_of_Persis,_Istakhr_mint.jpg

---

[29] *Photius' Excerpt of Ctesias' Persica,* Livius.
https://www.livius.org/sources/content/ctesias-overview-of-the-works/photius-excerpt-of-ctesias-persica/#34.

The rebels yielded to General Megabyzus, who took them to Artaxerxes I. When Artaxerxes saw Inarus, he wanted to rip his throat out for killing his brother, but Megabyzus intervened, explaining the deal he'd struck with Inarus. Artaxerxes relented, but his mother Amestris was livid that he allowed her son's killers to live. For five long years, she badgered Artaxerxes to allow her to take vengeance. Finally, Artaxerxes gave Inarus to her, and Amestris impaled him on three stakes and decapitated the fifty Greeks who had not left when they had the chance.[30]

Deeply aggrieved, Megabyzus left for his province of Syria, where he met up with the Greeks who had escaped Amestris's wrath. Forming an army of 150,000, he revolted against Artaxerxes, who sent General Usiris and 200,000 men to put down the rebellion. Megabyzus and Usiris, men who had once been comrades in arms, charged each other on their horses, simultaneously wounding each other. Usiris pierced Megabyzus's thigh with his spear while receiving injuries to his thigh and shoulder that knocked him off his horse. Megabyzus wheeled around and caught Usiris as he fell. He ordered his physician to treat Usiris and sent him back to Artaxerxes.

Artaxerxes sent another force against Megabyzus. This time, the men were led by Artaxerxes's nephew Menostanes, who received two arrow wounds from Megabyzus in his shoulder and head. Although not mortally wounded, Menostanes fled the battlefield with his men, and Megabyzus scored another brilliant triumph. At this point, Artaxerxes's brother Artarius (Menostanes's father) got involved. He traveled to meet Megabyzus.

"Megabyzus! We have a long history, and you have served our king and his father with great valor and distinction. Why throw everything away now, after your stellar career? Come to terms with my brother, the king."

"Artarius, I'm ready to make amends with my king Artaxerxes. But I can't bear the thought of returning to court and seeing the Queen Mother Amestris. That would drag up the horror of what she did to Inarus, who I vowed to protect. If I can stay in my

---

[30] *Ctesias' Persica.*

satrapy of Syria, I will make peace with my king."

Artarius carried his message to Artaxerxes, and even Amestris urged her son to forgive Megabyzus, as he was an influential and legendary war hero. What if he stirred up trouble with the Ionian Greeks? Artaxerxes pardoned Megabyzus but forced him to make one last trip to the Persian court to receive it.

When Cyrus the Great conquered Babylon, he permitted the Syrians, Medes, Jews, and other people who the Assyrians and Babylonians had relocated to return to their native lands. He returned the treasures taken from the Jewish temple and funded the temple's rebuilding in Jerusalem. Close to fifty thousand Jews returned to their homeland in Cyrus's time. There they encountered the Babylonians who'd been forcibly relocated centuries earlier by King Esarhaddon of Assyria.

These ancestral Babylonians governed the Persian satrapy of Israel. They stirred up trouble against rebuilding Jerusalem and its temple during the reigns of Darius, Xerxes, and Artaxerxes. Darius had researched Cyrus's edict and permitted the temple's completion. But Israel's governor Rheum sent a letter to Artaxerxes I, warning him the Jews had laid the foundation of Jerusalem and would soon finish its walls. "If they rebuild this city, the Jews will refuse to pay their tribute, and you will lose the province west of the Euphrates River."

Artaxerxes wrote back, "I ordered a search of the records and have found that Jerusalem has indeed been a hotbed of insurrection against many kings. Rebellion and revolt are normal there! Issue orders to have these men stop their work. That city must not be rebuilt!"[31]

However, in the seventh year of Artaxerxes's reign, he had a change of heart regarding Jerusalem; he was perhaps influenced by his Jewish cupbearer, Nehemiah. He wrote to Ezra, the Jewish priest and scribe, instructing him to beautify the temple in Jerusalem with silver and gold from the Babylonian treasury and voluntary offerings of the Jews.

---

[31] Ezra 1-4, Tanach: Ketuvim: Book of Ezra.

Fourteen years later, Artaxerxes's cupbearer Nehemiah received a visit from his brother Hanani, who lived in Jerusalem, where the situation was bleak. They had been allowed to finish the temple, but Hanani told Nehemiah that the city's walls and gates still lay in ruins. The next day, Artaxerxes was sitting with his queen and noticed something was troubling his cupbearer. "Why are you looking so sad?" he asked.

Nehemiah was terrified; one always had to have a cheerful demeanor around the king. But he told the king he was grieving his ancestral city. "What can I do to help?" Artaxerxes asked.

Nehemiah breathed a quick prayer, then replied, "Send me to Judah to rebuild Jerusalem's walls."

So, Artaxerxes agreed to send Nehemiah to rebuild Jerusalem's walls and gates. He also provided timber, sent armed troops with Nehemiah to guard him, and appointed him as governor of Judah.[32]

Even before Artaxerxes agreed to the Peace of Callias in 449 BCE, he preferred a war of subterfuge and bribery against Greece. Open combat cost him the lives of his citizens and a fortune in ships and other military costs. Artaxerxes ingeniously decided to exploit the ongoing tensions between Sparta and Athens. He funded the build-up of Sparta's military, paying for new ships for its navy. Meanwhile, he assuaged the Athenians' suspicions by sending his emissaries with gifts and flowery overtures. Then, he sat back and waited for the simmering conflict between Athens and Sparta to erupt.

He didn't have to wait long. In 460 BCE, hostilities broke out in southern Greece in the First Peloponnesian War. With Athens entangled in a war with Sparta and other cities, the time was ripe for Artaxerxes to annihilate Athens. He summoned Themistocles, who had been a helpful advisor in Greek affairs, to fulfill his vow to destroy Athens. When it came down to a direct attack on Athens, Themistocles had second thoughts. How would he go down in history if he betrayed his mother city? Instead of helping Artaxerxes, he committed suicide.

---

[32]Nehemiah 1-2, Tanakh: Ketuvim: Book of Nehemiah.

With his wife, Queen Damaspia, Artaxerxes I had only one son, Crown Prince Xerxes II. But with his concubines, he had seventeen other sons. His Babylonian concubine Alogyne was the mother of Sogdianus, and another Babylonian concubine Cosmartidene was the mother of Ochus. He had at least one daughter, Parysatis, by yet another Babylonian concubine, Andia. Parysatis married her half-brother Ochus while her father was still alive. Marriage between half-siblings was not taboo in ancient Persia and Egypt, especially in royal families. Artaxerxes I and his queen died on the same day in 424 BCE, perhaps of the same illness.

Crown Prince Xerxes II ascended the throne, ruling only forty-five days before his half-brother, Sogdianus, assassinated him while he was in a drunken sleep. Sogdianus usurped the throne but, despite heavy bribes to his military, only ruled six months before falling prey to two of his half-siblings: his sister Parysatis and his brother Ochus. Parysatis was savvy and scheming, and she guided her husband/half-brother Ochus in grasping the throne from Sogdianus and executing him by suffocating him in ashes.

This drachma coin depicts Darius II.

After usurping the throne, Ochus took the throne name Darius II, ruling for twenty years. He and Parysatis had thirteen children together, although all but five died in infancy, perhaps caused by problematic recessive genes from the brother-sister marriage. The Greek historian Ctesias, who lived in the palace as the royal family's physician, portrayed Parysatis as a powerful woman and

Darius's chief counselor in political affairs. Queen Parysatis was astute in identifying and eliminating anyone presenting a threat to Darius's rule.

In ancient times, any time a new king ascended the throne, rival nations usually tested his strength. The same was true for the countries within the expansive Achaemenid Empire; they would frequently revolt even when a legitimate king was crowned. When Darius II took the throne by murdering his brother, who had murdered their only legitimate brother, the empire was initially reluctant to accept him as their rightful ruler.

Various provinces revolted, including the Egyptians under Amyrtaeus, who founded Egypt's Twenty-eighth Dynasty. (Amyrtaeus was its only pharaoh.) Egypt successfully drove the Persians out of the Nile Delta, which was a crucial grain source for the Achaemenid Empire and a vital trade center. Even Darius's full-blooded brother Arsites rebelled against him and allied with the Greeks. Darius bribed the Greeks to hand over Arsites, promising he would spare his life, but Queen Parysatis convinced him to throw him into the ashes to suffocate.

King Darius II's son Artaxerxes II married Stateira, the daughter of an important nobleman, and her brother Terituchmes married Darius's daughter Amestris. However, Terituchmes loved his beautiful half-sister Roxana, a warrior with excellent spear-throwing and archery skills. He wanted to marry his sister, but he was already married to the king's daughter, so he conspired with three hundred accomplices to murder Amestris and take over the empire.

King Darius got wind of the plot, so he arranged for his friend Udiastes to murder Terituchmes. Queen Parysatis ordered the execution of Roxana and the rest of Terituchmes's family, including all the women except her daughter-in-law Stateira. She spared Stateira because Artaxerxes II deeply loved her and pled for her life, but Darius warned Parysatis that she would later regret that decision.

While murder and mayhem rocked the royal family, affairs in Greece opened the door for the Persians' involvement. They were still nursing their all-consuming desire to thrash Athens. Everything hinged around the handsome, dazzling, and audacious General

Alcibiades, who was accused of defiling the sacred statues around Athens. Alcibiades escaped to Sparta to avoid a death sentence but soon wore out his welcome with Sparta's king Agis by having an affair with his wife.

Alcibiades next fled to Ionia, putting himself under the protection of the Persian satrap Tissaphernes. He masterminded a coup d'état in Athens that overthrew its democracy, replacing it with an oligarchy (ruling council) of four hundred men in 410 BCE. However, Athens' pro-democracy navy was moored in Samos in Ionia and refused to accept the new government. Unaware of his political machinations, the sailors appointed Alcibiades as their commander. He led the renegade navy in triumph over the Spartan-Persian fleet at the Hellespont in the Battle of Cyzicus.

The Persians' heads were spinning; wasn't Alcibiades their ally? More than anything else, Alcibiades was an opportunist; his only loyalty was to himself. Before the Achaemenid Empire knew what was happening, the victory in Ionia goaded the Athenians into kicking out the oligarchs and restoring democracy. They sailed across the Aegean and brought the Ionians back under the Athenian Empire's control. This was when Darius II stepped in, proving himself a formidable commander-in-chief.

As his father had done before him, Darius financially supported Sparta. He commissioned his Phoenicians to build warships to replenish the Spartan fleet while reconquering most of the Ionian city-states with his own fleet. This move was the final break of the Peace of Callias. Darius II's second son Cyrus (the Younger) struck a deal with General Lysander of Sparta during this campaign. He assisted Sparta against Athens, supporting Lysander with his revenues from Anatolia. Cyrus helped make Lysander ruler of a joint Greece in exchange for assistance in a planned coup against his older brother after his father's death.

Lysander and his two hundred ships that had been provided by Persia, as well as his Spartan navy, went up against the Athenians at the Hellespont in the Battle of Aegospotami in 405 BCE. The unsuspecting Athenians pulled their ships on shore to dry the hulls, which would get waterlogged after a time. They knew Lysander was nearby, but he had refused to engage in battle in two recent episodes, so they were not overly worried. However, Lysander suddenly attacked, killing three thousand sailors and capturing or destroying their fleet—only six ships escaped.

Lysander then sailed to Greece, laying siege to Athens until it surrendered. Persian interference instigated Greece's Peloponnesian War, but Persian interference brought it to an end, with Sparta the victor. The Athenians handed over their naval fleet and dismantled their empire. Lysander tore down Athens' fortification walls, and Sparta demanded an enormous tribute. Athens would not present a threat to the Achaemenid Empire until Philip II and his son Alexander the Great united Greece decades later.

Just as the Peloponnesian War ended, Darius II fell ill in Babylon. He died in 404 BCE, and his oldest son, Artaxerxes II, succeeded him. However, credible rumors emerged that Darius's second son, Cyrus the Younger, planned to kill Artaxerxes II and steal the throne. Cyrus was arrested, but his mother, Parysatis, staunchly defended her favorite son and got the charges dropped. Cyrus left for his satrapy of Lydia and Ionia until things cooled down in Persia. The rumors were true, of course. But Cyrus bided his time until Artaxerxes's guard was down and circumstances were ripe for his overthrow.

Cyrus the Younger assembled a large army of about twenty-three thousand men, including ten thousand Greek mercenaries and a Spartan contingent. Under the pretense of campaigning against the Pisidian tribe in the Taurus Mountains, he instead marched southeast before Artaxerxes II realized what was happening and assembled troops to meet him in Babylonia. When the forces lined up against each other, Cyrus's main objective was not to defeat the opposing side but to kill his brother. If Artaxerxes was dead, he could take the throne.

To that end, Cyrus ordered his Greek commander Clearchus to move his men into the center, opposite Artaxerxes. That went against the classic Greek phalanx formation, which placed the most potent forces on each side, especially the right flank. Fearing the Persians would outflank them, Clearchus ignored Cyrus's order. Left with only thin support in the center, Cyrus charged headlong toward his brother but was cut down before he could kill him.

Artaxerxes II was now the unchallenged king of the Achaemenid Empire.

Chapter 10: Artaxerxes II

"Some armistice!" Lysander hissed as he watched the massive Persian brigade arrive with their warhorses. "Three months, he said! I'll negotiate for Greek independence in Ionia, he said! Instead, he's doubled his armament."

The Persian satrap Tissaphernes swaggered over to Lysander and Sparta's king, Agesilaus. "King Agesilaus, I command you to leave Asia immediately or prepare for war!"

The Spartans scowled at Tissaphernes's duplicity. What chance did their scanty force of eight thousand men have? But King Agesilaus was undaunted, even cheerful. "Tissaphernes, I am indebted to you! By committing perjury, you have brought heaven's hostility down upon yourself. Now the gods will smile on us Greeks."

The struggle over the Ionian-Greek colonies began another chapter between Persia and Sparta as they segued from allies to enemies to allies once again. Artaxerxes II reigned for forty-five years, focusing on infrastructure and building projects along with his busy domestic life that included over three hundred concubines and more than one hundred sons. Plutarch said he even married one (or more) of his daughters, but the Greek historians loved to insert drama and scandal that may or may not have happened. Artaxerxes had to deal with yet another Egyptian revolt and a rebellion of his satrapies, and he couldn't resist inserting himself into Greece's ongoing conflicts.

This gold daric coin features Artaxerxes II.

Marie-Lan Nguyen / Wikimedia Commons;
https://commons.wikimedia.org/wiki/File:Double_daric_330-300_obverse_CdM_Paris.jpg

After Persia's ally Sparta pulverized Athens, Sparta took over where Athens left off as the ruling power over the Greek world. Lysander exchanged the democratic governments in the Greek city-states for oligarchies, each led by a Spartan military governor loyal to him. He was essentially building a personal empire. Athens revolted against Lysander's "Thirty Tyrants" oligarchy and lost. But King Pausanias of Sparta allowed Athens to resume its democracy, reining in Lysander's unchecked power play.

Artaxerxes's father Darius had allied with Sparta against Athens, conquering most of the Ionian city-states in 412 BCE, with Persia holding overlordship. Artaxerxes II now seethed with displeasure that Sparta had sent men to support Cyrus the Younger's failed coup d'état. What's worse, Sparta instigated a revolt of the Ionian Greeks against the Achaemenid Empire. Constant warfare had decimated Sparta's warriors, and only thirty could join the resistance fighters. But Sparta's new king Agesilaus and Lysander assembled an army of two thousand newly freed helots and six thousand Greeks from allied city-states.

Lysander was in his element when they arrived on the Ionian coast in 396 BCE. He had spent much of his military career there and appointed most of the Spartan leaders. Feeling patronized and overshadowed, King Agesilaus determined to leave Lysander in Ephesus, away from Sparta, once they concluded their campaign. In Ionia, the Persian governor Tissaphernes asked for a three-month ceasefire while he sent ambassadors to Artaxerxes II to negotiate the independence of the Ionian-Greek city-states.

Xenophon, an Athenian who signed up as a mercenary with Agesilaus, said the Spartan king agreed to the armistice. Despite knowing that Tissaphernes had double-crossed him by sending for reinforcements, he kept his end of the bargain. When Tissaphernes ordered the Spartan force to leave Asia immediately, Agesilaus confidently ordered his soldiers to prepare for battle and warned the Ionian Greeks in the area to be ready for war. He sent dispatches to the rest of the Greek city-states in Asia to send their regiments.

Expecting the Spartan forces to attack his headquarters in Caria, Tissaphernes transported his infantry to Caria and stationed his cavalry on the Meander River. But Agesilaus led his army in the opposite direction, raiding the region of Sardis and accumulating treasure. It took three days for Tissaphernes to realize that Agesilaus wasn't coming to Caria; he then marched on Sardis. This delay gave the Spartans time to set an ambush; they killed six hundred Persians, sending the rest fleeing.

An irritated Artaxerxes decapitated Tissaphernes, replacing him with his vizier Tithraustes, who offered new peace terms. Tithraustes said the Ionian city-states could have autonomous rule if they paid tribute to Artaxerxes. He gave Agesilaus thirty talents to leave the area. But then, Tithraustes bribed Thebes and Corinth, former Spartan allies that had grown disgruntled with Sparta's imperialistic control, to fight Sparta. Another Persian satrap, Pharnabazus, also visited Greece to bribe the city-states to launch a war on Sparta. The bribery worked, and the Corinthian War raged for eight years, keeping Sparta distracted from Ionia.

Thebes allied with Athens, and Sparta recalled Lysander from Asia. He was to bring allies from northern Greece on his way to meet King Pausanias of Sparta in southern Greece to lay siege to Haliartus, Thebes' sister city. Arriving first and unaware that Theban troops were nearby, Lysander attacked Haliartus without waiting for Pausanias. The Thebans counter-attacked from the rear, killing Lysander, and the Spartans fled with the Thebans hot on their heels. Pulling one of their favorite tactics by suddenly stopping and whirling around, the Spartans caught the Thebans by surprise and killed many of them. Nevertheless, they did not take Haliartus, and neither did Pausanias when he finally arrived.

The Spartans exiled King Pausanias for arriving late to the battle. His young son Agesipolis became co-king with Agesilaus, who the Spartans recalled from Ionia. As Agesilaus was marching back overland, his navy, commanded by his brother-in-law Peisander, sailed from Cnidus in southwestern Ionia on its way back to Greece. But his fleet was suddenly attacked by a Persian-Phoenician fleet commanded by Pharnabazus and an Athenian fleet commanded by General Conon.

The panicked Spartan fleet reversed course, running aground and abandoning their ships to flee, only to be cut down by their pursuers. The Persians and Athenians captured fifty ships and killed Peisander. This catastrophe spelled the end of Sparta's navy and its dominance over the other Greek city-states, which would soon be reclaimed by Athens. Conon and Pharnabazus sailed to southern Greece to raid the Peloponnese coast. Pharnabazus funded the rebuilding of Athens' long walls in gratitude for their aid to the Persian campaign.

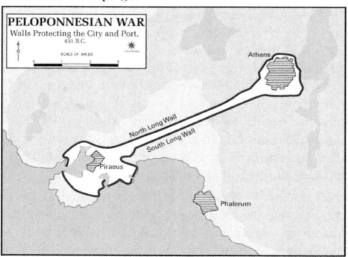

The walls surrounded Athens and extended seven miles to the port of Piraeus.
https://commons.wikimedia.org/wiki/File:Pelopennesian War, Walls Protecting the Ci ty, 431 B.C.,JPG

As King Agesilaus marched back to Sparta, a coalition of Athenians, Corinthians, Thebans, and other Greeks suddenly attacked. Both sides lined up in phalanx formations on the battlefield, but instead of steadily marching toward their adversaries, the Spartans ran at the coalition forces, which unnerved them so much they ran for the hills. Well, all except the Thebans, who circumnavigated the Spartan phalanx and pillaged their camp. The Spartans wheeled and charged the Thebans. Instead of running away, the Thebans tried to run *through* the Spartan phalanx to rejoin their allies. This suicidal mistake cost the lives of six hundred Thebans.

Through King Artaxerxes's influence, the Peace of Antalcidas ended the Corinthian War in 387 BCE. Persia was once again friendly with Sparta, abandoning its alliance with Athens. Athens was unwilling to come to the negotiating table, so the Spartans guarded the Dardanelles Strait, not permitting grain shipments to reach Athens until the city capitulated. Persia retained sovereignty over the Ionian-Greek city-states, and the rest of the Greek city-states regained autonomous rule. Artaxerxes guaranteed the treaty, promising to pour out his wrath on anyone breaking its terms.

The Nile Delta region of northern Egypt had revolted from Darius II, Artaxerxes's father, who failed to retake it. The year Darius died, Amyrtaeus, the leader of the Egyptian revolt, crowned himself pharaoh of Egypt. But while Artaxerxes was preparing a force to invade Egypt, he was distracted by his brother's attempted coup and then got involved with the Greek conflict. Once he brought the Greeks in line, Artaxerxes focused on Egypt.

Shortly after settling the Peace of Antalcidas, Artaxerxes II sent a campaign to Egypt. His satraps Tithraustes and Pharnabazus had served him well in the Greek conflict, so he sent them along with Abrocomas, the satrap of Syria, to bring Egypt back into the fold. Artaxerxes launched the campaign with 200,000 Persian troops, 500 ships, and 12,000 Greek mercenaries.

The Egyptian engineers set to work, blocking the Persians from sailing up the Nile and its tributaries by damming the rivers. They impeded the Persian infantry by flooding fields they needed to march across. Then, dissension broke about between Pharnabazus and the Greek mercenaries. Finally, the Nile flooded, and the

Egyptians doubled their resolve to defend their land.

After three years of brutal resistance from the intransigent Egyptians, the Persian force withdrew in disgrace. Egypt was now autonomous, ruled by several Egyptian dynasties until Artaxerxes II's son, Artaxerxes III, finally reconquered it. Not only did the Egyptians successfully fend off the Persians, but they also instigated rebellions in other satrapies of the Achaemenid Empire. Three successive pharaohs—Nectanebo I, Teos, and Nectanebo II—supported several satrapies in a breakaway attempt from the Achaemenid Empire.

In 372 BCE, the first satrap (governor) to revolt was Datames, who had once been Artaxerxes's bodyguard with distinguished service in battle. Artaxerxes appointed him as Cappadocia's satrap when his father, the previous satrap, died. He faithfully served Artaxerxes, who commissioned him to retake Egypt when Pharnabazus failed. However, Datames's enemies in the Persian court made him fear he would lose his position and probably even his life. Instead of invading Egypt, he retreated with his army to Cappadocia. Infuriated, Artaxerxes II ordered the neighboring satrapies, Lydia and Lycia, to snuff out the rebellion, but they could not overcome Datames's forces.

Ariobarzanes, the satrap of Phrygia, joined Datames in his rebellion in 366 BCE. Ariobarzanes, Pharnabazus's son, served as Phrygia's regent satrap. When his brother Artabazus attempted to claim his office, Ariobarzanes refused to give it up. Ariobarzanes received funding from King Agesilaus II of Sparta in his rebellion. Athens was also sympathetic to his cause. However, Ariobarzanes was crucified after his son, Mithridates, betrayed him to Artaxerxes.

Orontes I was the satrap of Armenia and son-in-law to Artaxerxes II, as he married his daughter Rhodogune. Artaxerxes was dissatisfied with a military expedition Orontes had led to Cyprus and dismissed him from Armenia's satrapy, sending him to Mysia in northwestern Turkey. Orontes gathered an army of mercenaries and linked up with Datames and Ariobarzanes but then betrayed them to Artaxerxes, expecting he would be exonerated and rewarded by his father-in-law.

Another rebel was Rheomithres, who joined the revolt in 362 BCE. He was sent by his cohorts to Egypt to request aid from

Pharaoh Teos (Tachos) of Egypt. He returned with fifty ships and five hundred talents. He was the hero of the insurgency until, like Orontes, he betrayed his fellow conspirators, chaining them and sending them off to Artaxerxes. Datames and many other rebels died in battle in 362 BCE, but Artaxerxes offered pardons to most who survived.

Meanwhile, Athens was experiencing a comeback in Greece after realizing how past misjudgments had nearly doomed the city. In 378 BCE, they launched the Second Athenian League, although it had significant differences from the first one. All of the city-state members got to keep local autonomy in a decentralized alliance. Athens encouraged democratic governments, and every city-state member had equal voting rights. This low-key approach began breaking Sparta's power.

Sparta disrupted Artaxerxes II's Peace of Antalcidas only five years after its enactment by imposing a Spartan garrison in Thebes in 382 BCE, as it was eager to quell Thebes' expanding dominion. Artaxerxes did not interfere at the time, probably because of his involvement in Egypt. General Pelopidas and other Theban government leaders escaped to Athens and plotted how to overthrow Sparta's hold. General Epaminondas stayed behind in Thebes, secretly training the city's young men in warfare.

Three years later, a dozen exiles, including Pelopidas, stealthily reentered Thebes and, with the help of the young men, killed the Spartan-appointed oligarchy and surrounded the Spartan fortress. The Spartans surrendered and left Thebes unharmed, but the move instigated a war between the two city-states. Sparta attacked the region three times in seven years. Thebes avoided major confrontations, employing guerilla tactics against Sparta. At the same time, Thebes' military leader Gorgidas trained the "Sacred Band," which consisted of three hundred full-time warriors, in military tactics, weaponry, and horseback skills.

Thebes decisively crushed Sparta's power over Greece at the epic Battle of Leuctra in 371 BCE. It almost ended in disaster for Thebes when the Spartans caught the city by surprise after a quick march north. By the time the Thebans realized the Spartans were coming, they barely had time to assemble to defend their city just seven miles away. The Spartans outnumbered the Theban infantry, but the Thebans implemented an innovative phalanx formation and routed the Spartans. This extraordinary and unanticipated victory elevated Thebes as Greece's new power.

Artaxerxes finally got involved by sending delegates to Delphi to form the Common Peace between Sparta and Thebes. However, negotiations fell through when Thebes refused to return Sparta's historical territory of Messenia, which lay between Thebes and the sea. Consequently, the Persian delegate Philicus, desiring a balance in power between Thebes, Sparta, and Athens, funded a new army for Sparta by recruiting two thousand mercenaries.

In 367 BCE, multiple Greek city-states sent emissaries to Artaxerxes II, attempting to gain his support. Artaxerxes advanced a new peace settlement in which Messenia would be independent and Athens had to give up its fleet. Nobody in Greece liked that idea except the Thebans. Sparta and Athens decided to support the rebel Persian satraps to destabilize the Achaemenid Empire, sending troops to help Ariobarzanes in Phrygia. Athens also sent military assistance to Pharaoh Teos in Egypt.

The aftermath of Artaxerxes II's bungled attempts to negotiate peace not only caused problems within his own empire, but Theban power also began to explode as they won multiple battles with their new phalanx maneuvers and fearsome long spears. They controlled large sections of the Peloponnese and invaded Macedonia, taking the king's son, Philip II, as a hostage. Little did they know the boy would learn their military tactics and then overpower them as an adult. Not only that, but he would also train his son, Alexander, who would one day conquer the Achaemenid Empire.

The queen mothers and chief wives of the Achaemenid kings exercised considerable influence over their sons and husbands. The king usually took his meals with one or the other, and Nehemiah, Artaxerxes I's cupbearers, mentioned the queen sitting next to her husband. The prominent royal women weren't hidden away in a harem somewhere but were active in court life. Several historians spoke of the royal women accompanying the Persian kings in military campaigns. Later in history, Alexander the Great captured King Darius III's mother, wife, and daughters at his camp adjacent to the battlefield.

Artaxerxes II's strong-willed mother, Parysatis, had been his father's chief advisor, and she continued to influence Artaxerxes, which put her into a rivalry with his beloved wife, Stateira. Stateira interacted with the ordinary people, making her popular with the empire's citizens. Bitterly jealous, Parysatis encouraged Artaxerxes to take many concubines and never missed a chance to insult Stateira. Finally, she murdered Stateira by smearing poison on one side of a knife and cutting a small roasted bird in half. She offered Stateira the side the poison touched while eating the other half. Artaxerxes couldn't punish his powerful mother, but he tortured her eunuchs and executed the servant who assisted her in the murder.

Artaxerxes II avidly engaged in building projects around the empire, especially in Persia. He restored the exquisite palace in Susa that Darius I erected and rebuilt Susa's fortifications. In the city of Ecbatana in Media, he built a new A*padana*, his grand audience hall, which featured enchanting columns supporting a roof but with three of its four sides open; it was a sort of elaborate veranda. He also decorated Ecbatana with charming sculptures. He built numerous temples to the goddess Anahita throughout the empire and, typical of the Persian kings, built his own tomb in Persepolis. It featured a bas-relief of himself and representatives from all the ethnicities of his far-flung empire.

This portrayal of Persepolis's Apadana may have mirrored Ecbatana's.
https://commons.wikimedia.org/wiki/File:Persepolis_Reconstruction_Apadana_Chipiez.jpg

According to Plutarch, Artaxerxes wanted to settle the matter of succession before his death so his heir wouldn't suffer the attempted coup that he did from his brother Cyrus.[33] His oldest son by his queen was Darius, but his younger son, Ochus, schemed to get his father's appointment as crown prince. He courted his half-sister Atossa, Artaxerxes's favorite daughter, thinking his father would want her to be the next queen. But Artaxerxes proclaimed his fifty-year-old son Darius as his heir to the throne.

But then Darius asked his father for Aspasia's hand in marriage; she had been Cyrus the Younger's consort. Finding this improper, Artaxerxes appointed Aspasia as a priestess to Anahita, which meant she had to be sexually chaste for the rest of her life. Distraught, Darius fell in with some conspirators who plotted to assassinate Artaxerxes in his bed. Learning of the plot, the king escaped by slipping into a hidden room behind his bed. He ordered Darius beheaded.

With Darius dead, Ochus's hopes of becoming crown prince had been renewed, but he still had two rivals. Ariaspes was Queen Stateira's only remaining son, and Arsames was the son of a concubine but his father's favorite. Ochus deceived Ariaspes into believing his father was planning to kill him, and in despair, he committed suicide. Artaxerxes wept for Ariaspes and suspected Ochus but couldn't prove it. Ochus then killed Arsames, and Artaxerxes II, who was already near to death, died of grief in 358 BCE.

---

[33] Plutarch, *The Parallel Lives: The Life of Artaxerxes* (The Loeb Classical Library edition)
https://penelope.uchicago.edu/Thayer/E/Roman/Texts/Plutarch/Lives/Artaxerxes*.html

Chapter 11: Artaxerxes III and the Second Conquest of Egypt

After eliminating the top contenders in his gory path to the throne, Ochus took the crown in 358 BCE, with the throne name Artaxerxes III. The Macedonian historian Polyaenus said Ochus colluded with the palace eunuchs, stewards, and guards to keep his father's death a secret for ten months while consolidating his rule. Meanwhile, he forged letters, supposedly from his father, naming Ochus as the heir. Once Ochus's subjects acknowledged him as king, he announced Artaxerxes II's death and pronounced a period of mourning. Yet, he still had over one hundred brothers who could challenge him. According to the Roman historian Justin, he massacred most of the royal males—eighty in one day. He even killed some of his sisters.

One year before this bloodbath, Philip II ascended the throne of Macedonia, a sprawling country north of Greek with little significance or power. In turmoil from a succession of assassinations within the royal family, it faced extinction from its strong and warlike neighbors. Philip spent his adolescence as a hostage in Thebes, then returned to Macedonia, highly trained in tactical skills and ready to teach new battle strategies to his military.

He introduced his deadly new weapon, the sarissa: a huge spear up to twenty feet long and weighing over twelve pounds. Philip used the sarissas in his terrifying new phalanx formation. Training his army was the first step in his jaw-dropping plan of swallowing up all of Greece. But that was only the beginning of his ambitions. His ultimate goal was to use a massive Greek coalition army to overpower the Achaemenid Empire and become its next king. Could Artaxerxes III (Ochus) withstand the challenge?

Plutarch said of Artaxerxes III, "In cruelty and blood-guiltiness, he surpassed all." The ancient accounts of Artaxerxes III agree that he was evil personified. However, the modern historian Leo Mildenberg argued that Artaxerxes III was the victim of bad press in ancient times. He pointed out that Artaxerxes III was a relatively benign ruler once he cemented his succession. The high-energy Artaxerxes III strengthened the empire, recouping its one-time prestige and power. Art, architecture, and coinage flourished during his reign in a cultural renaissance accompanied by economic prosperity.[34]

Artaxerxes Ochus brought renewed confidence and solidity to the empire, engendering increased local commerce and foreign trade. Greece's economy flagged during his reign, while Achaemenid trade in the western Aegean and Mediterranean Seas thrived. The Athenian orator Isocrates vehemently urged Philip II to invade the Achaemenid Empire, moaning, "The barbarians are faring better than the Greeks." (The Greeks called anyone who didn't speak Greek *bárbaros* or "babbler.")

Artaxerxes III governed his far-reaching empire as a confederation with a central authority. He strengthened the position of the satraps over their provinces almost to the point of political autonomy. A positive attribute was his ability to generate mutual trust with his satraps, which helped maintain stability within the empire. However, he did face several rebellions, and the first rebel was Artabazus, the satrap of Phrygia.

Artabazus's older half-brother Ariobarzanes had rebelled against Artaxerxes II, who executed him by crucifixion. The brothers were the sons of Pharnabazus II, whose second wife, Apame, was

---

[34] Leo Mildenberg, "Artaxerxes III Ochus (358 – 338 B.C.): A Note on the Maligned King," *Zeitschrift Des Deutschen Palästina-Vereins (1953-)* 115, no. 2 (1999): 201–27. http://www.jstor.org/stable/27931620.

Artaxerxes II's daughter, making Artabazus the king's grandson. Artabazus became Phrygia's satrap, but King Artaxerxes III, his uncle, wanted him dead. Artabazus had descended from Darius the Great on his father's side. With Princess Apame as his mother, Artaxerxes considered him a rival to the throne.

Realizing his peril, Artabazus preemptively rebelled with help from an army of Athenian mercenaries and partnered with Memnon and Mentor of Rhodes, his wife's brothers. Artabazus's daughter Barsine married her uncle Mentor; after he died, she married Memnon. With his Greek allies, Artabazus won a stunning victory in Phrygia against three neighboring satraps in 355 BCE, which the Greeks jubilantly labeled "a second Marathon."

Sputtering in rage, Artaxerxes Ochus demanded Athens pull their support from Artabazus. Fearing Persia's reprisal, Athens gave in, so Artabazus desperately recruited a Theban army of five thousand men, which triumphed again against Artaxerxes's forces. Artaxerxes III then resorted to bribing Artabazus's mercenaries and finally captured him. But Memnon and Mentor continued fighting on Artabazus's behalf and managed to free him.

Artabazus fled to Macedonia with Memnon and his large family. Philip II welcomed them graciously, and Artabazus became friends with his son Alexander (the Great). They stayed in Macedonia for almost a decade, and several historians recorded that Artabazus's daughter Barsine became Alexander's wife or mistress. The first was unlikely, as she was married to Mentor. Still, she may have been Alexander's mistress when Mentor was in Egypt, fighting as a mercenary for Pharaoh Nectanebo II. After she returned to Asia, Alexander later invaded. He captured her along with King Darius III's family, so she might have become his paramour then.

Nectanebo sent Mentor with four thousand mercenaries to fight for the Phoenician city of Sidon, which had revolted against Artaxerxes III. Mentor was an exceptionally skilled general who initially scored several victories until the Persians captured him in 346 BCE. Artaxerxes Ochus assessed the situation: he could kill the rebel or take advantage of his expertise. Artaxerxes offered Mentor clemency, then sent him back to Egypt to fight on the Persian side.

Mentor's sensational victories in Egypt brought about the pardons of his brother Memnon and his father-in-law Artabazus. Both men returned to Asia in 342 BCE, informing Artaxerxes III of Philip II's schemes to invade the Persian Empire. Twelve years later, Artabazus and his sons fought against the Macedonian-Greek invasion. After losing, Artabazus surrendered to his old friend Alexander, who made him an advisor and the satrap of Bactria.

Mildenberg noted Artaxerxes Ochus's graciousness toward Artabazus. "Ochus had to clean up after his father and deal with the rebellious attempts in the fifties. The few Persian rebels involved fled abroad or sought pardon at Susa after their complete failure. No revenge whatsoever was taken by Ochus, especially not against Artabazus, but modern historians still seem to take his generosity for granted."[35]

Artaxerxes Ochus's father's attempt to reconquer Egypt had ended in shameful failure, but he was determined to prevail. Diodorus said he was "unwarlike," so he likely stayed home but sent his generals to lead a military campaign into Egypt in 351 BCE, confronting Pharaoh Nectanebo II. But the pharaoh had heavy support from Greek mercenaries, and the Persian forces were inexperienced and overly cautious. The Achaemenid forces suffered a brutal loss after a year of war and retreated. Nevertheless, an unabated resolve to retake Egypt drove Artaxerxes, especially since his initial failure sparked contempt in the Phoenicians and Cypriots, leading to new revolts.[36]

On Lebanon's Phoenician coast laid Sidon, one of the world's oldest cities. It has been continuously inhabited since 4000 BCE. Fantastically rich from its sea trade, Sidon was also renowned for its glass manufacturing since at least the 8th century BCE, as well as purple dye made from the Murex trunculus sea snail. When Phoenicia fell to Persia, Sidon became the region's Achaemenid seat of government and military headquarters. The Sidonians grew

---

[35] Mildenberg, "Artaxerxes III Ochus," 212.

[36] Diodorus Siculus, *Library of History*, Volume II: Book XVI, Loeb Classical Library Edition. https://penelope.uchicago.edu/Thayer/E/Roman/Texts/Diodorus_Siculus/16C*.html.

increasingly irritated by the Persians' superiority complex and led the rest of the Phoenicians in a campaign for independence.

The Phoenicians allied with Pharaoh Nectanebo of Egypt against their common enemy of Persia. As maritime nations, both Egypt and Phoenicia had many ships for a coalition navy, and the Egyptians provided four thousand Greek mercenaries led by Mentor. Their hostilities against the Persians began by cutting down the royal park the Persian kings used in Phoenicia. They burned the horse fodder stores maintained for Persian wars and arrested the insolent Persian aristocrats who had made their lives miserable.

Fuming at the new insurgency in Phoenicia, Artaxerxes Ochus prepared for war, but this time, he would lead his men. He assembled 300,000 infantrymen, 30,000 cavalry, 300 warships, and 500 supply ships along with food, weapons, and siege engines. Typically, the Persian kings used the Phoenicians and Egyptians to man their warships, but in this case, he was fighting both countries, so he depended on Greek mercenaries. While Artaxerxes III was marching from Babylon to Phoenicia, the Persian satraps of Syria and Cilicia led their joint armies in the first attack on Phoenicia. General Mentor soundly defeated them and drove them out.

Meanwhile, inspired by Egypt and Phoenicia, the nine cities of the large island of Cyprus off Lebanon's coast declared themselves independent of Persia. Outraged, Artaxerxes asked Idrieus, ruler of Caria on Turkey's southwestern coast, to sail his infantry and cavalry to Cyprus. Idrieus sent forty triremes and eight thousand soldiers to Cyprus, which were commanded by Phocion of Athens and the deposed king Evagoras II, whose family had ruled Cyprus since the fall of Troy. Phocion and Evagoras collected so many spoils of war in their initial assault on the affluent island that the Syrian and Cilician troops rushed over to help fight and collect booty for themselves. This doubled the size of the Persian forces on the island, triggering panic among the Cypriot kings. All of them surrendered to Persia except the ruler of Salamis.

When Artaxerxes III arrived in Phoenicia with his mammoth army, Sidon's ruler Tennes realized his men couldn't possibly defeat the Persians. He struck a secret deal with Ochus: he would give Sidon over and fight with Artaxerxes against Egypt, where he knew the best harbors. Tennes left Sidon with five hundred soldiers and one hundred of the city's elite, who thought they were going to meet with the other Phoenician leaders.

Instead, Tennes handed the leading citizens to Artaxerxes, who executed them for instigating the insurgency. At this point, five hundred more of the Sidonian nobility, unaware of Tennes's duplicity, approached Artaxerxes waving olive branches to signify peace. Artaxerxes called Tennes over, saying, "Accepting the surrender of the Sidonians is not good enough for me. I need to strike terror into the rest of the empire, so no one else will revolt. My goal is to crush Sidon utterly. Make that happen!"

Artaxerxes Ochus commanded his archers to shoot the five hundred Sidonians waving olive branches. Meanwhile, Tennes plotted with Artaxerxes's Greek mercenaries to lead the king's forces inside the city, revealing how to get in. Tennes's double-dealing ended in his execution, as Artaxerxes didn't need him anymore. While awaiting the Persian assault, the Sidonian citizens burned their ships to prevent anyone from sneaking away instead of fighting.

But when they saw King Artaxerxes and his men had gotten inside the walls and were swarming the streets, they gave up all hope. After gathering their families and servants in their homes, the Sidonians barred their doors and burned down their houses. Forty thousand perished in the immolation, and much gold and silver melted in the flames. The other Phoenician cities immediately surrendered to Artaxerxes.[37]

Immediately after obliterating Sidon, Artaxerxes deployed his forces to Egypt with his Greek allies from Argos, Ionia, and Thebes. Artaxerxes believed he and his father had erred in not accompanying their generals in their failed attempts to retake Egypt. His father had a laissez-faire approach to the antagonism between his generals, and Artaxerxes felt his own generals lacked confidence and tactical skills. This time, he was a hands-on commander, one in firm control of his officers. Artaxerxes's leading general was his best friend and vizier, the eunuch Bagoas,

---

[37] Diodorus Siculus, *Library of History*, Volume II: Book XVI.

who would later murder him and most of his family.

While passing through the Sinai Peninsula, the army had to navigate the bogs of Barathra, losing many men to quicksand. The wind would blow the sand from the surrounding desert dunes over the surface of the deep swamp. The bogs appeared to be part of the desert until one stepped in and sank beneath the surface, unable to swim in the thick mire. After crossing the marsh, the men arrived at the city of Pelusium, where one of the Nile tributaries empties into the Mediterranean. It was the same city that Cambyses previously defeated with cats, dogs, ibis, and rams.

Pharaoh Nectanebo had fortified Pelusium with twenty thousand Spartan mercenaries, twenty thousand Libyans, sixty thousand Egyptians of the warrior caste, and countless warships that moored in the river. On the first day, the Persians' Theban allies rushed recklessly toward the city to prove they were better warriors than the Spartans. That day's battle was an inconclusive contest between the two Greek factions.

Despite having a formidable defense, Pharaoh Nectanebo II's overconfidence spelled his doom. He had always beaten Persia before, and he fully expected to this time. He refused to share the command with his highly experienced Athenian and Spartan generals. That night, the Persian Argive general crossed the river by boat, led by Egyptians whose families were held hostage by the Persians. He entered a secret canal and engaged in battle at the foot of the city walls, killing over five thousand of the Egyptian forces.

Aghast, Pharaoh Nectanebo fled south to the capital city of Memphis. The Persians then took Pelusium with their old trick of diverting the river until it was dry, then bringing siege engines right up to the walls. When the catapults broke the walls, the Greek mercenaries quickly repaired them with wood. This went on for several days until the Greeks realized that Nectanebo and the Egyptians had abandoned the city. They surrendered, and Artaxerxes allowed them to return to Greece with whatever of Pelusium's plunder they could carry on their backs.[38]

---

[38] Diodorus Siculus, *Library of History*, Volume II: Book XVI.

General Mentor and Bagoas conquered one Egyptian city after another, tearing down their walls and plundering the temples; the sacrilege instigated great hatred toward the Persians. Several decades later, the Egyptians welcomed Alexander the Great as their deliverer from Persia. Nectanebo II fled to Ethiopia with his family and as many possessions as he could carry. The stunning victory brought control of Egypt's trade ports and grain supply, leading to substantial economic growth in Persia.

This coin depicts Artaxerxes III as Egypt's pharaoh.
Classical Numismatic Group, Inc. http://www.cngcoins.com, CC BY-SA 3.0
<http://creativecommons.org/licenses/by-sa/3.0/>, via Wikimedia Commons;
https://commons.wikimedia.org/wiki/File:Artaxerxes_III_as_Pharao.jpg

In 340 BCE, the Achaemenid Empire experienced its first encounter with Macedonia when the two powers clashed in Thrace. Multiple tribes had ruled divisions of Thrace until it came under the control of the Achaemenid Empire under Darius the Great. After the Greeks expelled the Persians from Thrace, it was divided into four kingdoms. But now, King Philip II of Macedonia was conquering cities and setting up Macedonian garrisons in Thrace.

King Cersobleptes ruled Odrysian, the largest Thracian kingdom. He had been attempting to unite Thrace, which brought him into competition with Philip II. He lost a battle to Philip in

352 BCE and had to send his son as a hostage to Macedonia. Now, the Thracians were fending off another attack by Philip II of Macedonia at Perinthus, a strategic city on the Sea of Marmora, just west of the Hellespont. Artaxerxes had initially formed a treaty of friendship with Philip, but he was alarmed by Macedonian conquests so close to Persian territory and sent forces to aid Thrace.

The Achaemenid satraps successfully repulsed Philip II from the city of Perinthus; nevertheless, Artaxerxes's response uncharacteristically lacked tenacity. When Philip retreated, Artaxerxes Ochus did not pursue him, nor did he attempt to retake Thrace, which served as a buffer zone between Macedonia and the Achaemenid Empire's territories. His generals had proven that they could mobilize their forces quickly, so he seemed overconfident. Underestimating the menace that Macedonia was becoming, Artaxerxes's lackluster campaign allowed developments that later proved lethal to his successor Darius III and doomed the Achaemenid Empire.

After Artaxerxes's stellar success in retaking Egypt and snuffing out insurrections in Sidon, Asia Minor, and Cyprus, he enjoyed a stable and prosperous empire. It all came crashing down when Bagoas poisoned him. The historian Diodorus described Bagoas as grasping and treacherous, and indeed he was, but he was Artaxerxes III's closest friend. Artaxerxes admired Bagoas for his audaciousness and trusted him implicitly. He had appointed Bagoas vizier, making him second in the kingdom. But Bagoas morphed into a power-hungry megalomaniac.

Artaxerxes Ochus III's death from poisoning brought his son Arses (Artaxerxes IV) to the throne. Arses had older brothers, but Bagoas orchestrated events to crown him, expecting he could easily manipulate the youth and rule through him. During the two years of Artaxerxes Arses IV's reign, King Philip II of Macedonia completed his conquest of all of Greece in preparation to invade the Persian Empire.

Restless under the thumb of Bagoas, King Arses tried but failed to poison him and was, in turn, poisoned by Bagoas. Artaxerxes III had wiped out most of the royal males at the beginning of his reign. Bagoas poisoned all the remaining heirs, leaving no males alive in the direct line of Artaxerxes III.

Finally, Bagoas brought a young man he identified as the great-grandson of Darius II to the throne. But Darius III turned out to be too headstrong and savvy for Bagoas's liking. Time for another poisoning! But Darius wasn't going to be another one of Bagoas's victims. Suspecting murder was afoot, Darius handed his cup to Bagoas. "Drink a toast to me!"

Bagoas stared at the red wine in the golden goblet, desperately trying to think of a way of escape. But there was none. He lifted his head and raised the cup. "To the victor!"

As Darius's attendants carried Bagoas's dead body out of the room, he leaned back on his throne. He could now concentrate on ruling the empire and facing its greatest challenge: Macedonia.

Chapter 12: Darius III and Alexander the Great

In Babylon, two centuries earlier, Daniel the Seer had a vision where he was in Elam, at the river by Susa. He looked up to see a ram with two long horns, one longer than the other, although the longer horn had begun growing later than the shorter horn. The ram butted everything out of his way to the west, north, and south, and no one could stand against him. He did as he pleased and became very great.

Suddenly, a shaggy male goat with one enormous horn between its eyes appeared from the west, crossing the land so swiftly that he didn't even touch the ground. He charged in a rage at the two-horned ram, striking him and breaking off both his horns. Now the ram was helpless, and the shaggy goat knocked him down and trampled him. The shaggy goat grew increasingly powerful, but his large horn was broken off at the height of his power. Four prominent horns grew in its place.

As Daniel attempted to understand the vision, the angel Gabriel appeared. Terrified, Daniel fell with his face to the ground, but Gabriel helped him to his feet. "Son of man, the two-horned ram represents the kings of Media and Persia. The shaggy male goat represents the king of Greece, and the large horn between his eyes represents the first king of the Greek Empire. The four prominent horns that replaced the one large horn show that the Greek

Empire will break into four kingdoms, but none as great as the first."[39]

Now, it was 336 BCE, and Darius III paced back and forth on his balcony with a furrowed brow. He'd ruled the satrapy of Armenia, which had been awarded by Artaxerxes III for valor in battle, but he never imagined being king of the entire Achaemenid Empire. And what was he going to do about Philip II?

While Bagoas had been murdering the Achaemenid royalty, Philip of Macedonia conquered all of Greece except Sparta. The Greek city-states united under the League of Corinth, and with Philip II as their commander-in-chief, they declared war on the Achaemenid Empire. To them, it was a sacred war, punishment for the Persians desecrating and burning Athens' temples over a century earlier.

Philip's years of scheming and arduous work had come to fruition. Everything was in place to lead a mammoth Greek force into Persia. Philip had just sent an advance force of ten thousand Macedonian soldiers across the Hellespont into Asia. They had already taken the coastal cities from Troy to Miletus. Darius wiped the sweat off his forehead. Could he stop Philip?

Just then, Darius's vizier rushed in. "Sire!" he panted. "I have astounding news! Philip II is dead!"

"What? Dead? What happened?" Darius swung around, incredulous.

"Murder, sire! His jilted lover stabbed him to death!"

Darius laughed. "My nemesis was killed by a woman?"

"No, sire, his bodyguard. Philip was throwing a wedding for his daughter, and his bodyguard suddenly pulled out his dagger and stabbed him!"

"I can't believe my good fortune!" Darius exclaimed. "So, what does this mean? Is Alexander the king now?"

"Yes! And I believe the Macedonian threat is eliminated! Philip's army is confined to a small beachhead near Abydos. Who knows if the young Alexander wants to renew Philip's quest? And

---

[39] Daniel 8. Tanakh: Ketuvim: Book of Daniel.

if he does, could he? He's only twenty, and I doubt he can hold the Greeks together with his father dead. I've heard Athens, Thebes, and Thessaly have already pulled out of the League of Corinth, and Thrace has revolted."

Darius III might not have been so gleeful had he known more about Alexander. Yes, Alexander was only twenty, but the great philosopher Aristotle tutored him in his childhood, and his father, Philip II, schooled him on the battlefield through his teenage years. At age eighteen, Alexander scored an epic victory with his father against Athens and Thebes in the Battle of Chaeronea. He was already a brilliant general and a savvy statesman by the time he took the throne. He was even poised to lead his father's campaign against the Achaemenid Empire. But he first had to rein Greece back in.

Bringing Greece back in line took almost two years. First, the southern Greek states capitulated, apologizing for their defiance. Then, Alexander tamed the northern states, but Athens and Thebes revolted again while that was happening. Alexander leveled Thebes, enslaving its citizens, which influenced Athens to surrender. Once again, all of Greece except Sparta was united under one leader: Alexander. With over fifty thousand men and six thousand warhorses, Alexander marched toward the Hellespont with his canny veteran General Parmenion, crossing into Ionia in 334 BCE. Meanwhile, his fleet of 120 warships carrying a navy of 38,000 crossed the Aegean Sea.

Darius III stayed home in his palace in Persepolis, Persia, assuming that Alexander would only attack Ionia. Undoubtedly, his shrewd, battle-seasoned satraps could run the Greeks off. Darius never imagined that Alexander had set his sights on the entire Achaemenid Empire. But one of his generals, Memnon of Rhodes, knew better. Decades earlier, he had fled to Macedonia with his brother-in-law Artabazus when their revolt in Phrygia against Artaxerxes II had failed. He knew Philip II and Alexander personally, and he knew their plans and the Macedonian-Greek military's capabilities.

Memnon had already fought against Philip II's earlier advance forces that were sent to Ionia in 336 BCE. After Philip's murder, Memnon had defeated the demoralized Macedonians near the

Maeander River, hounding them back to Europe. Now, as he and the Persian satraps tracked Alexander's approach, he urged a scorched earth strategy. "Burn the fields, cut down the fruit trees, remove all supplies, and move everyone to the interior. If he's unable to feed his army, he'll be forced to leave. And send word to King Darius to get the Spartans to start attacking the other Greek cities so Alexander's forces will pull out and go home to defend their cities."

But the Persian satraps didn't entirely trust Memnon; after all, he was ethnically Greek. "Why would we destroy our own food sources and supplies? If we run away, we'll look spineless, which will spur the Greeks on. No, we'll march out to meet him at the River Granicus."

The Persian forces lined up on the high ridge on the eastern banks of the Granicus, awaiting the Macedonian-Greek forces. Alexander's men would have to wade through the water and climb up the ridge to engage with the Persians. The Persians had the advantage of being uphill, sending volleys of arrows that darkened the sun. They watched Alexander's army arrive, but it was late afternoon, so they didn't expect him to forge the river until morning.

Instead, Alexander's forces quickly moved into formation: cavalry on the flanks with the infantry in the center in the lethal Macedonian phalanx formation. His Bulgarian javelin-throwers, elite infantry, and archers were also on the right side. Suddenly, the cavalry charged across the river and up the bank. As the Persians engaged with the warhorses coming up the ridge, the rest of the army plunged into the river and waded across, fending off a hail of javelins and arrows.

Charles le Brun's portrayal of Spithridates's rear attack on Alexander.

Reaching the top of the ridge, Alexander immediately impaled Darius's son-in-law Mithridates in the face with his javelin. Spithridates, the Persian satrap of Ionia and Lydia, came up behind Alexander and levied a blow to his head with his battle-ax. His helmet split in two, but astoundingly, Alexander was uninjured. Spithridates raised his arm to strike again, but just then, Alexander's bosom friend Cleitus the Black ran Spithridates through with his spear.

The Greek infantry had made it across the river and charged up the hill with their lethal eighteen-foot sarissas. Already unnerved, the Persian cavalry fled to Halicarnassus while the Greeks decimated the Persian infantry in the center. In the aftermath of the Persians' appalling loss, most of the Ionian city-states under Persian control quickly surrendered, except Miletus and Halicarnassus, which were important Persian naval bases.

Alexander successfully laid siege to the two harbors, crippling the Persian navy.

Finally spurred to fight Alexander in person, Darius III led his colossal army out as Alexander approached Cilicia on the Mediterranean coast. Darius caught Alexander by surprise, coming up on his rear on the narrow coastal plain between the Gulf of Issus and the Nur Mountains. Alexander wheeled his forces around to confront Darius. His units quickly assumed the same formation they used at Granicus: the Macedonian phalanx in the middle, General Parmenion and the Greek cavalry on the left, and Alexander's cavalry and elite infantry on the right flank.

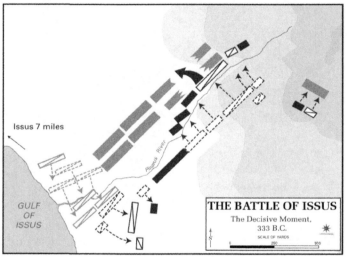

In the Battle of Issus, Alexander crossed the Pinarus River from the south.
https://commons.wikimedia.org/wiki/File:Battle_issus_decisive.png

The Persians lined up north of the Pinarus River, with their heavy cavalry on the right, next to the sea, and Darius with his Greek mercenary infantry in a phalanx position in the middle. His Persian infantry lined up on the left all the way into the foothills, some crossing the river and coming up on the Macedonian right flank. The Persian cavalry led the charge across the river, meeting General Parmenion's Greek cavalry.

While the two cavalries clashed on the beach, Alexander's right-flank cavalry plunged into the river at full speed, up the opposite bank and right between the Persians' infantry, breaking the lines. Meanwhile, the river's depth and strong current hindered

Alexander's Greek infantry with their heavy sarissas and armor. The Greek mercenaries on the north bank forced them into a temporary retreat.

But Alexander's cavalry charge disrupted the Persian infantry and enabled the right-flank elite Macedonian infantry led by Alexander on foot to cross the river without challenge. They also broke through the Persian line. Alexander then jumped on a horse and led his Companions (the Macedonian cavalry) in a charge at King Darius and his bodyguards. Shaking in terror, Darius wheeled his chariot and fled the field with his bodyguards.

At this point, Alexander realized Parmenion's cavalry and his center infantry were in desperate straits. Instead of chasing Darius, he shattered the Persian infantry from the rear, receiving a sword thrust to his thigh. At the same time, Parmenion doggedly resisted the Persian cavalry. Finally, the Persian forces caught on that King Darius had fled the scene. They paused briefly, glanced at the bristling Macedonian sarissas, and ran for the mountains with Alexander's forces at their heels.

The Battle of Issus was another crushing loss for the Achaemenid Empire. The people were demoralized over Darius abandoning his military mid-battle. What's worse, he left his women-folk behind. Alexander captured the Persian queen mother, the queen, and Darius's two daughters, who had accompanied the king on his campaign. He treated the royal women and girls kindly, later marrying Stateira II, one of the daughters.

In 332 BCE, Alexander worked his way down the Mediterranean coast. All the Phoenician cities except Tyre surrendered, completely incapacitating Persia's naval presence in the Mediterranean. Ancient Tyre resisted for seven months until Alexander's fire ships and siege towers brought it to its knees. He massacred all the able-bodied men and enslaved the women and children. While Alexander was in Phoenicia, he received a letter from King Darius offering peace terms: "I will give you my friendship, my daughter in marriage, a large payment for returning my women, and all of Ionia."

Alexander turned down the offer and continued to Gaza. His engineers told him they could not use their siege engines at Gaza because the city sat on a high hill. But Alexander refused to accept their prognosis.

Since the city, which was on a hill, was too high to hit the walls with their siege engine missiles, they built a slope next to it, rolled their siege engines up, and demolished Gaza's walls. Alexander was wounded again by a high-velocity arrow that pierced his shoulder through his shield. Alexander then entered Egypt, hailed as the conquering deliverer from Persia's oppression. Even the Persian satrap bowed to him and handed the treasury over.

King Darius wrote another letter to Alexander, offering even more magnanimous peace terms. "I give you half of my empire, my daughter in marriage, and a fortune in gold."

Alexander snorted. "I've already acquired a fortune from the cities I've conquered. I have both your daughters, and I want all the Achaemenid Empire, not half!"

The breakdown in peace negotiations led to the Battle of Gaugamela in today's northern Iraq. Darius arrived at the battle with double the men Alexander had, war elephants from India, and chariots with blades extending from the wheels. The Greeks and Macedonians had never faced off against elephants, nor did they have much experience with chariots. Still, they possessed more training and battle experience than the Persian forces.

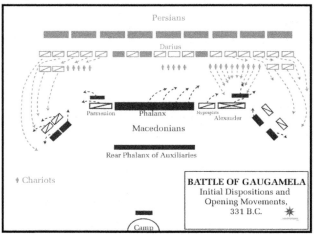

Darius attacked Alexander's right and left flanks in the opening of the Battle of Gaugamela, while Alexander focused on attacking the Persian center and left flank.
https://commons.wikimedia.org/wiki/File:Battle_of_Gaugamela,_331_BC_-_Opening_movements.png

King Darius again positioned himself in the center with his infantry. His cavalry from Ionia, India, Mesopotamia, Media, and Anatolia was on his left flank, accompanied by Greek mercenaries and the highly trained Immortals infantry. His left side held his cavalry from Bactria, Scythia, and other Central Asian tribes. Alexander used the same lineup he'd used all along. He rode with his Macedonian cavalry on the right flank, his infantry in the center, and Parmenion on the left side with the Greek and Thracian cavalries.

While Parmenion held the left flank steady as the Asian cavalry charged, Alexander's infantry marched forward in the middle in an ever-widening fanned-shaped phalanx position. Meanwhile, Alexander led his cavalry off to the far right to draw out Darius's left flank, which would leave the Persians' center exposed. His ploy worked. The Persians' middle line thinned, allowing the Greek infantry to penetrate it as the fierce Scythian cavalry charged his right flank in a vicious confrontation. The Scythians would have overpowered the Macedonians, but the Bulgarian javelin-throwers helped defeat them.

Darius then sent out his chariots with their blades sticking out from the wheels that could cut a man or horse off at the knee. But the Greeks and Macedonians simply stepped aside, opening a way for the chariots to pass through, then attacked the chariots from the rear. At this point, most of the warriors on both sides were engaged in hand-to-hand combat, but faced with the bristling Macedonian sarissas, Darius once again turned and raced off the battlefield.

Darius III fled the field (again), as portrayed in this ivory carving.

Similar to the Battle of Issus, Alexander raced to assist Parmenion's left flank, losing sixty of his elite Macedonian cavalrymen in the brutal conflict. Once Alexander's forces decisively won the battle, General Parmenion collected the loot, including the elephants that apparently weren't used in the fight. Meanwhile, Alexander pursued Darius, but he managed to slip away to the east. So, Alexander marched his troops into Babylon, where the people hailed him with great fanfare as the new king of Persia. Alexander made Babylon his headquarters for the rest of his short life.

King Darius escaped to Ecbatana with the remnants of his royal guard. He later met up with his Bactrian cavalry, two thousand Greek mercenaries, and General Bessus, the satrap of Bactria. Darius planned to recoup, gather a new army, and confront Alexander again. He decided to relocate to the flat plains of Bactria, where he could better use his cavalry in battle than in Media's mountains.

But his men began drifting away, fearful of another attack by Alexander before they had built up their forces. Finally, Bessus staged a coup, tied up Darius, and tossed him into an oxcart, just as Alexander arrived for a surprise attack. Bessus and his men impaled Darius with their javelins and raced off, leaving the Macedonians to find Darius bleeding out on the side of the road. Alexander had hoped to capture Darius alive. He sadly removed the signet ring from the last Persian king of the Achaemenid Empire and sent Darius's body back to Persepolis for a state funeral and internment in a royal tomb.

After arriving in Bactria, Bessus declared himself the new king of the eastern portion of the empire (Central Asia), taking the throne name Artaxerxes V. But his empire quickly unraveled. His compatriots fled the land, surrendered to Alexander, or suffered defeat. Even the Bactrians realized any victory against Alexander was hopeless. And what was the point? Alexander seemed to be keeping most of the local leaders in place and following the governmental system of the Achaemenid Empire. But if they protected Bessus, they risked Alexander's wrath.

Pragmatically, the Bactrians handed Bessus over to the Macedonians, who stripped him and took him to Alexander, naked and tied with ropes. Alexander followed the Persian protocol for regicide, publicly flogging Bessus and cutting off his nose and ears. He then sent him to Ecbatana, where Darius's brother oversaw his crucifixion.

With Darius III's death avenged, Alexander pressed east and conquered the rest of the Achaemenid Empire. He finally reached the Jaxartes River, the empire's easternmost boundary. The final campaign was brutal on his men, who were battle-weary and longing to return home to their families. It was also harsh on Alexander; an arrow pierced his fibula, breaking it, and then a rock hit him in the head, causing him to be unable to see or speak for a time.

Alexander adopted the Persian customs and clothing, which his men found weird. He also became increasingly erratic and mentally unstable, which was perhaps collective fallout from several head injuries. He even killed his close friend, Cleitus the Black, while drunk. In 327 BCE, he captured Roxana, a Sogdian princess, and married her. After Alexander's death, she gave birth to his only known child. Having crossed the Hindu-Kush Mountains to explore the Indian subcontinent, Alexander finally returned "home" to Babylon. He threw a wedding to unite eighty Persian princesses to his officers, joining the Macedonian and Persian elite together in a symbolic ceremony of his new cross-cultural empire. Alexander married Princess Stateira, Darius's daughter, and Parysatis II, Artaxerxes III's daughter, on the same day.

But in 323 BCE, Alexander fell ill with a fever and died two weeks later at age thirty-two, having won every battle in which he engaged. The Persian Empire fell into chaos after his death. Roxana murdered his Persian wives, and she and her son by Alexander were later poisoned themselves. Alexander's new empire now encompassed all of the original Persian Empire plus Greece, Thrace, and most of the rest of the Balkan Peninsula. How could one person rule three continents, and who should it be? Finally, his generals divided the empire, although the conflicts over this decision persisted for decades. Much of the Asian part of the Persian Empire lived on as the Seleucid Empire, which survived for nearly 250 years under Greek rule.

SECTION FOUR:
ANCIENT PERSIAN SOCIETY, CULTURE, AND GOVERNMENT

Chapter 13: Arts, Culture, and Religion

The ancient Persians left an impressive legacy of arts, culture, and religious tolerance. As a multi-ethnic empire, they embraced a myriad of cultures while retaining the core elements of the ancient Iranian ways. The Achaemenids were highly innovative, developing astounding new techniques in art and technology. An incredibly visual people who appreciated bright colors and intricate artwork, their fascinating art and architecture still capture the imagination.

When the Persians settled in ancient Iran, they became a multi-lingual people. They spoke their ancient Indo-Iranian language known as Ariya or Old Persian, but since they lived near and intermarried with the people of Elam, they also spoke Elamite. When they first arrived in Iran, they were pre-literate, so they adopted Elamite as their written language. However, under Darius the Great's reign or perhaps as early as Cyrus the Great, the Persians developed a written form of their ancient language. It was a cuneiform script written from left to right, with thirty-six phonetic characters and several logograms or pictographs.

The Achaemenid Empire used spoken and written Elamite for administrating and communicating with their far-flung provinces from the time of Cyrus the Great to Darius the Great. Clay tablets that recorded financial and administrative details of everyday life were in Elamite. However, grand inscriptions of the kings carved into rock were in three languages: Elamite, Old Persian, and the Babylonian dialect of Akkadian. In all likelihood, the Persians used Elamite, but it was not used in the rest of the empire. After 458 BCE, Elamite seemed to have died out, as it no longer appeared in documents. By the time of Artaxerxes II, inscriptions in Old Persian were so imperfect that it indicated scribes no longer understood or commonly used the language.

When Cyrus established the empire, people in Mesopotamia and the Levant (Syria, Lebanon, and Israel) spoke variants of the Semitic language group, mostly Babylonian-Akkadian, Aramaic, and Hebrew. Written Aramaic had the advantage of an alphabet. It was far easier to learn twenty-two letters representing phonetic sounds than to memorize around a thousand characters representing words in the cuneiform script. Spoken and written Aramaic became the lingua franca (common language) throughout the empire; by Artaxerxes I's reign, it replaced Old Persian and Elamite in administrative affairs.

In the northwestern part of the empire, Ionia was ethnically Greek, and its citizens spoke and wrote Greek. Darius I placed two stone monuments at the Bosphorus with inscriptions in Greek and Aramaic, implying that diplomatic relations with the Ionian Greeks used Aramaic and Greek. When communicating with mainland Greece, the Persians used the Greek language, often through translators.

Banquets for Persian nobility included golden drinking vessels and fluted bowls.
Photo zoomed in. Credit: Rosemanios from Beijing (hometown), CC BY 2.0
<https://creativecommons.org/licenses/by/2.0>, via Wikimedia Commons;
https://commons.wikimedia.org/wiki/File:Persia_-_Achaemenian_Vessels.jpg

The Greeks, especially the austere Spartans, thought the Persians were a bit over the top in their lifestyle, especially their enjoyment of fine wine, excellent food, and parties. When King Darius III was defending his empire against Alexander the Great, he brought along three hundred cooks and seventy wine filterers on his campaign. But even ordinary Persians enjoyed throwing elaborate parties for birthdays.

They would roast an entire horse, camel, or ox (or maybe all three if they were rich). An important rule to remember was never talking with one's mouth full during a meal; this was the height of rude behavior. The festivities could continue for days, and after eating the roasted meat, they savored an endless assortment of desserts. The Persians sneered at the Greeks, who didn't ordinarily eat desserts, saying they left the table hungry. After eating an array of sweet delicacies, they enjoyed wine and music.

Since the Persians lived in a hot desert climate, they stored their food and wine underground in brick chambers to keep it cool. The ancient Persians were wine connoisseurs and heavy drinkers. The Greeks, who always drank their wine watered down, found it scandalous that the Persians drank wine at full strength. Herodotus wrote that getting drunk was an essential part of decision-making for Persian leaders:

"If a crucial decision is to be made, they discuss the question when they are drunk. The following day, the master of the house where the discussion was held submits their decision for reconsideration when they are sober. It is adopted if they still approve it; if not, it is abandoned. Conversely, any decision they make when sober is reconsidered afterward when they are drunk."[40]

Herodotus also wrote about the Persian custom of proskynesis or going prone on their faces before royalty or other superiors:

"When the Persians meet one another on the roads, you can see whether those who meet are of equal rank. Instead of greeting by words, they kiss each other on the mouth; but if one of them is inferior to the other, they kiss one another on the cheeks, and if

---

[40] Herodotus, *Histories*, 1.133.

one is of much less noble rank than the other, he falls down before him and worships him."[41]

After conquering the empire, Alexander the Great adopted many Persian customs, including demanding his military officers practice proskynesis. The Greeks were accustomed to democracy and felt Alexander was developing into a megalomaniac by expecting them to throw themselves at his feet.

The ancient Persians highly valued speaking the truth. They considered a person righteous if they steadily lived in honesty and integrity. Their insistence on not lying and consistently telling the truth caught the Greeks' admiration. Herodotus said that a Persian boy spent his childhood learning three essential concepts: how to ride a horse, shoot an arrow, and speak the truth. The Persians considered lying a huge disgrace, even a cardinal sin. They felt one should not go into debt because owing money to someone often led to lying.

Lying could sometimes earn the death sentence, and it could send someone to the Persian idea of hell. They believed the righteous truth-tellers would go to the House of Song and Good Thought, where they would see the god Ahura Mazda on his throne and the heavenly lights. But the foolish liars went to the House of the Lies, the home of the daevas (demonic deities) of chaos and disorder who are incapable of discerning truth from lies. There they would suffer in miserable darkness.

Cyrus the Great said nothing about his personal religion, but after conquering Babylon, he publicly worshiped Babylon's chief god Marduk. Perhaps it was a way of pleasing the Babylonians and legitimizing his rule over them. On the Cyrus Cylinder, he spoke of being blessed by Marduk. "Marduk, the great lord, bestowed on me as my destiny the great magnanimity of one who loves Babylon, and I every day sought him out in awe."[42]

Cyrus also restored the temple of Jerusalem that Nebuchadnezzar had looted and destroyed, returning the temple

---

[41] Herodotus, *Histories*, 1.134.

[42] Cyrus Cylinder, trans. Irving Finkel (The British Museum).
https://www.britishmuseum.org/collection/object/W_1880-0617-1941

treasures and paying for its restoration. "The LORD, the God of heaven, has given me all the kingdoms of the earth, and he has appointed me to build him a Temple at Jerusalem, which is in Judah."[43]

Cyrus's general policy, which set the tone for his successors, was benevolence toward conquered people and support for their religious systems. He worked to correct injustices perpetrated against the people or their gods by previous rulers. He returned cult images the Babylonian kings had brought to Babylon from other cities and repaired temples throughout the empire. Cyrus and the other Achaemenid kings displayed extraordinary religious tolerance for the diversity of religions practiced throughout the empire's vast reaches. All the people within the realm were free to worship whatever gods they chose.

Herodotus noticed that the Persians had no idols of their gods. He observed the Persian gods didn't have human-like, fallible natures. By contrast, his own Greek gods got married, had children, cheated on their spouses, deceived and fought each other, and were quite human in nature. He said the Persians would climb the highest mountains to offer sacrifices to their chief god and also offered sacrifices to the sun, moon, earth, fire, water, and winds.

During the Achaemenid era, the Zoroastrian religion became popular in Iran and spread throughout the empire. Zoroastrianism emerged from the ancient Vedic religion that also gave birth to Hinduism. The followers of the Vedic religion did not have idols or temples. They sacrificed animals to a sacred fire and drank an intoxicating juice from the soma plant, which had a hallucinogenic effect.

A Vedic priest named Zarathustra (Zoroaster in Greek) had an epiphany while offering sacrifices. The god Ahura Mazda appeared to him; following that vision, Zarathustra began teaching that Ahura Mazda was the supreme god. By his holy spirit Spenta Mainyu, Ahura Mazda created the earth, humans, and everything good. Six other spirits, the Amesha Spenta, created the rest of the universe.

---

[43] Ezra 2:2, Tanakh: Ketuvim: Book of Ezra.

However, the toxic evil energy of Angra Mainyu introduced chaos into this new creation, so goodness and light must combat evil and darkness.

Zoroastrianism was somewhat monotheistic in worshiping one supreme god, yet they had multiple minor deities with the same names as the Vedic, Iranian, and Hindu gods. The priests sang and prayed to the Amesha Spenta and the yazatas (lesser divine entities). Artaxerxes II prayed to Ahura Mazda but also Mithra, the sun god, and Anahita, the water goddess, building temples to her in Babylon, Media, and Persia. This was apparently the first time that cult images appeared in Persian temples.

This image may represent the goddess Anahita, who was worshiped by Artaxerxes II.
Photo cropped. Credit: Carole Raddato from Frankfurt, Germany, CC BY-SA 2.0
<https://creativecommons.org/licenses/by-sa/2.0>, via Wikimedia Commons;
https://commons.wikimedia.org/wiki/File:Head_and_left_hand_from_a_bronze_cult_stat
ue_of_Anahita,_a_local_goddess_shown_here_in_the_guide_of_Aphrodite,_200-
100_BC,_British_Museum_(8167358544).jpg

Ancient Persians who practiced Zoroastrianism did not bury or cremate their dead but practiced "sky burials." They placed the bodies of their deceased on a mountain for the vultures to eat. They thought burying bodies that would decay defiled the earth. Once the skeleton was picked clean and bleached by the sun, they gathered the bones and placed them in lime pits. The custom of sky burial is a remnant of primordial Vedic beliefs, and it is still practiced today by the Zoroastrians in India and the Tibetan and Mongolian Buddhists.

As Herodotus noted, ancient Persians generally worshiped in the open air, usually on a mountain top, and did not often build temples. However, several temple structures dating as far back as the 14th century BCE have been found in eastern Iran, Afghanistan, and Turkmenistan. None of the sites had cult images (idols), which were not part of the Persians' early religion. They did have evidence of fire worship, which was part of the ancient Vedic worship.[44]

The Persepolis Fortification or Foundation Tablets (506 and 497 BCE), which were found at the foundation level of the city's defensive walls, reference the worship of both Elamite and Iranian gods, describing priests and rituals but not mentioning temples. Darius the Great boasted in an inscription about rebuilding the *ayadana* (temples) destroyed by Gaumata the Magi, who impersonated Cambyses's son Bardiya. However, Darius did not mention where the temples were or what gods were worshiped. Xerxes I wrote that a temple existed for daeva (demon) worship in his empire, which he destroyed, purifying the area. But we have no idea what lands and which temples.

A temple found in Sistan in eastern Iran was built during Cyrus the Great's lifetime but was abandoned after about a century. The mudbrick structure was square, with rooms in each corner and three large altars in the courtyard's center, hinting at a triad of gods. Ashes and burned bones indicate animal sacrifices, which the ancient Zoroastrians practiced, as did Vedic worshipers and other religions. Two square tower-like structures in Pasargadae, the principal Achaemenid capital in Cyrus's day, appear to be temples.[45]

When the nomadic Persians arrived in Iran, the ancient cultures they encountered influenced their artistic and architectural styles.

---

[44] Michael Shenkar, "Temple Architecture in the Iranian World before the Macedonian Conquest," *Iran & the Caucasus* 11, no. 2 (2007): 169–71. http://www.jstor.org/stable/25597331.

[45] Michael Shenkar, "*Temple Architecture*," 172-8.

The Persians were assimilators who borrowed from the cultures of Iran and cultures throughout the empire, blending these ideas into a distinctive Persian look. Their appropriation of other customs spurred Herodotus to comment, "The Persians adopt more foreign customs than anyone else."

The city of Persepolis near the Zagros Mountains displayed a brilliant example of Persian architecture. Cyrus the Great chose the location for his religious center or ceremonial capital. He designed the elegant buildings of the new city he envisioned, but Darius the Great began carrying out Cyrus's plans. Darius initiated the building of five halls with grand entrances, and his son Xerxes finished most of the construction.

The highlight of Persepolis's architecture was its lavish Apadana, the king's hall where their subjects lay tribute at their monarch's feet and received gifts. Bull figures rested at the top of majestic sixty-five-foot columns that supported the roof. Two lofty staircases adorned with bas-reliefs led to the northern and eastern ends of the hall. The reliefs showed the empire's various ethnicities wearing their distinctive clothing and presenting tributes to the king, including a hippopotamus from the Egyptians. Exquisite gardens encompassed the Apadana.

Xerxes also built the Gate of All Nations in Persepolis. It was a splendid hall in an eighty-two-foot square graced by four fifty-four-foot columns. It served as the gateway into the city's Western Wall for visiting kings from other countries and satraps from around the empire. Two lamassus (celestial winged bulls with human heads) guarded the threshold from evil.

Lamassus, human-headed bulls, stood guard at the Gate of All Nations.
Photo modified: zoomed in. Credit: David Holt from London, England, CC BY-SA 2.0
<https://creativecommons.org/licenses/by-sa/2.0>, via Wikimedia Commons;
https://commons.wikimedia.org/wiki/File:Iran_2007_081_Persepolis_Gate_of_all_Nation
s_(1731628479).jpg

The energetic King Darius I also rebuilt Susa, Persia's summer capital, forming exquisite gardens designed by Cyrus the Great. Enameled carvings of brightly colored animals and palms embellished the palace and the Apadana. Two of the reliefs were especially interesting. One creature had a lion's body with wings and a man's head. Another striking image was a white unicorn against a bright blue glazed tile background. It had eagle wings, a lion's tail, and a spiraled horn.

This unicorn adorned the Apadana in Susa.

Cyrus the Great was buried in a free-standing tomb in Pasargadae, but four Achaemenid kings' tombs were carved on a high cliff northwest of Persepolis. Inscriptions identify that Darius I was buried in the first tomb. The others are probably Xerxes I, Artaxerxes I, and Darius II. Each tomb has an entrance in a cross shape opening into a small room where the sarcophagus lay, with bas-reliefs on the cliff face displaying that king and some event in his life.

The Persians were renowned for their landscape gardens dating to the early Achaemenid dynasty. Cyrus the Younger reportedly told General Lysander that he gardened every day when he wasn't on military campaigns. Lysander visited Cyrus the Younger's garden that he designed in Sardis, admiring its rectangular symmetry, lovely trees planted in rows, and scents wafting in the air. Persian gardens featured pavilions, fountains, pools, and sunny areas combined with areas to relax in the shade. The gardens were often connected to an indoor courtyard that was separated by vaulted arches.

The Persians developed remarkable technology for accessing water in their arid lands to maintain their prized gardens. More importantly, they had water for consumption and growing food. Their qanat irrigation system brought water up from an underground aqueduct rather than river systems like the Mesopotamians and Egyptians did. The underground system permitted long-distance water transport without much evaporation, and it was resistant to floods, earthquakes, and destruction by enemies. Tapping into the underground aquifer provided a relatively steady water source even in a drought. The Persians built the qanat system with a sloping tunnel coming up from aquifers with intermittent vertical shafts bringing the water aboveground.

This artistic rendition is of the Persepolis palace garden.
https://commons.wikimedia.org/wiki/File:Persepolis_T_Chipiez.jpg

The indefatigable Darius the Great built the Royal Road of the Achaemenids, an intercontinental network that traveled 1,500 miles from Persia to the Aegean Sea. It took ninety days to travel from Susa to Sardis on foot. Branches of the road extended as far south as India and Egypt, east into today's Afghanistan, north into today's Turkey, and west to the Hellespont and Europe. The Royal Road was not just for land travel but also connected rivers, canals, and seaports and included a channel that ran from the Nile to the Red Sea.

The Oxus Treasure of gold and silver crafts discovered at the Oxus River showcased the Achaemenid Empire's exquisite artwork. The Oxus River ran between today's Afghanistan and Turkmenistan, the Persians' ancestral homeland. The jewelry, coins, figurines, and other items were hidden by temple priests in the riverbank for protection during an uprising and were never recovered. An unusually dry season lowered the river level and exposed the treasure trove in 1880.

The intricate craftsmanship showcased spectacular metallurgy skills, hinting at Egyptian and Assyrian influences. Many of the elegant pieces appear to be cut from sheet gold. The treasure points to the significant production of silver and gold ornaments in the Persian Empire, which encompassed many of the ancient world's artistic hubs.

This miniature Oxus River golden chariot showed exquisite precious-metal skills.
BabelStone, CC BY-SA 3.0 <https://creativecommons.org/licenses/by-sa/3.0>, via Wikimedia Commons; https://commons.wikimedia.org/wiki/File:Oxus_chariot_model.jpg

The Achaemenid Empire merged numerous cultures spanning three continents into one superpower. The Persians respected all cultures and religions, encouraging a society where everyone could appreciate and learn from the multiple ethnicities that mingled together. They blended that knowledge and skill into their own distinctive culture, which influenced architecture, technology, and art for centuries to come. Persian culture lives on in a lively, unique blend of ancient and modern innovations.

Chapter 14: Military Tactics

The Persian military machine was the Achaemenid Empire's backbone. It served not only to expand the empire through conquest but also to maintain order in the far-flung provinces and protect the border regions from invasion. Beginning with the Persians and their Median kinsmen, the military transformed as it conquered new nations and assimilated new warriors with novel skills and tactics. The Achaemenid military was no longer a Median-Persian army but an international force that rocked the ancient world.

The Achaemenid Empire (559–330 BCE) started with a military of up to 150,000 troops of Medes and Persians. They conquered new regions and made alliances with others, acquiring tens of thousands of new warriors. The army's smallest unit was a ten-man squad called a dathaba. Ten dathaba squads formed a company called a satabam, and ten of these formed one-thousand-man regiments called hazarabam. Ten of these regiments comprised a division called a haivarabam. Uniforms of assorted colors identified the various units.

The Achaemenid Empire's military fell into three categories: part-time soldiers, full-time professionals, and the elite division, which Herodotus called the Immortals. The Sparabara warriors fought during the military season between spring planting and the fall harvest. They were farmers, herders, or craftsmen when they weren't on a military campaign. However, they were well-trained in archery and other battle skills from adolescence.

The drawing depicts three ethnicities (among many) in Xerxes's army: a Persian flagbearer on the left, an Armenian in the middle, and a Cappadocian on the right.
https://commons.wikimedia.org/wiki/File:Soldiers_of_Xerxes_army.png

The Sparabaras wore quilted linen armor and were experienced with the ten-foot "apple bearer" spear, named after its bronze counterweight. The Sparabara used these long spears in the front line of the Persian forces. Typically, they held their large rectangular wicker shields next to each other to form a wall with the spears sticking out to impale any attackers. Behind them, the javelin-throwers hurled their weapons while archers fired arrows over their heads. The wicker shields stopped arrows but were a poor defense against Alexander the Great's eighteen-foot sarissas.

Cyrus the Great quickly realized he needed a full-time military to deal with internal and external threats and long campaigns in distant lands. He formed a professional land army called the Spada, which included infantry, a cavalry of warhorses, camels, and a few chariots. The professional army had warriors from other parts of the empire. The Persians later hired Greek mercenaries, who formed a substantial portion of their forces; they received free food and one gold daric a month in pay. Although the Achaemenid military used citizens from around the empire and Greek mercenaries, it favored the Iranian tribes, who provided more soldiers but paid lower tribute. Next to ethnic Persians, the Medes provided the second-largest force, including many of the empire's generals. The Bactrians and other eastern Iranian tribes also contributed many fighting men.

Among the professional forces was an elite division that Herodotus called the "Immortals." They were highly trained infantrymen with some cavalry who maintained precisely ten thousand men. More trained men were in reserve; if an Immortal was wounded, seriously ill, or killed in battle, a reserve soldier immediately filled his spot. The Immortals also served as the imperial guard.

The Immortals were the Persian elite division of the Achaemenid military.
Pergamon Museum, CC BY 2.0 <https://creativecommons.org/licenses/by/2.0>, via Wikimedia Commons; https://commons.wikimedia.org/wiki/File:Persian_warriors_from_Berlin_Museum.jpg

Most Immortals were Persian, but they included some Medes and other Iranians. The Immortals wore bronze helmets and either bronze breastplates or scale armor: small plates of metal, leather, or horn in overlapping rows. Their warhorses also wore bronze protection on their heads, chests, and withers. A bow would be hooked over their shoulder, and they would carry a quiver of arrows. They also fought with short spears, swords, slings, and daggers. While most armies ran at each other screeching war cries, the Immortals were eerily silent as they marched toward the opposition. The enemy would feel a slight tremor under their feet as ten thousand men marched their way, but all they could hear was a slight jangle of weapons and a steady thud of feet. This psychological tactic unnerved the enemy forces so much that they sometimes fled without fighting at all.

Camels, mules, and wagons followed the Immortals, transporting their servants, concubines, special food, and supplies. The glazed tile reliefs in Persian halls portray the Immortals wearing ankle-length tunics, but these outfits were almost certainly for ceremonial functions since they would be cumbersome for warfare. They probably wore close-fitting pants or patterned leggings with short tunics on the battlefield as the regular Persian soldiers did.

Persian boys from leading families began military training at age five and other youths at age fifteen. They were schooled in riding and grooming horses, running, archery, javelin throwing, and sword fighting. They developed discipline through repeated drills, long marches, and meager meals. They joined the active military at age twenty, and professional soldiers retired at fifty. The part-time soldiers served when they were called up for military campaigns or individual battles. Each satrapy had its own army that could quickly deploy to meet an urgent need in the region.

From their earliest days, the Persians and Medes were expert horsemen, so a lethal cavalry division always accompanied their infantry. Cyrus the Great increased his cavalry from about 10 percent of his forces to 20 percent in his later years. Xerxes I marched on Greece with an elite cavalry of 1,000 leading the way; farther back was 100,000 regular cavalry. The Achaemenid military fought against Alexander the Great with over ten thousand horsemen. From descriptions of various battles, an elite cavalry regiment of one thousand seemed to persist from Xerxes I to Darius III; these soldiers were most likely Persian noblemen on horses from the Persian heartland.[46]

---

[46] Michael B. Charles, "Achaemenid Elite Cavalry: From Xerxes to Darius III," *The Classical Quarterly* 65, no. 1 (2015): 14–34.

The Persian charioteer units used four horses to pull two-man chariots heavier than the Babylonian and Egyptian chariots. One man guided the horses while the other fought with spears or arrows. Persian chariots had scythes attached to the wheels that could slice off legs or sever arteries. When the satrap Pharnabazus unexpectedly encountered an army of Greek soldiers, he killed one hundred men, putting the rest to flight with only two scythed chariots and four hundred cavalrymen.

Cyrus the Great commonly used camels to carry luggage on military campaigns. However, he placed them on the frontlines in the Battle of Thymbra, terrifying the Lydian horses that had never seen or smelled camels and stampeded off the field. Over six decades later, Xerxes used thousands of Arab archers on camels in his second invasion of Greece. King Darius III positioned fifteen war elephants from India on his center frontline when facing off against Alexander at the Battle of Gaugamela. They horrified the Greek troops so much that Alexander made a special sacrifice to the god of fear; however, no accounts mention the elephants' use in the actual battle.

The Persian, Elamite, Median, and Scythian archers in the Achaemenid military struck terror in their opponents. They used the immensely powerful composite bow made of wood, horn, and animal sinew laminated together with animal resin. These bows launched lethal three-bladed arrows with copper alloy tips. Although capable of hand-to-hand combat with spears, swords, and battle-axes, the Persians preferred to fight from a distance with their superior archery skills. The archers often wore their quivers on their hips for rapid reloading and could shoot and reload up to ten arrows in a minute. A division of 10,000 archers could launch as many as 100,000 arrows in a minute.

http://www.jstor.org/stable/43905638.

This ivory carving depicts a Persian cavalry archer at the Battle of Gaugamela.
Luis García, CC BY-SA 3.0 <https://creativecommons.org/licenses/by-sa/3.0>, via Wikimedia Commons; https://commons.wikimedia.org/wiki/File:Batalla_de_Gaugamela_(M.A.N._Inv.1980-60-1)_04.jpg

The Persians adopted the sagaris battle-ax or war hammer from the Scythians. It had a long thin handle almost two feet long with either a blunt metal hammer-head or a heavy cutting blade. It was lightweight enough to be used one-handed on horseback or on foot, but it could also pierce armor and helmets.

Combat engineers often won battles for the Persian forces. In Babylonia and Egypt, they diverted rivers into irrigation canals so troops could wade across otherwise impassable rivers or roll siege engines up to city walls. The engineers would march ahead of the Achaemenid forces to build or repair bridges and roads. They had been building boat bridges long before Xerxes's one-mile bridge across the Dardanelles Strait. Darius I's engineers constructed a 2,500-foot boat bridge over the Bosphorus. Xenophon reported a bridge of thirty-seven boats on the Tigris River and seven vessels on the Meander River.

The Achaemenid Empire had an astonishing communication system. Suppose a satrapy revolted or was invaded in the western part of the empire. In that case, the news could quickly reach the king in Persia, allowing him to deal with the emergency without delay. On horseback, couriers charged down the Royal Road, changing out their steeds at regular intervals at the way stations. They used fire signals from towers on mountain tops. The use of light and mirror signals in the Aegean Sea enabled the navy to receive news of the outcome of battles on the Greek mainland within hours.

Cyrus the Great and his successors used siege engines that were twenty-seven-foot-high mobile towers on a rolling cart. Eight oxen pulled each tower, which held twenty soldiers. The tower's height enabled the archers to shoot from the top parapets and get their arrows over the city walls. They could also launch fire missiles. The siege engines were also used on the battlefield to shoot arrows or heavier missiles from the high, protected towers.

The support team for the massive Achaemenid armies was a vast undertaking, with baggage trains, supply ships, cooks, doctors, and other elements needed to accommodate tens of thousands of warriors. Part of the support team went ahead of the army to scout out drinking water, places to camp, and fields for the horses, mules, and camels to graze. In addition to their triremes, which had no holds for food and other necessities, the Persian navy deployed supply ships to carry up to five hundred tons. They also used transport ships to carry thirty horses at a time.

Did Xerxes really invade Greece with a million-man army? Some sources report as many as three million people, including the support team and navy. At the time, the Achaemenid Empire had an estimated population of almost fifty million people, so one million men could be possible. However, the logistics of feeding one million men for a months-long campaign far from home is mind-boggling. The accounts do mention they often ran out of drinking water and that the army starved on the way back to Asia.

The Persian military typically began a battle by sending out the cavalry to disrupt the enemy lines. The horsemen threw javelins, discharged arrows, and attempted to outflank the opposition. They tried to herd their adversaries together into one clump, making them an easy target for their archery division, which could shoot thousands of arrows a minute. If the enemy scattered rather than cluster together, the cavalrymen and charioteers could easily pick them off.

This tactic required enough flat ground where the cavalry and chariots could easily maneuver. It also helped to have an undisciplined adversary that wasn't highly mobile. When the Persians fought the Scythians, they often lost because the entire Scythian force was on horseback and could move swiftly into various formations. The Persians struggled with battles on Greece's mountainous, rocky territory where the horses couldn't maneuver well. The Greeks found ways to get around the Persians' favored strategy of long-distance combat with cavalry and arrows. They would fight from the mountains or force the Persians to fight on tight battlefields where hand-to-hand combat was the only option.

The Persians' ancestral homeland was landlocked Central Asia, but the Achaemenid Empire launched the world's first imperial navy. Unaccustomed to ships, they took advantage of the Phoenicians, who had surrendered to Cyrus the Great without a struggle and been mostly loyal citizens of the empire ever since. The Phoenicians were seafaring people from prehistorical times and experts in shipbuilding and sea warfare. The Persians also used Egyptian and Greek mercenaries to build and man their ships.

The first Achaemenid king to use a navy was Cambyses in Egypt's conquest. After this, the empire's navy exercised power in the eastern Aegean Sea, Black Sea, Mediterranean Sea, and the Persian Gulf. The navy also operated in smaller vessels in the Tigris, Euphrates, Nile, and Meander.

Their first ships were called triremes and measured about 120 feet in length and 15 to 20 feet wide and could carry up to 300 men. The name came from the three rows of oars that propelled the ship along with one square sail. The draught (the part under water) was shallow, only about three feet deep, permitting the sailors to pull them ashore easily, which they often did. At top speed, which the ships could reach in thirty seconds, they could travel about twelve knots an hour and had excellent agility at sea in ship battles. A bronze battering ram like a long tapering pike projected out from the bow, which was used to impale and slice open the hulls of enemy ships. The sailors used grappling hooks to snare enemy ships. Most ships had two catapults to hurl rocks or fiery projectiles at the adversary. The Persian triremes used 170 oarsmen and carried other marines for combat.

They had to beach their ships every few days to dry out since they got waterlogged, which sometimes became inconvenient if the enemy was nearby. The Achaemenid navy later incorporated other vessels. These included the larger quinqueremes, which allowed for additional men and weaponry, and the smaller penteconters and triaconters, which were more maneuverable and better for river travel.

The Achaemenid naval bases were centered on Phoenicia's coast, the island of Cyprus, Cilicia on the mainland just northeast of Cyprus, and Cyme in Ionia. They also had a naval base on the Shatt al-Arab, where the Euphrates and Tigris Rivers met to flow into the Persian Gulf. Smaller bases included Halicarnassus on present-day Turkey's southwestern coast, Tripoli in northern Lebanon, Samos in Ionia, and the Nile Delta (when Egypt wasn't revolting). The Achaemenid Empire also had trade settlements along the Persian Gulf and the Arabian Sea, including Oman, Bahrain, Yemen, and the Indian subcontinent.

During the Achaemenid navy's inception under Cambyses, the fleet had about three hundred triremes, with around fifty-one thousand rowers. During the reign of Darius the Great, the navy doubled to six hundred triremes and was a decisive factor in the conquest of Ionia and Thrace. Under his son Xerxes, Persia's navy vessels doubled again to 1,200 warships, 3,000 transport ships, and at least 36,000 crewmen.

But the navy suffered an apocalyptic loss to the Greek coalition navies at Salamis, losing many ships in addition to the ones lost in an earlier battle and two storms. The Achaemenid navy never fully recovered. Under Xerxes's son Artaxerxes I, the empire's navy experienced another catastrophic loss of two hundred ships at the Eurymedon River, which spelled the end of its presence in the Aegean Sea. Another humbling defeat occurred in 450 BCE at Cyprus.

Despite ultimately being conquered by Alexander the Great, the Persian military reigned as the world's premier war machine for over two centuries. Through military conquests, it spread from a modest province in today's Iran to cover three continents, the largest empire yet seen in the ancient world. Their conquests were remarkable for the Persians' warfare skills and their humane treatment of conquered people who submitted. Aware of the Persians' benevolence, many regions under attack from the Achaemenid Empire were more likely to surrender than resist to the bitter end.

Chapter 15: Rule, Governance, and Economy

The Achaemenid Empire established the world's first successful attempt at large-scale globalization, bringing together diverse ethnicities and nations from three continents into one political entity. Through trade and serving together in the military, the various ethnic groups blended with and learned from each other. The Persian kings encouraged sharing ideas and customs, promoted an elevated level of autonomy in local governments, and orchestrated a thriving economy.

The Persian kings ruled over their colossal empire with surprisingly modest use of control. Cyrus the Great set an example of tolerance and open-mindedness, which led to the Achaemenid Peace (*Pax Achaemenica*). The stability was markedly different from the preceding conflicts between Middle Eastern states, especially the three centuries of brutal dominance under the Assyrian Empire.

Cyrus was known for treating conquered monarchs kindly, often offering them a position within his court or as governor over their own kingdom or another realm. His respect for the various religions and cultures won the esteem of the conquered people, leading to a peaceable rule. One issue he confronted was the ancient rivalries between different nationalities that now made up his empire. Cyrus dealt with this by respecting each ethnic group but encouraging the exchange of ideas by serving together in the military and interacting with other groups in commerce. As Cyrus's biographer Reza Zarghamee noted, "Cyrus seems to have understood that people are driven by certain basic needs: the preservation of social order and local autonomy."[47]

The core elements of the Achaemenid Empire's administrative system included a structured state with interconnected provinces. Its road network encouraged trade and communications and allowed for the quick movement of military troops, which contributed to relative peace and prosperity. Xenophon, a Greek who fought as a mercenary for Cyrus the Younger, considered Cyrus the Great a model of statecraft who "eclipsed all other monarchs" and inspired his subjects to please him.

The remarkable tolerance exercised by Cyrus and his successors was a matter of political expediency. If they kept the people content, revolts were less likely. The Achaemenid kings developed a sustainable political concept and set a standard of statecraft that future rulers adopted. After conquering the Achaemenid Empire, Alexander the Great essentially left the preexisting government in place.

The one area that tested the Achaemenid rulers' tolerance was revolts. When satrapies rebelled, the punishment was swift and severe. The Persian kings considered insurgencies a personal afront, a failure to acknowledge their divine right to rule and their benevolence toward their citizens. Even if it took decades and the efforts of multiple kings, as it did with Egypt, the kings were relentless in bringing rogue nations back into the fold.[48]

Five capitals functioned as administrative centers of the mammoth empire under Cyrus the Great. He continued using the cities of Babylon, Susa (Elam's ancient capital), and Ecbatana (Media's capital) and made Sardis (Lydia's capital) the administrative center of the western satrapies. He also built Pasargadae as his primary capital. It was located in Fars Province,

---

[47] Reza Zarghamee, *Discovering Cyrus*, 12.

[48] Maria Brosius, *A History of Ancient Persia: The Achaemenid Empire* (Hoboken, NJ: Wiley Blackwell, 2020), 1-2.

where he and his son Cambyses were buried. Darius the Great later added Persepolis as a capital. Why so many capitals? The king constantly moved about the empire when not on military campaigns, reinforcing the bond with his subjects. Also, seasonal weather made some locations more appealing at certain times of the year.

Persepolis's Tachara palace was for ceremonial use but probably not the king's residence. *Hansueli Krapf, CC BY-SA 3.0 <https://creativecommons.org/licenses/by-sa/3.0>, via Wikimedia Commons; https://commons.wikimedia.org/wiki/File:Tachara,_Persepolis.jpg*

Interestingly, in some capital cities like Persepolis, archaeologists haven't been able to find a structure that served as the king's private living quarters. The grand Apadana halls stood as a place to hold court but with no place for the king and his entourage to sleep, eat, or relax. We know that Persepolis burned during the time of Alexander the Great, so perhaps it mainly had wooden structures that the fire consumed. However, another theory is that the kings stayed in elaborate tents or pavilions as they moved about, which would link them to their nomadic past.[49]

Courtiers and servants orbited around the king within the Persian royal court as he administered economic, military, political, and religious affairs. He would meet with his advisors to determine the best course of action, receive homage from visiting dignitaries,

---

[49] Ali Bahadori and Negin Miri, "The So-called Achaemenid Capitals and the Problem of Royal Court Residence," *Iran*, (2021) DOI: 10.1080/05786967.2021.1960881.

and host feasts for his nobles and even for the ordinary people.[50] He would also interact with his family: the queen mother, his queen, his brothers and sisters, his concubines, and his children, who numbered in the hundreds with some of the later Achaemenid kings.

A high official called the "Master of a Thousand" ruled over the king's inner court, which held the king's family, personal slaves and servants, royal bodyguards, and the highest-ranking nobles. Anyone who wanted an audience with the king had to go through him. One official who regularly reported to the king was his chief spy known as the "King's Eye." The king's cupbearer was nearly always in his presence; he was a servant but also a confidante.

In the outer court, the cooks, bakers, wine stewards, grooms, translators, administrators, and doctors kept busy with their tasks. The outer court workers came from around the empire. Royal eunuchs, who had been castrated in adolescence, served in many functions, often as high as the king's vizier, military generals, and advisors. They served as bodyguards and servants in the harem and as translators and messengers traversing between the inner and outer courts.

The Persian king sat on a high-backed throne with lion feet, resting his feet on a footstool. Most people who entered his presence had to prostrate themselves and kiss his feet. The king had an inner circle of officers. The Book of Esther speaks of seven princes or close advisors to the king who were Persians and Medes. They were possibly kinsmen and ranked highest in the kingdom. They met with the king regularly, and he always asked for their advice.[51]

The queen mother was the highest-ranking female at court, outranking even the queen. Darius the Great's mother, Irdabama, is recorded as administrating her private estates, overseeing the purchase and distribution of food, and commanding the court officers. She even served as the king's deputy in his absence. She traveled throughout the kingdom with her entourage, often

---

[50] Esther 1:1-8, Tanakh: Ketuvim: Book of Esther.
[51] Esther 1:13-14.

independently of the king. A royal tent city accompanied the king and his family on military campaigns. At the center of the royal tent complex was the king's tent, which faced east and was surrounded by the tents of his mother, wife, and daughters. His sons and other male relatives would usually serve as generals and camped with their men.

When Persia conquered new regions, the king or a top general would linger for a bit to set up the new administrative structure and appoint government leaders. The appointed governor (satrap) might be the same leader as before, or the king might select one of his sons or a favored officer he wanted to honor. Once everything was in place, the king and his military would head to their next destination, leaving the running of the province (satrapy) to the newly appointed satrap. The everyday lives of the citizens continued much as they had before.

Cyrus the Great had twenty-six satrapies under his centralized government, and Darius the Great increased the satrapies to thirty-six. The satrap or "protector of the province" was the top leader of a satrapy or region. The local satrap collected taxes, acted as the "supreme court" judge for criminal and civil cases, kept the roads maintained and safe from bandits, and appointed and supervised local officials.

A military general who answered to the king would recruit and train a local army for the satrapy. This force protected the province and could be called up by the king for military campaigns. A state secretary kept track of records and administrative affairs and reported both to the satrap and the central government. One of his duties would be overseeing the collection of taxes and tributes. While each satrapy had a high degree of autonomy, the "King's Eye" would send his intelligence-gathering officials around the empire to monitor any brewing situations.

The Old Persian word "dāta" meant law and was used to refer to the immutable "Law of the Medes and Persians,"[52] the king's law for the empire, and divine law. Xerxes spoke of the Persian deity

---

[52] Esther 1:19 & Daniel 6:6-15, Tanakh: Ketuvim: Book of Esther & Book of Daniel.

Ahura Mazda's law,[53] and Artaxerxes referenced the Hebrew "Law of the God of Heaven."[54] Xerxes said the person who obeyed both the king's law and divine law "becomes happy while living and blessed when dead."

The Persians believed the king's right to rule and all legal authority were divinely ordained. Beginning with Darius I, references to the king's law appeared in Babylonian records documenting tax payments and trials before a judge who had to follow the king's law. Darius introduced a new law code based on Persian law that impacted the empire's legal and judicial systems. Any decrees made by the king carried the force of law.[55]

The Achaemenid law code differed from earlier Middle Eastern court procedures. People could be found guilty or innocent in ancient times based on one person's oath or trial by ordeal. An example of an ordeal from ancient Babylon's Code of Hammurabi was for a woman to throw herself into the river if someone accused her of adultery. If she drowned, she was guilty, and if the wife survived, she was innocent. Trial by ordeal for certain crimes pervaded ancient law codes. By contrast, Achaemenid law required the presentation of rational evidence of guilt or innocence in court, such as multiple witnesses. Another change in the legal system was that a woman's testimony was now accepted in court, pointing to women's enhanced status in society.[56]

A stellar communication system was critical for keeping the central government informed of events in the empire, which stretched from the Indian subcontinent to the Aegean Sea. The Royal Road spanning Central and West Asia aided military movements and trade and enabled the speedy Persian *pirradazish* postal service. A letter sent from Persia could arrive in Sardis in seven days.

---

[53] Roland Kent, *Old Persian: Grammar, Texts, Lexicon* (New Haven: American Oriental Society, 1950), 151-2.

[54] Ezra 7:12-26, Tanakh: Ketuvim: Book of Ezra.

[55] "Dāta," *Encyclopaedia Iranica.* Vol. VII, Fasc. 1 (2011): 114-15. https://www.iranicaonline.org/articles/data.

[56] "Achaemenid Judicial and Legal Systems," *Encyclopaedia Iranica,* Vol. XV, Fasc. 2 (2012): 174-77.

Over one hundred relay stations along the way allowed horses and postal carriers to switch off. Herodotus was so impressed with the Persian postal service that he penned the words now chiseled in stone over New York City's Eighth Avenue Post Office doors: "Neither snow, nor rain, nor heat, nor gloom of night stays these courageous couriers from the swift completion of their appointed rounds."

The Achaemenid Empire comprised about three dozen satrapies with diverse local economies. Regions like Ionia, Babylonia, Egypt, and Phoenicia had well-developed and wealthy economies based on sea and river trade and centuries of advanced civilization. Other areas were decentralized and emerging from subsistence farming or herding communities. Some regions' economies and populations had been devastated by drought or incessant warfare.

Throughout the empire, the main economic activity was agriculture, especially grains like barley or wheat and vegetables and fruit like cucumbers, peas, apples, and dates. Grapes were grown for wine, which was a popular economic commodity. Persia, Media, and northern Mesopotamia raised much livestock, providing dairy products that were popular around the empire. Fishing was also a prosperous economic endeavor.

Many of the regions conquered by Persia already had a land distribution system in place, with part of the land owned by nobility, part by the temples, and part privately owned. The latter was often divided into small family-owned plots and more extensive plantations worked by tenant farmers. Two changes the Achaemenid rulers introduced were accurate land measurements and land redistribution. The most productive lands were divided between the king, nobility, wealthy businessmen, and (in Egypt and Babylonia) the temples.

The land allotted to the king provided herds for meat. They also grew grain and other items consumed by the royal family and their entourage. Some of the "king's land" was farmed by and for the military. Part of military training for adolescent youths included agricultural skills; the soldiers tilled the land themselves when not on military campaigns or rented the plots out. Some of the "king's" property belonged to the queen, royal princes, and other nobility like the satraps. Accounting records documented sheep and wine sent to the queen and shepherds herding the crown's flocks, which numbered in the thousands. Records show that Darius II's wife, Queen Parysatis, owned fields in the Nippur region of Babylonia, which she rented out to a family business.

The crown also owned some of the workshops and craftsmen enterprises. For instance, Phoenicia produced and exported glassware and purple dye. The Egyptians, Babylonians, and Ionians produced clothing from cotton and linen. The workshops owned by the crown produced goods or services for the royal court and included more than sixteen thousand workers, including stone masons, carpenters, winemakers, weavers, and other specialists.

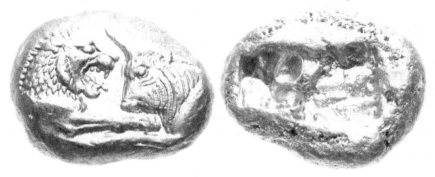

Sardis minted this gold lion and bull Croeseid coin circa 561–546 BCE.
Classical Numismatic Group, Inc. http://www.cngcoins.com, CC BY-SA 3.0 <http://creativecommons.org/licenses/by-sa/3.0/>, via Wikimedia Commons; https://commons.wikimedia.org/wiki/File:Kroisos._Circa_564-53-550-39_BC._AV_Stater_(16mm,_10.76_g)._Heavy_series._Sardes_mint.jpg

The ancient world began using minted coins in a flat, round shape with a picture on one side about a century before Cyrus the Great's reign. They originated in Lydia, which eventually became part of the Achaemenid Empire, but coinage had yet to extend to Persia when Cyrus rose to power. In very ancient times, the Mesopotamians used talents, minas, and shekels for currency; they weren't coin-shaped but rather pieces of silver or gold of a specific weight. The Persians adopted this currency but continued to use their ancient bartering system.

When Cyrus conquered Lydia and befriended its king, Croesus (after nearly burning him to death), he decided to use coins in his empire in 546 BCE. He adopted the Lydian coinage already in place: the lion and bull Croeseid coinage, which were minted in Sardis, Lydia (which became the Achaemenid capital for the western satrapies). Sardis continued to mint the empire's new coins, and the empire accepted coins from Greece as legal currency and vice versa.

By 500 BCE, Darius the Great introduced new coinage: the gold daric and silver siglos. Instead of the double reverse punch of the original coins, he used a single reverse punch. He replaced the lion and bull with the king's image, one running with a bow and spear. One gold daric, roughly equivalent to the Babylonian 8.33-gram shekel, equaled 20 silver sigloi or 25 Greek drachmae.

Darius the Great changed the coinage to gold darics like this one with his image.
Classical Numismatic Group, Inc. http://www.cngcoins.com, CC BY-SA 2.5 <https://creativecommons.org/licenses/by-sa/2.5>, via Wikimedia Commons; https://commons.wikimedia.org/wiki/File:Daric_coin_of_the_Achaemenid_Empire_(Xerxes_II_to_Artaxerxes_II).jpg

When their city-states or countries fell to the Achaemenid Empire, the most drastic change the people experienced was having to pay tribute to Persia. Under Cyrus the Great and Cambyses, the satraps paid tribute, usually in the form of gifts. These were generally the area's specialty, like precious metals, gemstones, timber, cloth, horses, or food items like dried fish, dried fruit, or grain. The tribute's amount depended on the satrapy's wealth, whether they were Persian or kinsmen to Persians and whether they surrendered quickly or forced Persia into a long, expensive siege.

Some satraps paid a money tax in lieu of or in addition to "gifts." Payment in silver increased under Darius the Great, who instituted a standardized, coordinated tax system in 519 BCE. Taxes were based on precise measurements of each satrapy's land, how fertile it was, and what each harvest produced in an average year. The territories on the outskirts of the empire generally paid more in goods than in silver. Interestingly, even though silver and gold coins were in use, the satraps paid the taxes with silver talents.

The three stunningly wealthy provinces in the Indian subcontinent paid almost one-third of the entire empire's tribute: eight tons of gold dust plus elephants, ivory, and teak. Affluent Babylon had to feed the military for four months plus pay one thousand silver talents. Egypt, Libya, Cyrene, and Barca provided 120,000 measures of grain and 700 silver talents. The Iranian satrapies had relatively low taxes. Elam paid three hundred talents, and Media paid four hundred, but they also provided many men for the military, which seemed to factor into the taxation rate. Persia did not pay taxes but did pay tribute, mainly sheep and other livestock.

The entire Levant (Syria, Phoenicia, Israel, and Cyprus) paid only 350 talents annually, despite Phoenicia's astronomical wealth. These countries had surrendered almost immediately to Cyrus the Great. Phoenicia had been an enormous asset in the empire's naval affairs, as it constantly built ships and manned them. The wealthy Ionian-Greek city-states only paid four hundred talents a year for the entire area. Perhaps the Persian kings didn't want to rock the boat with the volatile area, as the Greeks were just across the Aegean, ready and willing to help their kinsmen against Persia. The Ionian Greeks also contributed many men to the military, especially naval crews. The city-states of Anatolia had relatively modest taxes; Phrygia paid 360 talents, and Lydia and Cilicia each paid 500 talents.

The Persepolis reliefs featured the empire's citizens presenting tribute to the king.

Some neighboring regions who were allies but not part of the empire sent tribute; for instance, Arabia sent one thousand talents of frankincense annually. The Achaemenid Empire also collected trade tariffs, and the slave markets had to pay taxes on their sales. Unlike the Assyrian Empire, which bled people dry with high taxes, the Achaemenid tax and tribute system was sustainable. The satrapies could pay the annual amount without great suffering. However, the disastrous wars with Greece emptied the Persian coffers, and the Persian royalty grew increasingly lavish in their lifestyles. These changes meant higher taxes for the citizens, sparking an increase in revolts by the disgruntled people and vulnerability to Alexander the Great's invasion.

Conclusion

The Persian Empire's legacy has endured throughout the millennia. The Achaemenid Empire played a decisive role in the history of its day in the Middle East, Central Asia, and the Balkan Peninsula. It successfully implemented a centralized government, with satraps holding a remarkable degree of local autonomy. Its capable and efficient administrative system was unmatched in the world's history up to that point, and it managed to maintain stability and peace in a vast and diverse empire. It developed outstanding infrastructure throughout the entire Middle East: a trans-empire road network, canals connecting key waterways, and a speedy postal system.

The Achaemenid Empire also ruled over a multi-ethnic, multi-cultural empire that was ahead of its time in respecting all ethnicities and giving all people freedom of religion. Its rulers even restored and rebuilt temples of various faiths. By contrast, the Athenians executed Socrates for "impiety" because he said the Greek gods were morally compromised and that humans could only have a moral compass with a rational and perfect god.

The Achaemenid Empire set a standard of orderly political administration that Alexander the Great adopted. One could even say the Persians gave the Greeks and Macedonians the idea of a multi-continent, multi-cultural empire. Previously, the Greeks existed as independent city-states and were constantly warring with each other. The Achaemenid Empire forced them to unify for survival. When Philip II of Macedonia saw what a unified Greece could do in self-defense, he conceived the idea of using it to swallow up the Achaemenid Empire.

The Achaemenid Empire's efficient and effective bureaucracy significantly influenced its Middle Eastern, Macedonian, Greek, and Iranian successors. Its multifaceted heritage survived throughout the succeeding Seleucid, Parthian, and Sassanid Empires. After Alexander the Great died suddenly in 323 BCE, his Macedonian generals split up the empire. General Seleucus first got Babylonia and then began a ruthless expansion program that grabbed everything from Syria to Afghanistan, forming the Seleucid Empire in the process.

Seleucus continued with the Achaemenid tolerance of all religions and cultures. However, Koine Greek became the lingua franca, as the steady immigration of Greeks into the empire brought the Hellenistic culture and the rise of a political class led by Greek elites. Nevertheless, the Macedonian and Greek emigrants also absorbed the Persian customs and technologies, forming a Greco-Iranian cultural blend that surged ahead in science, math, and the arts.

The Seleucid Empire's political structure continued the Achaemenid system of a centralized government, with the satraps exerting power over a decentralized administration. It left Iran to its own devices for almost a century, with Persian kings running Persis (Persia proper) who paid tribute to their Seleucid overlords. However, the Seleucid ruler Antiochus I (r. 281–261 BCE) appointed Andragoras as the satrap over all of Iran. He was probably ethnically Iranian, but the Persians and other Iranians resented the loss of autonomy.

The Parthian tribes of northeastern Iran rebelled against the Seleucids in 247 BCE. Their growing power, coupled with the Seleucid Empire's struggles with Rome, Armenia, and Egypt, eventually led to the empire's collapse. Under the new Parthian Empire, the Persians and other Iranian tribes had local autonomy as vassal kingdoms, paying tribute to the Parthian kings, who claimed to be the Achaemenid Empire's heirs. The Parthian kings maintained the satrapy system with states outside of Iran.

King Ardashir I of Persis overcame the Parthians and established the Sassanid Empire in 224 CE. It ruled for four centuries, restoring Persian rule over much of the Achaemenid Empire's previous territory, from the Mediterranean to Pakistan. Like the Achaemenid rulers, the Sassanids tolerated all faiths and cultures; however, they intentionally elevated the Persian culture over the Greek ways. They also had a centralized government with a decentralized administration of the shahr districts, which were like the earlier satrapies.

When the Sassanid Empire fell to the Islamic Arabs in 651 CE, its elevated level of state and administrative traditions and its cultural heritage were passed to the Islamic caliphates. The Ottoman and Safavid Empires adopted the Achaemenid Empire's organizational principles. Its influence can still be seen in today's Middle Eastern governments. Persia remained a significant Middle Eastern power until its decline in the 19th century CE and recently has been regaining its regional ascendency. Maneuvering through ongoing social, economic, and political challenges, the resilient Iranian state has expanded its regional leverage and influence.

Cyrus the Great and the Achaemenid Empire still loom larger than life in the minds of today's Iranians. Before the Achaemenid Empire, the Iranian tribes were vulnerable to oppression from foreign powers. Cyrus preserved Persian freedom and cultural identity and made their land the greatest empire yet seen. Today's Iranians consider him the father of their people and the founder of Iran's first unified state. They remember Cyrus's story and the great Achaemenid Empire with extraordinary pride.

The Iranians consider Cyrus a hero, a likable leader, and a role model of benevolent rule. He was a man ahead of his time. It is no wonder why a proposed peace initiative between Iran and Israel in 2021 was named the Cyrus Accords. It celebrated the bond of friendship going back to when Cyrus released Israel from the Babylonian Captivity in 538 BCE.[57]

---

[57] Karmel Melamed, "Cyrus Accords' Old Seeds of Peace: Iran & Israel's Forgotten Friendship," *The Times of Israel*, April 4, 2021.
https://blogs.timesofisrael.com/cyrus-accords-old-seeds-of-peace-iran-israels-forgotten-friendship/.

A spontaneous tradition has emerged in the past two decades. Thousands of Persians gather at Cyrus the Great's tomb to honor him on "Cyrus the Great Day." The unofficial holiday falls on the seventh day of Aban, the day in October that Babylon fell to Cyrus. In one recent gathering, as hordes of people frequently broke into song, a celebrant explained the crowd's sentiment. "We pay tribute to a king who respected people everywhere, no matter what their religious or ethnic background."[58]

[58] Alijani Ershad, "Thousands in Iran use King's Anniversary to Protest against Ruling Regime," *France 24: The Observers*, April 11, 2016. https://observers.france24.com/en/20161103-iran-cyrus-king-regime-protest.

Part 2: History of Iran

An Enthralling Overview of Iranian History, Starting from the Ancient Persians through the Persian Empire to Modern Iran

Introduction

Located in western Asia, sandwiched between the Caspian Sea in the north and the Persian Gulf in the south, at the crossroads of the Levant and the rest of the Asian continent, Iran is arguably one of the most conveniently placed countries in all of Eurasia. Officially known today as the Islamic Republic of Iran, the country has a population of more than eighty-five million people and is the sixth-largest landmass in all of Asia. Iran is an important regional and global actor and has played a big role in Middle Eastern politics for a long time. Due to its geographic location, this area has long been a meeting point of ancient civilizations, resulting in a diffusion of cultures, traditions, customs, and lifestyles and giving birth to a history unlike no other.

However, despite its rich culture, compelling history, and definite identity, much of the Western world tends to associate Iran with religious fanaticism, old-fashioned political structures, and an innate hatred toward the West. Still, these ideas are relatively new, as they were generated largely after the events of the Iranian Revolution of 1979, when a democratic regime was replaced by an Islamic theocracy. The theocracy greatly altered the Iranian way of life and still continues to function to this day.

What many people don't know or rather don't acknowledge is the fact that civilization in Iran has existed for thousands of years, transforming and adapting to changes around the world until finally producing the modern 21st-century sovereign state that is the

Islamic Republic of Iran today. One cannot find a lot of places where life goes back as far as it does in the area occupied by Iran and its peripheries today. It is for this reason that the study of the history of Iran is necessary.

The focus of this book is to provide an in-depth overview of the history of Iran, along with the causes and consequences of each important event in the country's past. It aims to narrate history in a captivating way and provide a solid background on the subject. Throughout the chapters, we will discuss the main developments and key figures in Iranian history and how they affected its society, culture, and politics throughout the ages, starting from ancient times to the 21st century.

The first part of the book will be concerned with covering the ancient history of Iran up until the medieval period. We will discuss the origins of the peoples who inhabited the region thousands of years ago and talk about the establishment of the first prehistoric settlements in the area. Then, the book will move on to ancient Persia. We will explore the formation of the famous ancient Persian Empire and many of its greatest rulers, as well as its eventual conquest by Alexander the Great and the reign of Hellenism in the region. This era is one of the most vital parts of Iran's history, as it contributed greatly to the formation of the Iranian people's identity and ultimately led to the arrival of Islam in the 7th century CE.

The middle part of the book will discuss the history of Iran during the medieval age, starting from the Islamification of the area, first under Muhammad and later under several Arabian caliphates that would emerge as dominant regional actors in the early Golden Age of Islam. We will also cover the global developments that shaped medieval Iran, including the infamous conquests of the region by several Central Asian hordes, namely the Mongols and the Timurids, from the 13th to the 16th centuries. This part of the book will conclude by discussing the emergence of the Safavid dynasty, which ruled Iran for almost 250 years. During the Safavid era, Iran became one of the largest and most powerful empires in Eurasia and went through a series of sociopolitical and cultural changes that would greatly affect its legacy.

The final part of the book will examine the final three hundred years of Iranian history, starting from the Qajar Era, which lasted from 1797 to 1925 and led to the birth of modern Iran. The early modern history of Iran is well known for its high levels of cultural diffusion and socioeconomic development. Then, we will discuss the democratization of Iran with the White Revolution and the important processes that took place immediately after the end of World War II. This will be followed by the reactionary Islamic Revolution and the installation of a theocratic regime that largely backtracked many of the advancements made in the previous decades.

Diving into the history of Iran is not necessarily an easy job, as its dense events require adequate coverage. Thus, you will experience just that: an overview of Iran's most important political, social, and cultural developments that ultimately resulted in the creation of modern-day Iran.

Chapter 1: Iran: What You Need to Know

Geography

The geography of Iran is dominated by mountainous regions that practically surround the country and the small portions of flatter land in its territories. The Zagros Mountains, stretching almost from the Caucasus to the Persian Gulf, is the largest mountain range in the region. The Elburz Mountains are located in the northern part of the country, south of the Caspian Sea, with several peaks reaching ten thousand feet or higher. The famous Damavand Peak is located there; it rises higher than eighteen thousand feet and is one of the most pivotal parts of Persian mythology and culture. In the east, the country is divided from Pakistan and Afghanistan by smaller ranges that sandwich the heart of the country, making Iran one of the highest countries in the world today, with an average elevation of about 4,280 feet.

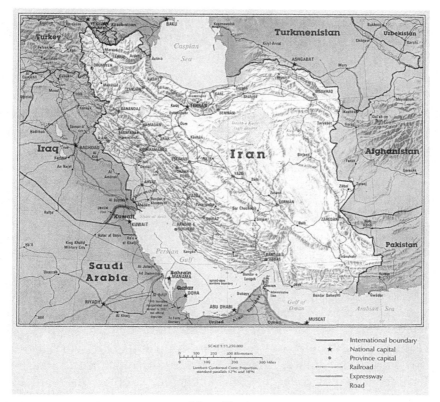

Map of Iran.
https://commons.wikimedia.org/wiki/File:Map_of_Iran.jpg

The proximity of so many different ranges—commonly referred to as the Iranian Plateau, which geologists believe have emerged rather recently when compared to others throughout the world—causes the region to be very active seismologically, something that has been shown many times in different chronicles throughout Persian history. At the heart of the Iranian Plateau lie the deserts of Kavir and Lut, in Iran's north and southeast. These two deserts are extremely hot and windy and are considered to be some of the most inhospitable places in the world. Nobody lives in them. In fact, the majority of Iranian lands are useless for dwelling, as Iran is made up of dry terrain and shallow soil. There is a lack of water, and the land is unfit for agriculture.

Still, despite these disadvantages, Iran is rich when it comes to natural resources. Ever since ancient times, the inhabitants of Iran have been familiar with the abundance of different metals in the country, like iron, zinc, copper, and lead. Modern Iran is famous for its reserves of coal, natural gas, and oil, which are the main reasons behind the country's emergence as a powerful nation during the past century.

The People of Iran

Historians and anthropologists believe that the term "Iran" was first used during the 3rd century BCE by a local ruler who referred to his empire as *Iranshahr*. The name derives from the Aryans, a subset of Indo-European peoples who slowly migrated to India and Iran and organized themselves into the first settlements and tribal societies in Iran beginning in 2000 BCE (the Indus Valley already had its own developed civilization). Therefore, there is good reason to suspect that "Iran" is a modification of the word "Aryan" and means something along the lines of "land of the Aryans."

However, in its common usage, the word "Iran" only really became prominent in the 20th century, as the country had largely been referred to as Persia. "Persia," on the other hand, is derived from "Parahshe," a term used by the Semitic peoples of Mesopotamia to refer to the Zagros Mountains. It perhaps means the "land of the horses." After the Aryan (or Iranian) tribes started dwelling in the Zagros region, it is likely they adopted this name for themselves and thus became known by it to their neighboring societies. The ancient Greeks called the inhabitants of the region "Persians" and their land "Persia." For the rest of history, up until the 20th century, the name stuck. Although the terms "Iran" and "Persia" are not exactly synonyms, with the latter originally referring to the lands of the Zagros and the former deriving from the Aryan peoples who would gradually settle in the region, they do have similarities and have been commonly used to refer to the same people and land.

The situation is less complicated when it comes to Iran's demography. Today, the country is mostly made up of three ethnically distinct groups based on languages: Iranian, Turkic, and Semitic. The Persian language is the most widely spoken language in the country today. The modern Persian language developed from Old Persian due to the assimilation of cultures and peoples. It now combines elements of Arabic with the more local Pahlavi language. Together with the Kurdish dialect, which is spoken by well over 10 percent of the country's ethnically Kurdish population, the Persian language makes up the largest linguocultural group of Iran today.

Then, there are the ethnically Turkic peoples, who arrived in the region from Central Asia but would eventually migrate westward to settle mostly in Anatolia. Still, about a fourth of the Iranians speak a version of the Turkish language today. Finally, a small minority of Iranian citizens are made up of Semitic peoples, who speak Arabic languages and are mainly concentrated in the region of Khuzestan in the western part of the country.

When it comes to Iran's religion, it should come as no surprise that the majority of the country is Muslim. The Shi'a Muslims make up about 89 percent of the population, while about 10 percent are Sunnis. This makes Iran the largest country with a Shi'a majority. Due to the historical hostility between the two groups, Iran has poor relations with neighboring states, most of whom are dominated by Sunni Muslims. The remaining 1 percent of the population is made up of Christians, Jews, and members of the Zoroastrian religion.

Political Geography

Being the seventeenth largest country in the world, modern-day Iran occupies an area of about 628,000 square miles, stretched mostly over its rugged, dry lands, mountains, hills, and inhospitable deserts. Due to the harsh physical geography of the region, Iran has always struggled with problems regarding connectivity. The mountain ranges only have a few passes, and going through them has long been associated with great risks due to their desolate, remote locations at high altitudes. Before the development of modern infrastructure, deserts posed similar obstacles. There was no effective way of avoiding them, especially since Iran only has one river that can be used for transportation—the Karun—and even that does not cover much of the country.

Connectivity was so ill-developed that it would take about six months to travel across the country from east to west during medieval times; in comparison, Europe and the countries of the Levant rarely experienced such hindrances. Difficult terrain made it almost impossible to implement a cohesive infrastructure, as the engineers would struggle to find their way around the rough and unbalanced geography of the region to build a good system of roads and railroads.

The lack of connectivity was an obstacle when it came to a centralized political system. Since it was largely impossible for people, resources, and information to travel through the plateau quickly, political unity was often challenging. Different regions and provinces emerged throughout Iranian history that not only largely governed themselves but also developed their own customs, traditions, and societies.

As of now, the largest administrative divisions within Iran are called provinces, of which the country has thirty-one. Similar administrative units have been present throughout history in various forms, but their essence has always been the same. The eastern and northeastern part of the country is known as Khorasan, which, with its relatively easier-to-navigate geography, was the main entry point of the Central Asian peoples into Iran.

In the north, there are the provinces of Golestan, Mazandaran, and Gilan, which all border the Caspian Sea. For that reason, they have some of the most unique characteristics in all of Iran. They are very densely populated and produce a variety of goods that the rest of the country cannot, like citrus, tea, cotton, and sea products. For centuries, these areas had been considered the most remote, as the people lacked the means to significantly connect the regions with the rest of the Iranian provinces, something that resulted in social and cultural differences, which still exist. Another fertile region of the country is in the northwest. The province of Azerbaijan (not to be confused with the Republic of Azerbaijan, which is located just north of it) has perhaps the strongest sense of regional, distinct identity due to its proximity to the culturally different Caucasus.

In the southwest of the country, there is the region of Fars—the center of the ancient Persian civilization. It is often called Persia proper or Persis. It was where most of the power of ancient Persia was concentrated, including the magnificent cities of Persepolis and Pasargadae, two of the five capitals during the Achaemenid Empire. Over time, its political and economic significance declined, as the center of Persia gradually shifted more northwest. Fars still remains one of the more iconic provinces of modern-day

Iran, with the ruins of its ancient cities being prominent tourist attractions.

We have already briefly touched upon the province of Khuzestan, which lies in the westernmost part of the country, bordering the historically important lands of Mesopotamia. As the gateway to the west, Khuzestan always held special political importance in the eyes of Iran's rulers. Nowadays, it is one of the most ethnically and culturally diverse places in Iran, hosting the majority of the country's Arab population.

Finally, to the southeast, there are the least developed provinces of Iran: Kerman, Makran, Baluchistan, and Sistan. Bordering modern-day Pakistan and being remotely placed from the center of the country, it is not surprising these lands received the least attention from Iranian rulers. Life never managed to thrive in these provinces compared to other areas due to the tough climate conditions.

Briefly on the Socioeconomic System

Last but not least, it is necessary to go over the socioeconomic structure of Iran, as it, together with all the other factors mentioned above, has shaped the lives of the Iranian people throughout history.

The main thing to understand when it comes to Iran's economy is that, unlike its Mesopotamian neighbors in the west, for example, who are blessed by the abundance of fertile lands and fresh water, the vast majority of Iranian land is absolutely unfit for agricultural activity, at least when it comes to harvesting crops. Due to the lack of natural vegetation and the extremely hot temperatures, the ancient peoples who first inhabited Iran were largely nomadic tribes. They regularly moved around with their cattle and horses to find enough grazing land for the animals.

Unlike the plains of Central Asia, Iran has much hillier terrain, which means the nomads had to put in extra effort to survive. To avoid the harsh climates of the seasons, they would move to the hills during the summertime, where the temperatures would be relatively lower, and then return to lower altitudes during winter for the same reason. Still, despite all the hardships, nomadic pastoralism (and especially "vertical" pastoralism, as described above) was a common economic activity in ancient times.

Naturally, this provided the Iranian tribes with food and other necessary products, like leather and wool, which would be used to make clothes, shelters, and other equipment. As pastoralism became more and more important for survival, and as the number of people living in a tribe grew, neighboring tribes usually united to better control their herds, which would normally be spread out over large amounts of land. Throughout time, these tribes became masters of the local geography and acquired other skills to help them survive, like horse riding and archery. Then, slowly, the different tribes became the most important contributors to the militaries of the Iranian states.

Interestingly, tribal pastoralism continued to be a prominent activity in Iran in one shape or another all the way up until the 20th century. In the 1930s, for example, there were still certain tribes in the most remote areas of Iran that largely enjoyed independence and autonomy from the central government. However, with the significant advancements in technology in all fields of life in the age of modernization and globalization, the importance of nomadic tribes has drastically decreased. Many finally adapted and settled down in rural or urban areas throughout the country.

An absolutely crucial development that shaped the ancient Iranian economy was the invention of the qanat: an underground canal that made it possible for the Iranian population to farm crops near whatever scarce water resources were available, like small streams. The system of qanats, which was designed and established all throughout the country, was a game changer, utilizing the slopes of the Iranian Plateau to transport clean water from high to low ground while at the same time minimizing water loss due to factors like evaporation (this was because the water ran underground). It was a remarkable feat of ancient engineering and required constant effort to maintain. Otherwise, the people would have to deal with damage, erosion, and leaks.

Over time, the qanats became an instrumental part of Iran's life, and the network slowly expanded to cover all of Iran's water needs. Today, their remains can still be observed in the more rural areas of the country. They are easily identifiable because of the distinct row of holes that run along the canals, which were once used to check the condition of the qanat while it was still functional.

The construction of qanats fell under the responsibility of the rich landowners, who employed peasants to work their lands. Although agriculture was never Iran's strong side, with the harvests producing much less than that of the more fertile neighboring regions, this sort of agricultural enterprise was the main drive behind Iran's social hierarchy up until the early modern era. The system was not quite feudal, at least to the levels found in Europe, but it essentially operated in a similar way. Members of the higher classes would basically own the lands on which peasants resided and worked. The landowners would give a small minority of the income from these lands to the workers, taking the vast majority for themselves. In turn, as in other societies, the landowners provided the workers with protection and also funded and oversaw the construction of the qanats, which were just as important to a member of the elite as to a peasant.

Obviously, with modernization, the urbanization levels in Iran rose dramatically, with more and more people moving into larger urban centers. This has contributed to the decrease in domestic food production, as the agricultural lifestyle became less prevalent (which was already not that prevalent in comparison to other countries of similar size). Today, agriculture makes up about 25 percent of Iran's economy, and the country mostly produces very niche fruits and vegetables, like apricots and raisins. Still, when compared to the level of population growth, food production has not kept up, and the country has to import about a fourth of its food supplies from external markets.

Chapter 2: From Prehistoric to Ancient Times

The Rise and Fall of the Elamites

It is speculated that the first, most primitive permanent settlements appeared in Iran by about 7000 BCE after millennia of climate changes made the plains not only suitable for living but also quite similar to what they look like today. During the Neolithic period, the first Iranian settlements are thought to have been present in the central part of the Zagros region. The archaeological site of Tepe Sialk, which is dated to about 6500 to 5000 BCE, is one of the most important examples of a Neolithic settlement in this area.

For the next two thousand years or so, there was a drop in the number of new settlements in the area, as the people gradually moved toward the nomadic pastoral lifestyle mentioned in the previous chapter. Interestingly, archaeological evidence suggests the settlements that were not abandoned grew in size.

However, scholars do not yet know what caused this drastic change in lifestyle. It likely had to do with a sudden change in the climate, perhaps rendering the efforts to pursue settled agricultural lives more difficult, especially at this early stage when agriculture, as a whole, was still developing. Many historians have also suggested that people from Iran also moved slowly toward the west to the much richer lands of Mesopotamia, where living conditions were better.

The lack of suitable lands for agriculture was made up for by the fact that Iran was rich when it came to natural resources. It seems the prehistoric peoples were already aware of this as early as perhaps 5000 BCE, as people in the Iranian Plateau started using copper tools, replacing bones and flint as primary materials. Although copper was the most abundant and most widely used during this period, archaeological evidence suggests the people of the plateau near the modern-day cities of Isfahan, Kerman, and Qazvin also mined and used other metals, such as lead, gold, and silver.

One of the most advanced settlements was Shahr-e Sukhteh, located in the easternmost modern-day region of Sistan near Lake Hamun and the Helmand River. Dating back to c. 4000 BCE and probably lasting up until 1300 BCE, Shahr-e Sukhteh thrived as one of the richest and biggest cities in Iran and its surroundings, reaching a population of no less than eight thousand people at its peak. Due to its proximity to water sources, which also provided the settlement with fish, and due to the abundance of different minerals in the area, like lapis lazuli, Shahr-e Sukhteh remains one of the most prominent examples of an urbanized Iranian society in the prehistoric era.

The neighboring civilizations in Mesopotamia managed to reach new levels of urbanization and development, recording their lives and transitioning to the first state-like societies in ancient times. The first Iranian peoples never managed to attain similar heights. Those groups who resided in the western part of Iran, for example, the Urartians and the Lullubi, have been mentioned in some Mesopotamian writings, which means they did have some sort of contact with the Mesopotamians. Even so, they could never quite catch up to them when it came to their overall quality of life.

However, there was a group of people who could compare. They are considered to have been the first Bronze Age Iranian civilization. These people were the Elamites, and they would eventually arrive and dominate the region of Khuzestan from the southern part of the Iranian Plateau. Unlike other Iranian peoples, the Elamites managed to invent their own unique language and writing system quite early after their arrival, by about 3000 BCE, although historians have failed to fully decipher the earliest forms of their language. In the texts of their neighbors, namely the

Babylonians and the Akkadians, the Elamite state seems to have been one of the most prominent kingdoms in the region by about 2700 BCE. It existed throughout much of modern-day Iran and probably developed a large trading network that connected the eastern and westernmost settlements, including Shahr-e Sukhteh.

Up until about the mid-630s, it seems that the Elamite Kingdom went through three different periods: the Old (2400–1600 BCE), the Middle (1500–1100 BCE), and the Neo-Elamite (1100–600 BCE). Throughout this time, the kingdom reached new heights of development and dominance in southeastern Iran, challenging the neighboring states for power and control over the city of Susa, which emerged as an important regional center. In fact, at its peak, the Elamite Kingdom even managed to attack and sack the city of Babylon in c. 1175 BCE, famously taking one of the Code of Hammurabi pillars and transporting it to Susa.

Despite becoming the "first Iranian empire," the Elamites were finally destroyed by the Assyrians in 639 BCE when Assyrian King Ashurbanipal captured Susa. Eventually, the remnants of the empire would be taken over by the ethnic Iranians, who, by that time, slowly started to move into the central and southern parts of Iran in increasing numbers.

Nevertheless, the Elamite Kingdom's contributions to the development of trade and proto-Iranian culture, as well as its role in forming a relationship with the more advanced peoples of Mesopotamia, make it one of the most important parts of ancient Iranian history.

The Avestans and the Birth of Zoroastrianism

By 2000 BCE, the Aryan group from the Indo-European peoples had arrived in Iran, settling down permanently and eventually giving the place its name. Their arrival coincided with the decline of several civilizations in the Middle East, the Mediterranean, and the Indus Valley. Historians believe that the Aryans invaded and conquered these peoples in many instances, slowly replacing other cultures with their own, including in the Iranian Plateau.

The Aryans who inhabited Iran are generally divided into two groups. The first group was the Aryans, who lived in the western part of the plateau. They would eventually speak the Old Persian language, while the other group spoke a completely different language known as Avestan. They dwelled in the east. Since much less is known about the history of the Avestan Iranians than their counterparts in the west, it is perhaps better to briefly talk about them here and then move on to the Aryans of the west, who would eventually give birth to the ancient Persian civilization.

The name "Avesta" refers to a collection of sacred texts, hymns, and scriptures of the Zoroastrian religion. The cradle of the Avestans is thought to be the Airyanem Vaejah lands in eastern Iran, modern-day Pakistan, and Afghanistan, so the description is quite broad. Airyanem Vaejah is described in Zoroastrian and Avestan scriptures as the center of the world and the birthplace of the legendary Zoroaster, as well as the home of the sacred Hara Mountain, which holds a special place in Zoroastrian mythology. Historians speculate the territories mentioned above were the actual dwelling of the Avestans.

The history of the Avestan people is divided into two parts: Old and Young Avestan. Many cultural and social developments took place during the transitional stage between the two periods. The Old Avestan period was characterized by a simple social structure, low levels of urbanization for the time, no literacy, and limited trade and contact with other peoples. On the other hand, the Young Avestan period saw an adaptation to agricultural and pastoral lifestyles (with the cow considered to be a sacred creature), the creation of settlements, and the establishment of early forms of family-dominated social structures without many hierarchical levels. The Young Avestan society was largely divided into three classes: warriors, priests, and herdsmen. It was a rather primitive yet useful division.

The Avestans are the most known for their culture, namely their religion, Zoroastrianism. In fact, the great prophet Zoroaster, a central figure in the formation of the religion, is believed to have appeared among the Avestans. This belief has become prominent rather recently among historians. Traditionally, the birthplace of Zoroaster was thought to have been a place called Ray near modern-day Tehran. It is believed he was born sometime in the 6th or 7th century BCE, about two and a half centuries before Alexander the Great's conquest of Persia. The Avestan scriptures and the Gathas, the oldest texts of Zoroastrianism (believed to have been written by Zoroaster himself), suggest the great prophet was born in the Airyanem Vaejah region. This idea is reinforced by the similarities between the Gathas and the Vedas (the famous texts of the Hindu religion in India) and seems more logical due to the relatively close proximity between the two places.

According to Zoroaster, the deity he worshiped, the one true god, was called Ahura Mazda, the "Wise God." At the time, other ancient Iranian religions, just like in many other places throughout the world, emphasized the holy nature of astronomical objects, like the sun and the moon, and worshiped the personifications of natural phenomena, like the wind and rain. This was something Zoroaster went against. He proclaimed that his visions had revealed to him the only transcendent Being, the Creator of all and "the First Father of Righteousness." Ahura Mazda was supposed to be the god who created the earth, the stars, the moon, and every living thing. Angra Mainyu, on the other hand, was the "evil twin" of Ahura Mazda, and he was the source of all evil and darkness. The struggle for humans was to follow the way of Ahura Mazda and live a good and righteous life, praising and celebrating his majestic nature.

Zoroastrianism would soon become the central belief of the Iranian culture and would come to shape the region forever. It built on the older religions and, in a way, advanced them by making the struggle between good and evil the main point of the religion. Zoroaster left a lasting influence not only on Iran and its people but also on other cultures the religion came into contact with.

The Medes

The Avestans are a significant part of ancient Iranian history, although not a lot is known about them due to their remoteness from other advanced, literate societies of the time. We know much more about the people who settled in the northern and southwestern parts of Iran. In about the 9th century BCE, ancient Mesopotamian writings speak of the Medes people, who dwelled south of the Elburz Mountains in the western part of the Iranian Plateau, much closer to the more developed ancient civilizations than the Avestans. A lot of archaeological evidence in this area supports this claim, as different ancient Median settlements have been found and thoroughly excavated.

The Medes are significant in Iranian history because they were one of the first Iranians to consolidate into proto-state-like formations, along with the Elamites to their south. Historians believe the reason behind the advancement to a more cohesive political structure from a primitive nomadic tribal society stemmed from their contact with their expansionist western neighbor, Assyria. The Assyrian Empire was one of the most powerful military factions in ancient Mesopotamia, and its need for metals and horses is likely to have been the reason behind its expeditions east into the Iranian territories as early as c. 881 BCE.

For the next century, different Assyrian kings dominated the Medians, prompting the latter to unite into a predominantly anti-Assyrian faction in order to resist the invaders. Eventually, the Assyrian records tell of a man by the name of Daiaukku, who managed to unite the Median people with the objective of rebelling against the Assyrians and driving them out in the late 8th century BCE. This coincides with the accounts of Herodotus, who mentions that a man named Deioces became the first king of the Medes and ruled for nearly fifty years. He became popular for his efforts to defeat the Assyrians.

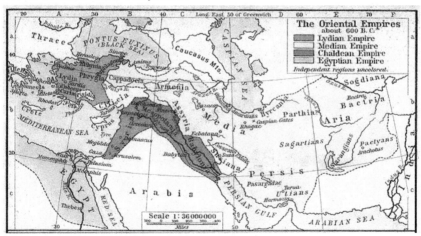

The Median Empire at its greatest extent.
https://commons.wikimedia.org/wiki/File:Median_Empire.jpg

The Medians followed in the footsteps of Daiaukku and started their long struggle for liberation from the Assyrian yoke. Eventually, Cyaxares, the grandson of Daiaukku, ascended the

193

throne in c. 625 BCE and managed to not only defeat his rivals but also make the Median Empire one of the strongest and most prosperous in the ancient world at the time. In his accounts, Herodotus tells how Cyaxares completely restructured the Median army, adopting elements from Scythia and Assyria, which made it more professional and mightier. He also united other Iranians, like the Persians, into a coalition. Cyaxares formed an alliance with Babylonia, the enemy of the Assyrian Empire. Then, in the late 7th century BCE, he defeated the Assyrians with the help of his allies and took over their lands, together with Babylonia.

What makes Cyaxares's reign so legendary is the fact that by his death in c. 584 BCE, he had expanded to the east and to the west. He destroyed the Kingdom of Urartu in Armenia and invaded and took over lands in eastern Anatolia before concluding peace with the ancient Lydian Empire, which ruled western Anatolia.

The rule of King Cyaxares marked the absolute zenith of the Median Empire, which would start its gradual decline after the accession of Cyaxares's son, Astyages. At its greatest extent, the Median Empire controlled a huge territory, including most of modern-day Iran, provinces in northern Mesopotamia, Greater Armenia, western Anatolia, and territories in the east.

Chapter 3: The Persian Empire

From Achaemenes to Cyrus the Great

South of the Medes, in the historical province of Fars or Persis, between the Polvar and Kur Rivers, another people group emerged by c. 700 BCE. They were called the Persians, and they would eventually come to dominate the neighboring lands and form legendary empires, making them the "real" ancestors of Iran. The different tribes are thought to have been consolidated by the legendary figure Achaemenes, who emerged as their leader and is the founder of the Achaemenid dynasty, which ruled Persia and its people for centuries.

Just like their Median neighbors to the north, the Persians were quite active, making frequent contact with the people that surrounded them. For example, the Persians fought with the Elamites against the invading Assyrians in c. 670 BCE. King Teispes, the son of Achaemenes, eventually took over the Elamite capital of Anshan. After expanding the realm, he divided its control between his two sons, Cyrus I and Ariaramnes. We know of this from several Assyrian records that mention Cyrus I to have been the ruler of Anshan in c. 640 BCE. Cyrus's son, Cambyses I, would later accept Median suzerainty since his reign coincided with the rise of the Medes under Cyaxares. Cambyses married his granddaughter, Mandane, during the reign of King Astyages of the Median Empire. Thus, by the early 6th century BCE, Cambyses I, the fourth generation of the Achaemenid dynasty, was the ruler of

Anshan and its surrounding lands. But it would be his son, Cyrus II, who would emerge as one of the most memorable rulers in the ancient era.

When Cyrus II succeeded his father in 559 BCE, the Median Empire had already destroyed and taken over many of the western kingdoms, which alarmed the Babylonians. The Babylonians were allies of the Medes, although the Babylonians had grown wary of the growing power of their allies. Historians believe the Babylonians encouraged Cyrus to join them in their cause to undermine Median power, resulting in the young king's revolt against his grandfather, King Astyages of the Medes, in c. 550 BCE. Astyages marched on Anshan with a large army to crush Cyrus but was eventually defeated, although history is not exactly clear how (it probably had to do with the fact that a large portion of his forces switched sides and defected to Cyrus). Somehow, perhaps with the help of the Median nobility, Cyrus was able to imprison Astyages and capture the Median capital of Ecbatana. With his victory, Cyrus was essentially able to unite the Persian and the Median realms, declaring himself to be the "king of kings and the king of the lands." Since Cyrus was a descendant of royal dynasties from both the Medes and Persians (he was the son of King Astyages's daughter Mandane of the Medes and the son of Cambyses I of the Achaemenid dynasty), he managed to secure his position as a legitimate ruler of both kingdoms and proceeded to build an empire unlike any other of his time.

In about a year, Cyrus II of Persia invaded and conquered the Iranian peoples in the regions of Hyrcania south of the Caspian Sea and in Parthia in northeastern Iran. Then, he turned his attention to the west, where King Croesus of the Lydians sought to take over the central and eastern Anatolian provinces, which had previously been under the control of the Median Empire. Cyrus defeated Croesus by 547 BCE, taking the Lydian capital city of Sardis on the Mediterranean and all the other territories formerly under the suzerainty of the Lydian king.

The ten-year period of Cyrus's reign between the conquest of Lydia and the subsequent conquest of Babylonia is relatively unknown, although historians believe that Cyrus either stopped expansion or consolidated his power in eastern Iran. Thanks to Herodotus, what is known is that in 539 BCE, Cyrus II invaded

Babylonia, defeating its unpopular King Nabonidus and laying siege to the ancient city of Babylon. Cyrus and his forces emerged victorious from the siege, claiming Babylon and all its surrounding lands. He expanded the borders of the Persian Empire to include Mesopotamia.

During his time as king, Cyrus single-handedly defeated all the major factions of the ancient Middle and Near East and laid the foundations for a vast and powerful Persian Empire. For his deeds, he has come to be remembered in history as Cyrus the Great, a title he gained not only because of his conquests but also because of his wisdom and ability to govern. In addition to being a great warrior and tactician, Cyrus was a benevolent and tolerant ruler. He never took away the freedoms of the people that he conquered. For example, once he defeated Nabonidus and seized control of the Babylonian lands, he encouraged the practice of different regional religions, something the Babylonian kings had long prohibited.

Not much is known about the final years of Cyrus's life, as well as the details of how he actually managed his kingdom. Still, Cyrus the Great is mostly remembered for his magnificent achievement of forging the Persian Empire and making it a regional powerhouse in the Middle East.

Persia after Cyrus

Cyrus II would be succeeded by his son, Cambyses II, in 530 BCE after dying while fighting some nomadic tribe at the age of seventy. Cambyses II's rule would be relatively short compared to that of his father, only ruling for eight years. Overall, his reign seems to be rather mysterious and controversial, with his biggest achievement being his conquest of Egypt in 525 BCE. Just like with his father, not much is known when it comes to how Cambyses actually governed the empire, with most primary sources depicting his campaign of Egypt and his supposed disgracing of the local religion. The young king died on his journey home to Persis, although the exact cause of his death is unknown.

After the death of Cambyses II, Persia found itself in a period of instability and turmoil. Although the details of what transpired still remain unknown because of contrary narratives from the era, the general picture still remains the same. Apparently, as Cambyses started his journey back to Persis from Egypt, his brother, Smerdis, pressed his claim to the throne. However, in reality, according to both Herodotus and the only other source of information available that depicts the situation (the Behistun Inscription in western Iran), Cambyses had already secretly murdered his real brother. The claimant was an impostor. Still, his appearance resembled that of the king's brother so much that even members of the royal family believed him. In fact, it is very likely the pretender was a man by the name of Gaumata, a cunning Magian priest, who seized the opportunity and managed to become the Persian ruler in 522 BCE. Historians don't have a lot of information about the Magi, but they were priests in Zoroastrianism and other pre-Avestan religions.

Gaumata would only sit on the throne for a very short time, as members of the royal court and the Persian aristocracy eventually found out the truth and deposed him. Darius I assumed the throne. Just like Cyrus, whose daughter he married, he would eventually come to be known as "the Great." According to the Behistun Inscription, which Darius commissioned and which depicts the events of defeating the usurper, Darius not only took down Gaumata but also reversed many of the pretender's decisions, destroying the temples he had built and restoring old practices in the sanctuaries. Herodotus claims that Darius proceeded to brutally suppress all Magians after assuming power and that his actions forever caused strife between the Magians and the Zoroastrians, as well as the people of Persia and the Medians.

It has also been speculated that Smerdis, or, as he is referred to in Old Persian, Bardiya, was the true brother of Cambyses and that Darius technically usurped the throne when he deposed him. Regardless of what happened, by the end of 522 BCE, Darius I emerged as the king of Persia, starting a long and prosperous reign that would forever affect the country's history.

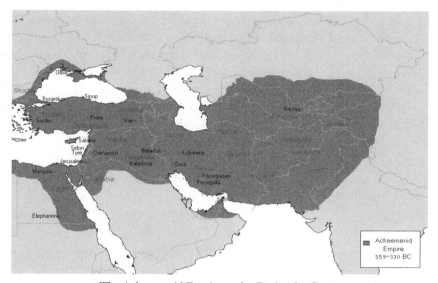

The Achaemenid Empire under Darius the Great.
https://commons.wikimedia.org/wiki/File:Achaemenid_Empire_559_-_330_(BC).png

After becoming king, Darius had a rather difficult task ahead of him. Cyrus the Great had managed to conquer the neighboring peoples and lay the foundations for the Persian Empire, so Darius had to firmly assert his dominance over his many subjects, something that he achieved rather marvelously. Due to the power struggles, different revolts broke out in Persia, which the new king eventually dealt with, suppressing eleven rebellions in total and mercilessly defeating every challenger. Not only that, but Darius also managed to expand the Persian borders even further by conquering the Libyan territories on the North African coast. He also crossed into Europe and took control of southern Thrace and asserted Persian control in the east, reaching western India.

At its greatest extent, the Persian Empire under Darius I is believed to have ruled nearly fifty million subjects and stretched three continents, from North Africa to the Indus River and from the Caucasus to Mesopotamia. Darius I earned his title "the Great" because of his excellent administrative policies, which would completely transform the way the empire was governed, contributing to the creation of a stronger, more cohesive system that was decentralized enough to allow regional rulers large autonomy but gave Darius the respect as the one true "king of kings and lands."

The Persian territories were divided into twenty separate provinces called satrapies. Each had local governors called satraps and paid taxes and yearly tributes to the king. Satraps would be personally placed by the king and his court and were always of noble descent. Persis, the central province of the empire, was excluded from this system, as it was under the direct governance of Darius himself and was exempt from taxes. What is interesting in this system was that there was technically no capital city for the empire, a place where most of the power would be centralized. The main reason behind this was probably the fact that Darius was always on the move, with his court following him everywhere he went. Instead of one capital city, there were four major cities: Persepolis, which was a ceremonial center; Babylon; Ecbatana, the former Median capital and the king's summer residence; and Susa, the former Elamite capital and the king's winter residence. The king would probably spend the different seasons in these four cities in times of peace. He constantly moved around and visited them, often personally overseeing the administrative issues of each and creating a stronger sense of the monarchy in his subjects.

Just dividing the vast lands of the empire into different satrapies was not enough, as Darius recognized the need to travel efficiently from one place to another. Thus, during his reign, he started to greatly expand and improve the existing road system in his realm, building the famous "Royal Persian Road," which connected Sardis to Susa and stretched for over 1,600 miles—an incredible feat of ancient logistics and infrastructure. A more cohesive and advanced road system was key to regional connectivity and allowed faster travel times for merchants, goods, messengers, and armies.

Along the new roads, Darius established different stations at set intervals where travelers could rest and spend the night. He also established what was essentially a postal service. Royal messengers traveled great distances and could stop after getting tired at one of the stations along the roads. They could entrust their message to another royal messenger who was stationed there at all times, ensuring that no time was lost when it came to the exchange of information. Needless to say, it was an amazing improvement that required a great deal of attention and organization to maintain.

Darius also sought to improve water travel, issuing the construction of various new canals, such as the one that ran from the Nile Delta to the Red Sea and whose construction was personally commissioned by Darius when he traveled to Egypt in 497 BCE.

The economic reforms of Darius the Great are just as impressive. After nearly a century since the Persian Empire existed, Darius would see that the empire started to use the same currency—the daric—which went a great way in regulating the Persian economy. This was followed by the implementation of a cohesive measurement system. The main reason behind this was to mint coins of similar weight and shape to determine their overall value. Both gold and silver darics were minted throughout the empire. The new road system and the monetary reform boosted domestic and foreign trade and commerce.

Throughout history, the reigns of truly great monarchs almost always contained at least some form of cultural development or renaissance, and Darius the Great was no exception. Persian culture thrived during his rule, something that was a result of the stability, prosperity, and peace that characterized Darius's later years as king. Unlike his predecessors, Darius put a great emphasis on all things Persian and was a great promoter and supporter of the culture. The writing system of Old Persian is thought to have been finalized by him, and the fact that there are many accounts of his rule is a testament to that.

Crucially, however, Darius was the most prominent Persian monarch to recognize that Persians were a part of a larger group of peoples—the Aryans (Iranians)—and he referred to himself both as a Persian and an Aryan. His tomb, located some eight kilometers northwest of Persepolis, famously reads, "I am Darius the great king, king of kings, king of countries containing all kinds of men, king in this great earth far and wide, son of Hystaspes, an Achaemenid, a Persian, son of a Persian, an Aryan, of Aryan lineage."

This Persian cultural revival is also characterized by the construction of numerous magnificent sites, temples, and castles, which were all commissioned by Darius and bore varying degrees of importance. In his endeavors to build these architectural landmarks, the accounts tell of Darius using different materials from different parts of his empire—a detail that further confirms high levels of connectivity and trade. For example, the great palace he constructed in Susa used lapis lazuli, stone, gold, and ebony, which were imported from places like Bactria, Elam, Lydia, and Egypt. It is likely that craftsmen and artisans from these provinces traveled to Susa to help build the palace. Persepolis, a major center of Persian culture, was built during his reign. The city was surrounded by great walls and hosted administrative, financial, and ritual complexes of great magnitude. Due to his struggle against the Magians, Darius is also considered the first ruler who essentially made Zoroastrianism a proto-official religion of the realm, although his successor, Xerxes, definitely contributed to it.

From early on in his reign, Darius realized the dangers that were innate with being in charge of such a vast and diverse empire. The different revolts he had to deal with in his early years as king demonstrated this. Thus, to avoid potential uprisings and challenges to his rule, Darius made sure to improve the military and also assert his legitimacy in the realm. As the Behistun Inscription suggests, Darius overpowered Bardiya thanks to the help of loyal Persians. Darius believed that he could rely on the Persians the most, as they had supported him for many years. Thus, the Persians constituted the bulk of his army. Darius created the famous Immortals, which was an elite unit of entirely Persian warriors that numbered ten thousand men.

Then, Darius made sure to underline his supreme rule over his subjects, as well as the fact that he was the one true "king of kings." He reminded his people of his royal descent from Achaemenes, essentially the founder of Persia, and stressed that he was the rightful heir to the throne, perhaps trying to suppress any beliefs that he had usurped power from Bardiya. According to the Behistun Inscription, Darius claimed that he had a divine right to rule Persia, something granted to him by Ahura Mazda, and that he had demonstrated his power and military prowess by defeating the usurper Bardiya and by emerging victorious from many of his battles.

The Behistun Inscription tells us a great deal about how Darius essentially legitimized himself as the true ruler of Persia by combining four of the most important qualities: royal blood, favor of the one true god, military prowess, and justice and virtue. In fact, long after Darius's reign, these four qualities were considered essential for any ruler of Iran.

Darius the Great was the brightest point of the ancient Persian Empire, transforming it from a state built solely upon expansion to a stable, prosperous realm. It was perhaps the most advanced and strongest empire by the time of his death in 486 BCE.

The Struggle for Greece

Xerxes I ascended the throne in 486 BCE after the passing of Darius I, marking the beginning of a very influential era for Persia. During Xerxes's reign, the empire saw itself trying to expand its borders farther to the west in the Greek lands of Thrace and the Peloponnese. By the time of Persian expansion into western Anatolia and southern Thrace, the Greek states perceived the prospect of joining the empire in different ways. Some recognized that becoming a part of a larger empire would bring economic benefits, bolstering trade and commerce between Greece and the east. Others believed the Persian Empire, which had grown in power exponentially and was undoubtedly stronger than Greece, which was divided between different rival city-states, was a definite threat to everything Greek, from its vibrant culture to its economy.

Back in 490 BCE, after Darius defeated the Scythians and established control over southeastern Thrace, he declared Persian suzerainty over all of the Greek lands. Some city-states, namely Athens and Sparta, resisted. The Greeks achieved a close but significant victory at Marathon against the Persian army that had been sent to "punish" them, prompting Darius to abandon hopes for an invasion of Greece. Darius could not and did not make time for another invasion, instead deciding to adopt a friendlier policy toward Greece and even welcoming and employing many Greeks.

With the accession of Xerxes, the Persian foreign policy toward Greece changed once again. The new ruler viewed the conquest of Greece as a project that had been started by his father and that he had to complete. Xerxes planned an invasion soon after becoming king, launching his campaign in 480 BCE after assembling a much larger force than what was available for the Greek city-states. Crossing into Thrace, the Persian army and navy followed the Aegean coast and entered Greece through Macedonia without much resistance. Famously, the Persians defeated a small but fierce Spartan-led force at Thermopylae after struggling against them for three days in the narrow passes of the mountains.

After Thermopylae, the Greek cities fell one by one, including Athens, which the Persians sacked in late 480 BCE. What saved Greece from utter destruction was the decisive naval victory against the Persian fleet at Salamis. Thanks to the efforts of Athenian general Themistocles, the Greeks lured and trapped the Persians in an advantageous position. With his fleet suffering heavy losses, Xerxes's chances of capturing all of Greece were significantly reduced, and he was forced to retreat to Sardis, essentially abandoning the invasion, which would be finally put to an end by the Greeks after their victory at Plataea.

While Persia's inability to subdue Greece might seem strange at first, and rightfully so, the impact it had on the development of both sides is disputed by historians. Most believe that Persia's defeat in both campaigns against the Greeks marked the beginning of a slow decline of Persia, leading to its ultimate conquest at the hands of Alexander the Great nearly 150 years later. Xerxes had poured a lot of money and resources into the offensive; that money and resources could have been used to further build up the lands the Persian king already controlled. It certainly appears that the struggle for Greece was not merely just another border war for Persia.

However, as some historians have depicted, the Greco-Persian Wars were not a conflict between "the west and the east." The motives behind Xerxes's invasion were materialistic just as much as symbolic: yes, it's true that he did want to finish the conquest started by his father, but it is also true that Greece was one of the richest places in the ancient world. Taking control of the wealthy Greek cities would bring great prosperity to the Persian crown. If anything, the war is a great testament to proving that numerical advantage is not always sufficient. The Greek armies were some of the best in the world; they were very disciplined, organized, and professional and were certainly the main reason behind the successful efforts of resistance against the Persians, who relied less on tactics and more on overwhelming the enemy.

Still, the unsuccessful campaign had an effect on Xerxes, as well as on the whole empire. For the next fifteen years, Xerxes decided not to embark on another daring military campaign, instead devoting his attention to court politics and building Persian cities, especially Persepolis. It is speculated that court intrigue was the reason for his demise. Xerxes was assassinated in 465 BCE and was succeeded by relatively weaker kings who rarely pushed expansionist policies. The ineffective changes implemented in the decades following Xerxes's assassination by subsequent rulers, starting from Artaxerxes I, caused great discontent among the different peoples of the empire. Tax rates increased, and corruption skyrocketed. The discontented populace rose up against the Achaemenid rulers time and time again, and the king dealt with the insurgents ruthlessly.

By the time Artaxerxes III became the king in 359 BCE, the situation had gotten out of control. Constant revolts had resulted in the loss of Egypt, and the court was engulfed in intrigue and schemes. Rival factions, with varying levels of actual legitimacy, pressed their claims to the Persian throne, prompting the new king to murder tens of his kin to assert his dominance as the true ruler. By the end of his reign, King Philip II of Macedon had emerged as a major power. He defeated the Greek city-states, including the long-standing rivals of Persia: Athens and Sparta. The Persians tried to stop Philip's rise to power and the Greek unification, but instead of getting involved militarily, they operated from behind the scenes, trying to exert their influence on the warring factions by different means, like bribing or blackmail.

Artaxerxes died a year later after the unification of Greece under Philip, in 337 BCE, likely having been poisoned by his doctor. The throne went to Darius III, the grandnephew of Artaxerxes. Darius only became king because his great-grandfather had slain so many of his kinsmen. Darius III would confront the biggest challenger to the Persian Empire. His name was Alexander the Great, the son of Philip II.

How exactly Alexander managed to put an end to the Achaemenids is a long and intriguing story. A thorough coverage of the event requires diving deep into intricate details to present the viewpoint of both sides; it deserves a book of its own. Since we have a lot of history to cover, here is the short version. Alexander the Great marched on the Persian positions, defeating them in three major battles in Anatolia: Granicus (334), Issus (333), and Gaugamela (331). He effectively drove the Persians out of the peninsula and Mesopotamia.

Alexander the Great conquered Egypt, Babylon, Anatolia, and Armenia with relative ease, thanks to the superiority of his phalanx and hoplites. He had defeated the bulk of the Persian army by the time he reached the Iranian Plateau. Darius III was forced to flee to the east but was eventually betrayed by his own satraps, who had long grown hostile toward the kings in Persis. By taking all the major provincial centers in the following years, Alexander the Great put an end to the Persian Empire. He seized all its lands and started a period of Hellenization in Iran, as well as the rest of the Near East.

Chapter 4: A New Era

Hellenistic Iran

By the time of Alexander the Great's death in 323 BCE, he had created the largest empire in the ancient world, having taken over all of the territories formally under the Achaemenids. His realm stretched from Macedonia to the northwestern border of India. This marked a marvelous achievement. He was the most powerful man in the world. It also had great implications for the Greek culture, which Alexander spread throughout his conquered lands. The four-hundred-year or so period that started after his death marked a golden age for the Greek culture, as it would come to dominate the lives of diverse territories. This period would come to be known as the Hellenistic period, with the ancient Greek word *Hellas* being used to refer to Greece. Hellenism shaped the future of the lands it reached and greatly influenced the social and political processes that would take place during the period.

When it comes to discussing the history of Hellenistic Iran, it has to be mentioned that Iran, or Persia, as an independent state, did not exist for a long time after Alexander's conquest. Two years after his unexpected death, in 321 BCE, several of his generals met up in Triparadisus, modern-day Lebanon, to discuss the matters of succession. The territories were divided into different satrapies, stretching from Greece to Persia, with individual commanders in charge of them. Technically, Alexander's half-brother, Philip Arrhidaeus, and his son, Alexander IV, were named as his heirs.

However, for the next few centuries, the lords of the satrapies largely operated on their own, not being subject to whoever was the "king" in Macedon (the homeland of Alexander).

What these satrapies and their rulers shared in common was their Greek origin. Throughout the years, they would slowly Hellenize the lands that were traditionally non-Greek. This resulted in one of the most amazing cultural phenomena of ancient times, as the Greek culture fused with the many eastern cultures. Not only did the Greek language, although often modified, become the most widely spoken language in the east, sort of like the first "common tongue," but the Greek gods were also worshiped throughout the satrapies. Elements of local religions were combined with the Greek religion, which gave birth to a lot of unique details in the lives of ordinary people. That's why the word "Hellenistic" is different from "Hellenic," with the latter meaning Greek while the former refers to the mix of Greek and eastern cultures.

The successor Hellenistic kingdoms.
https://commons.wikimedia.org/wiki/File:Diadoch.png

The different Hellenistic satrapies developed differently, with some managing to gain more power than the others and basically emerging as kingdoms of their own with their own hereditary dynasties. Several of them are particularly important. There was the Ptolemaic Kingdom, which included the lands of Egypt and the North African coast. It was founded by General Ptolemy and grew to become a powerful kingdom, lasting until 30 BCE before its conquest by Rome. The Kingdom of Pergamon was ruled by the Attalid dynasty, which controlled lands in western Anatolia and lasted for 150 years. The Kingdom of Bactria lay at the easternmost border of the Hellenistic world and included Central Asian, western Indian, and eastern Persian lands. It was known as the "land of the thousand golden cities." And then there was the Seleucid Empire, a state that had been expanded by its founder and the first satrap, Seleucus I of Babylonia, to include almost all of the former territories controlled by the Achaemenid dynasty. The Seleucid Empire would be the largest surviving satrapy from Alexander the Great's empire, reaching its peak in the mid-3rd century BCE. It would control almost all of ancient Iran, Mesopotamia, eastern Anatolia, and the Levant.

Parthia

Thus, the Hellenistic Seleucid Empire was still in possession of Iran in 238 BCE when a confederation of tribes that dwelled southeast of the Caspian Sea came together and rebelled. They were probably of Scythian origin. United by their king, Arsaces, these tribes were known as the Parthians. They had come to Iran around the same time as the Medians and the Persians. We know of the Parthians thanks to the extensive Greek and Roman accounts of their rise to power; no actual Parthian historical records have been found.

In any case, it is known that after the unification of the more primitive tribes under Arsaces, the Parthians slowly took over the bordering Seleucid territories and emerged as significant regional actors by the 2nd century BCE. Their rise was also aided by the decline of the Seleucids, as the empire was involved in constant wars in the west against Ptolemaic Egypt and Rome and in the east against the Indians. In 155 BCE, Mithridates I of Parthia finally decided to expand westward. His long campaign ultimately resulted in the capture of the city of Seleucia in Mesopotamia in 141 BCE.

In the following decades, the Parthians consolidated their rule over the Iranian territories and became rivals to ever-expanding Rome, something that was proven in 53 BCE when they defeated the Romans at the Battle of Carrhae in southeastern Anatolia with fewer men. Thanks to their nomadic origins in the plains of Central Asia, the Parthians were masters of horse warfare, excelling in open battles by utilizing both light-mounted archers and heavy cataphract horsemen to outmaneuver and crush the slow-moving, heavy Roman infantry.

During this period, the Parthian Empire reached its greatest extent, essentially having taken over all of the past Seleucid and Achaemenid territories, including Bactria, Persia, Mesopotamia, the South Caucasus, and parts of eastern Anatolia. For the next two hundred years, the Parthians were the biggest threat to the Romans, the latter of whom had greatly expanded their holdings and essentially conquered the western part of Alexander's empire.

With their culture still deeply rooted in their Central Asian tribal origins, the Parthian culture is especially interesting when considering its relationship with Hellenism, as it contains elements from both. Unlike other peoples, the Parthians did not have their own language and writing. They used Greek when communicating and in inscriptions on their coinage. The Parthian religion is largely thought to have been Zoroastrianism, but that is not to say the Parthians were intolerant of other religions within their borders, especially if one compares them to the Romans, who are infamous for the persecution of religious minorities.

The Rise of the Sassanids

The Parthian Empire reached the height of its power during its conflicts with Rome, which would last until 218 CE when the two sides agreed to a peace treaty. Although the Romans never truly found success when battling the Parthians, the situation was slowly deteriorating domestically for the Parthians. The ruling Arsacid dynasty of Parthia had suffered several decades of unfortunate events by the turn of the 3rd century CE, including various plague outbreaks in the eastern regions of the empire and the depletion of natural resources, mostly metals, due to their constant usage during wars. In addition, the political structure of the Parthian Empire was not as strong and advanced as it had been, for example, in Rome. For centuries, the Parthian kings had been dependent upon western expansion to fill their treasuries and maintain their dominant position over their subjects.

Thus, the internal struggles culminated in the year 205 when the upset population of Persis revolted against the king. Even after the destruction of the Achaemenids by Alexander and the subsequent occupation of Persian lands by the Seleucids and the Parthians, Persis remained one of the most autonomous regions. Then again, the political structure that extended over the Hellenistic lands after Alexander's death was not really cohesive in most places, so this fact should come as no big surprise. Before the revolt, for example, Persis still largely spoke Old Persian (Pahlavi), while the rest of the ancient Persian provinces had switched to Hellenistic Greek.

The revolt that started in 205 marked the beginning of the end for the Parthians. A local garrison commander named Ardashir led the rebels against the neighboring lands of Persis and defeated those lords who were still acceptive of Parthian suzerainty. Ardashir managed to significantly consolidate his position. Parthia was still unstable when King Artabanus V took the throne. At some point, he sent the main Parthian forces to war with the Romans in the west. The king had to stop his campaign to try to crush the rebels, but it was too late.

In 224, Ardashir and his supporters defeated Artabanus V. Two years later, they captured the capital city of Ctesiphon on the Tigris River. Having defeated most of the pro-Parthian lords of the realm, Ardashir was crowned the new king of kings, marking the beginning of a new Persian empire under a different dynasty. By this point, it had been more than five hundred years since the destruction of the Achaemenids by Alexander the Great.

Ardashir founded the Sassanid (Sasanian) dynasty, which would rule over Iran for the next four hundred years. The name "Sassanid" derives from a man called Sasan, who was either Ardashir's father or grandfather and is thought to have been somehow connected to previous rulers of Iran either directly by blood or to establish a sense of legitimacy. In any case, the Sassanids often claimed to have been descended from the legendary dynasty of the Kayanians, which is mentioned in the Zoroastrian texts. Although no clear line between them and the Sassanids can be traced, the narrative of the new king of kings coming from the same province as the Achaemenids certainly must have seemed attractive to the people.

Ardashir was succeeded by Shapur I in 240, who built upon the conquests of his father and further expanded the Sassanid Empire. Throughout his reign, Shapur I would struggle against Rome in Anatolia and the Levant. After being driven back from Antioch and forced to sign a peace treaty three years later, Shapur renewed his struggle with Rome for Syria in 258, this time emerging victorious and even managing to capture large parts of the Roman army, including Emperor Valerian. For hundreds of years, the Sassanids and the Romans continued to fight over contested provinces.

In a broader sense, the conflict between Rome and Sassanid Iran can be interpreted as a clash of cultures, especially when it came to places like Armenia, which was a major region where both parties had their own interests. The records show that during Shapur's reign, Zoroastrianism was the "official" religion of the Sassanids, and the Persians would force their conquered subjects to convert. Armenia was no different. It was invaded and conquered in the 250s by Shapur, and the Sassanid king installed his son as the ruler of the province and forced its population to convert. The Armenians resisted, and with the help of the Romans, they were able to drive out the invading Persians from their lands twenty years later, reinstalling the old Parthian Arsacid dynasty at its head. Armenia accepted Christianity as its official religion, something that angered the Sassanids even more since they saw Armenia as their sphere of influence. Eventually, Rome and Persia would divide Armenia into two, with the eastern part of the country becoming Zoroastrian Sassanid vassals, while the west went under the protectorate of Rome (which, by that time, was the Byzantine Empire).

In addition to being a very capable military power, Sassanid Iran is especially significant in history due to the developments it undertook regarding its societal structure, which was far more advanced and cohesive than the previous Iranian empires. The Letter of Tansar is the main source historians use when discussing Sassanid sociopolitical life. The letter is thought to have been written by a 3rd-century Zoroastrian priest during the reign of Ardashir and then revised a couple of centuries later under King Khosrow I Anoshirvan. The letter is considered to be propaganda, as it depicts King Ardashir as a noble and honest man who restored the true Zoroastrian religion, which had been disgraced during the time of the Parthians. It may have served as a sort of justification for Ardashir's rebellion against Parthia, as well as the "official" proclamation of Zoroastrianism as the one true faith of the Sassanid state.

In addition to outlining the importance of Zoroastrianism, the Letter of Tansar also divides society into four classes, with the priests at the top, followed by the warriors, then by scholars, and finally by artisans. This hierarchical division was integral to Sassanid Iran. Although it was not as strict as the Indian caste system, it was still very much respected and allowed for limited social mobility. It was the ruler's duty to not only ensure that each class prospered in its own regard and remained stable but also that the higher classes did not use their privileges unjustly to oppress people who stood lower than them in the hierarchy. This detail further underlines the fact that one of the main qualities of ancient Iranian kings was considered to be a sense of honor and justice and that the strength of the monarchy directly resulted in the strength of its people.

The importance and status of Iranian kings are clearly demonstrated in their magnificent and often over-the-top titles. The full title for Shapur I, for example, was "the Mazda worshipper, the god Shapur, king of kings of Iran and non-Iran, of the race of gods, son of the Mazda worshipper, of the god Ardashir, king of kings of the Iranians, of the race of gods, grandson of Papak, king of the empire of Iran. "It is clear that the Iranian kings placed a lot of emphasis on their noble ancestry and their divine status, which was given by Ahura Mazda. While this phenomenon is not unique to Iranian culture, as the notion of a god bestowing the right to rule to a sovereign is present throughout the world, the Sasanian kings perhaps pushed it one step further. They believed the king had a special visible divine aura called *farr*.

The Sassanid era marked a period of development in all aspects of life in Iran, as the kings became more and more involved in everyday matters of the realm, perhaps with the objective of establishing a sense of closeness to the population, something that would result in more support and loyalty from their subjects. The first Sassanid monarchs founded new cities and expanded the irrigation systems to facilitate agriculture throughout the realm, building upon the advanced infrastructure created by Darius the Great. These measures boosted Iran's urban life and increased the economy by encouraging more regional trade. The seizure of more of the realm's undeveloped lands positively affected the Sassanid royal family's revenue and contributed to more centralization of power.

Zoroastrianism was firmly established as one of the foundations of the Sassanid rule. Throughout the age of Hellenization, after Alexander the Great's conquest of Persia, many of the Zoroastrian shrines and temples were either damaged or replaced by regional cults that contained elements of different cultures, something that was backtracked after the establishment of the Sassanid monarchy. Although the empire was still ethnically diverse, the Sassanid rulers pushed for more centralization of power and resources; they believed that the practice of one religion in the realm was instrumental in this endeavor. Thus, the cults that had appeared during the Parthian Empire were almost fully replaced by the 5th or 6th century.

Soon after its inception, the Sassanid state developed a hierarchical structure for the Zoroastrian priests, with the king being in charge of appointing the chief priest, who was at the very top. Tansar, the author of the letter discussed above, is thought to have been the first chief priest under Ardashir. His writings speak of a special relationship between the state and religion, claiming the unity of "Church and state ... born from one womb, joined together, and never to be sundered."

One of Zoroastrianism's most important achievements was the collection of ancient religious texts and hymns, which had been orally transmitted for many centuries. Different Sassanid rulers compiled the Zoroastrian Avesta and oversaw their recording in various different scripts, both to incorporate the ancient Iranian dialects in which the texts had been historically spoken and to make it accessible for the speakers of the common Pahlavi (Middle Persian) tongue. This policy encouraged religious learning and also pushed for the establishment of one formal spoken language throughout the realm, something that would further centralize Sassanid rule. Nonreligious scholarship was promoted in this period as well, leading to the creation of one of the first national historical epics, *Khwaday-Namag* (the Book of Rulers), which was commissioned and supervised by the king's court and the Zoroastrian priesthood.

The Iranian legal system also saw improvements during the Sassanid era. The system placed a lot of emphasis on justice, namely on the king as the promoter and guarantor of justice in society. All subjects of the empire respected the law, regardless of their social status. Under the king's supervision, courts were established all throughout the realm, and the practice of law was mainly based on Zoroastrian principles. Different trials were recorded and used as examples for future instances of similar crimes. All of these practices were finally compiled together by the early 7th century in *The Book of a Thousand Judgements*, which essentially served as the empire's legal code.

Finally, the Letter of Tansar underlines King Ardashir's efforts to define boundaries between the Sasanian aristocracy and the common people. It seems that the distinctions between the two classes constituted a major part of Sassanid society. Not only were the nobility much more powerful, but they also conveyed their status in everything, from their distinct attire to property. They rarely interacted with members of the lower classes, and marriage between the two was forbidden. However, the truth of the matter was that the nobility continued to increase their wealth, power, and influence, something that soon became a problem for the Sassanid royal family.

Khosrow I

By the end of the 5th century, the Sassanids were faced with a series of challenges, just as it inevitably happens to all vast empires, regardless of their size or power. Before then, the empire had mostly been involved in struggles against the Romans over their bordering territories, having already established a somewhat consolidated center in the east. The South Caucasus and Greater Armenia were the main points of contention between the two sides, but under King Kavad I, the Sassanids were confronted with a major domestic sociocultural problem. For decades, members of the lower social classes, those who were not part of the nobility or aristocracy, had experienced worsening living conditions. It should come as no surprise that they were upset about their social standing.

They found their champion in Mazdak, a Zoroastrian priest who quickly gained a lot of followers and led the push for reforms in Iranian society. Mazdak and his supporters demanded that the conditions in which the majority of the population lived be improved, protesting the inequality and their exploitation by the aristocracy. They believed that ruthless, unequal competition gave birth to evils in the world and wished to at least reduce the gap between the two extremes of Sassanid society. Mazdak proposed to divide and redistribute the lands, which were the main source of income for nobles, so that more people assumed land ownership and grew their wealth. In addition, he pushed for the increased role of women in Iranian society, something that was untraditional.

Interestingly, King Kavad I, who did not nearly have as good of an eye for ruling as some of his predecessors, liked Mazdak's proposals at first, at least in theory. He wanted to gain more support from the peasants and reduce the power held by the aristocrats. Eventually, however, the accounts of the time suggest that Kavad was overpowered by the Zoroastrian clergy and the nobility. Amidst the political chaos that ensued, he lost his power.

In the struggle for succession, the priests and aristocrats proceeded to help install one of Kavad's sons, Khosrow I, as the new king. They probably influenced him to adopt an anti-Mazdakian attitude. Khosrow I murdered members of the royal family upon his accession, and he also summoned Mazdak to the capital city of Ctesiphon in 528. Mazdak likely thought the king wanted to discuss the different views he held regarding the social structure of the realm, but Mazdak was imprisoned and executed. For months following Mazdak's execution, his supporters were brutally suppressed by Khosrow's regime. Khosrow emerged as one of the most stalwart defenders of traditional Zoroastrianism and gained a lot of favors from the Sassanid nobility and the Zoroastrian clergy for his actions.

Khosrow I's reign would see the further strengthening of the Sassanid monarchy, something the king thought was absolutely necessary after a period of instability in the realm. He chose to ameliorate the administrative system of the realm, introducing a new tax system based on land ownership, which the king implemented after months of conducting land surveys and censuses. This reduced the power held by the biggest aristocratic families of the realm and guaranteed a new source of income for the royal treasury. Members of the *dehqan* (landowning class) profited greatly from Khosrow's reforms, emerging as a strong middle class and becoming a valuable part of the economy. They also comprised a large portion of the Sassanid army and were able to become one of the king's most favored social groups. Khosrow I also invested a lot in the modernization of Sassanid infrastructure and financed the repairs of many of the old roads that connected the major cities with each other.

Khosrow I is remembered in history for his decision to renew the war with the Byzantines, who had, in a way, recovered from their own unstable period and reemerged as a strong regional actor under Emperor Justinian. For about twenty-two years after the launch of the Sassanid invasion in 540, Khosrow's forces managed to penetrate the Byzantine lands and gained control of Antioch and some of the northeastern Anatolian provinces, giving the Sassanid monarch access to the Black Sea.

In 562, the two sides agreed to a peace deal. However, Khosrow followed up his success with even more military triumphs, defeating some of the factions that surrounded the Sassanid Empire. In the east, with the help of the Turks, he drove back the White Huns. In the Caucasus, he defeated the Khazars, who had been strategic allies with the Byzantines and were a thorn in the side of Sassanid interests in the region. And last but not least, he successfully defended the Arabian Peninsula from an Abyssinian Ethiopian attack, managing to establish Yemen as a Sassanid protectorate. By the 570s, when the war with the Byzantine Empire resumed, the Sassanids were clearly in a more favorable position, although the lack of commitment from both sides produced inconclusive results.

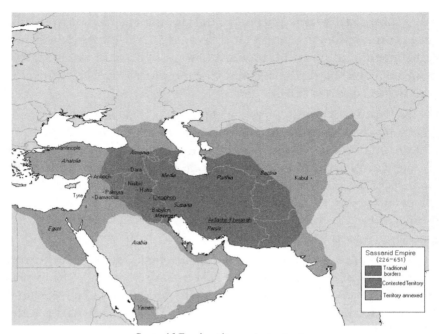

Sassanid Persia at its greatest extent.
https://commons.wikimedia.org/wiki/File:Sassanid_Empire_226_-_651_(AD).GIF

For his contributions to the realm, Khosrow I has come to be known as Anoshivan (Anushirvan), roughly translating to "of an immortal soul." He was the sort of ruler that only ascended the throne once in a generation. His policies touched almost every aspect of Sassanid life, and his reign was a symbol of prosperity and dominance for the empire.

Still, as history has demonstrated many times, almost immediately after Khosrow's death, the Sassanid Empire descended into another period of chaos, and the future of the realm came into question. This time, the insurgents emerged in northeastern Iran and mainly consisted of the Parthian nobility, which was discontent due to Khosrow's reforms that had weakened their power. The succeeding Sassanid rulers found themselves in a constant fight with the Parthian nobles until King Khosrow II Parviz finally defeated the rebellion in 602. The Sassanid ruler was able to follow up his victory by capturing a lot of territories in the Levant and even reaching Egypt by 619. His reign eventually came to a gruesome end after he was deposed by domestic rival forces in 628.

In short, Khosrow I would be the last great Sassanid ruler, and the empire would never reach the heights it did under Khosrow Anoshirvan again. Instead, in the late 600s, Iran would find itself confronted with a socio-historical phenomenon that would leave a permanent mark on the nation: the birth of Islam.

The Arab Conquest

Overall, it can be argued that the history of Iran can be separated into two huge eras: the pre-Islamic period, the history from the emergence of the first Iranian civilizations to the demise of the Sassanids, and the Islamic period, which began in the 7th century and has persisted for nearly 1,500 years. The reason behind this separation is the sheer cultural, social, and political transformation Iran would experience after the Arab conquest and its subsequent Islamification. The most obvious difference would be, of course, the replacement of Zoroastrianism with Islam as the new state religion, which would have massive cultural and social consequences, resulting in almost the complete disappearance of Zoroastrianism in the following centuries.

The beginning of the Islamic era would also see the destruction of the Sassanids—one of the most influential dynasties the country had ever seen. In short, social and political changes of such magnitude rarely happen in the world, but when they do, they tend to leave an impact that lasts for centuries. And the birth of a new religion called Islam can certainly be considered one of those developments.

Before we get to the Arab conquest, which introduced Islam to Iran, we should briefly go over the history of Arabia. It is important to understand that unlike Iran, where the original nomadic, horse-centered tribal life gradually transformed into a full-fledged state-oriented civilization, the peoples of the Arabian Peninsula were much slower to adopt similar changes to their lifestyle. Much of Arabia, even by the time of the Sassanids, was still nomadic, although permanent settlements and towns were established in some parts. The relationship between the ancient Persian rulers and the Arabs was largely hostile. The nomadic Arab tribes frequently launched invasions in the bordering Mesopotamian lands, which attracted them because of their wealth.

Thus, the Iranian rulers had to defend Mesopotamia not only

from the Romans but also from Arab raiding parties that plundered the Mesopotamian countryside time and time again. Sometimes, the Arabs posed an even bigger threat. For example, during the reign of Shapur II, they ventured out on one of their most daring expeditions and laid siege to the Sassanid capital city of Ctesiphon, which was located right in the center of the Mesopotamian lowlands. The Arabs would sometimes raid the Iranian Gulf coast. There had to be some form of Iranian naval presence to defend the region from these incursions.

To deal with the looming Arab threat, the Sassanid rulers commonly befriended an Arabic dynasty, establishing their lands as sort of a buffer state between the Sassanid realms and the dangerous Arab territories. Having a powerful ally to the south was helpful in greatly reducing the number of serious Arab incursions by the year 600. It also sometimes helped against the Byzantines as well, as the Sassanids' allies often launched raiding parties of their own to target the Christians.

Obviously, a major development that greatly affected the relationship between the Arabs and the Persians was the birth of Islam and its emergence as a major influential regional religion by the mid-600s. Of course, dissecting Islamic beliefs and principles in great detail is beyond the scope of this book, but what we need to understand is that the teachings of Prophet Muhammad gained a lot of traction very quickly. Thanks to the efforts of the revered military commander Khalid ibn al-Walid, the Arabic tribes from the southwestern Arabian Peninsula to the borders of Mesopotamia were united under the banner of Islam. The Arab tribes all around the peninsula swore allegiance to Abu Bakr, the first caliph of the Rashidun Caliphate—the Arabic state that emerged as the successor of Prophet Muhammad upon his death in 632. Abu Bakr was also the ruler of Medina and essentially all of the Muslim world.

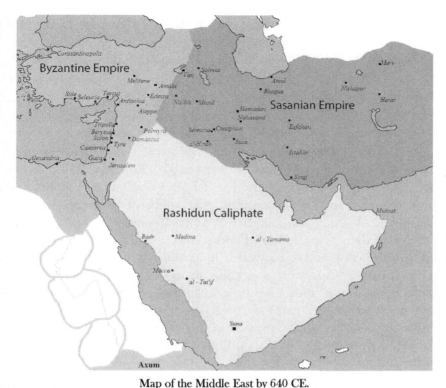

Map of the Middle East by 640 CE.
https://commons.wikimedia.org/wiki/File:IslamicConquestsIroon.png

All this coincided with the decline of Sassanid Iran after the death of Khosrow I Anoshirvan. Succession wars and the existence of rival noble families that acted according to their own interests weakened the realm, something that did not go unnoticed by the emerging Arab war machine. Beginning in early 634, the Arabs under Khalid ibn al-Walid launched their first incursions into Sassanid-controlled Mesopotamia but were repelled by the Sassanids under their new king, Yazdegerd III, who crushed the incursion at the Battle of the Bridge in October.

However, the Arabs did not give up. They continued to skirmish with the Sassanid forces in Mesopotamia and eventually launched another full-scale assault in 636, this time under their new caliph, Omar. They managed to break the Sassanids at the Battle of Qadisiya in early 637 and gained direct access to the rich Mesopotamian cities, which were theirs for the taking. The already disorganized Sassanid state was unable to resist the Arab invaders. Ctesiphon, or al-Mada'in, as the Arabs called it, was besieged and taken without much difficulty. While the Sassanid army fled to central Iran, the Arabs followed up their capture of Ctesiphon with a series of victories at Jalula and Nahavand, taking over all of Sassanid-controlled Mesopotamia and parts of the western province of Khuzestan.

Thus, the 630s was the period where the Arabs emerged as a power to be reckoned with, and the caliphate grew, for the first time, outside of the peninsula and penetrated the lands of the Levant. The people who remained in the conquered Mesopotamian towns converted to Islam. Caliph Omar was faced with the dilemma of continuing the offensive into the Iranian territories. At first, the caliph was reluctant, and he had a good reason to be. The Iranian Plateau was a dangerous place and unknown to the Arabs. However, he could not allow the Sassanids to regroup and assemble a sizeable army, especially since he had good momentum after his various victories against the Sassanids. Omar's men were particularly motivated after the capture of Nahavand Castle, which was one of the most important victories in the Arab-Persian war. In the end, the caliph chose to take the fight to the enemy.

So, in early 642, the Arabs finished all the necessary preparations for the capture of Persia. The Sassanids were still disorganized from the chaos of the past forty years and were not prepared to mount a defense that could overpower the Arab conquerors, something that Omar realized and decided to use to his advantage. The defeat at Nahavand had further demoralized the Sassanids, and Yazdegerd had fled to the east, perhaps in the hopes that the Arabs would be unable to reach him. After thrusting through the province of Hamadan to the heart of Iran, the Arabs took control of the central city of Isfahan, essentially splitting the Sassanid territories into two. Once that was done, they launched campaigns in Azerbaijan and Fars to take control of the lands. By 650, all of western and central Iran had fallen into Arab hands. Yazdegerd remained in the east. He was still nominally the ruler of the empire, but in reality, he was unable to assemble a force large enough to resist the Arabs. He eventually died in 651, murdered by his own people in the city of Merv in northern Khorasan. The Sassanid Empire had come to an end.

Following their conquest of western Iran, the Arab forces quickly invaded the eastern Iranian provinces with little to no resistance. Instead of putting up a fight, many in Khorasan gave up, capitulating to their invaders to avoid unnecessary bloodshed and destruction. The fight for Sistan in the southeast was more difficult for the Arabs, but they eventually defeated the final resisting parties and took over all of the Sassanid lands. By early 660, the Rashidun Caliphate, the first Muslim state, had established itself as one of the most powerful empires of the old world, controlling Arabia, the Levant, parts of eastern Anatolia, the South Caucasus, all of Iran, and even some of the lands in Central Asia. The Arab conquest of Sassanid Persia was complete.

Islamic Iran

The era of Islam in Iranian history started with the destruction of the Sassanid Empire and the Arab conquest of Persia. Despite the Arabs' quick and successful invasion, it would take the invaders a couple of decades before they could establish firm control over the Iranian territories. There were a number of sociocultural differences between the two peoples, and the Iranians stubbornly refused to accept the Arabs as their suzerains. Nevertheless, the Islamification of Iran started, and this massive change would forever alter the course of Iranian history.

Persia slowly converted to Islam, more easily in some places than in others. Historical records suggest it had been exposed to the religion, at least to some degree, before the Arab conquest. Supposedly, during the lifetime of Prophet Muhammad, the first Persian to ever accept Islam was Salman Farsi (Salman the Persian), a figure who is thought to have personally met the prophet in Medina in the early days of the caliphate. After becoming a Muslim, Salman Farsi retained a close relationship with the leaders of the caliphate and might even have been appointed as the governor of Ctesiphon once it was taken over by the Arabs.

Thousands of Iranians joined the Arabs during their conquest of the Sassanid territories, especially after the fall of Mesopotamia. This can be explained by the fact that the main motivation behind the Arab conquests of the 7th century was not to force the conquered people to convert to the newly formed religion. The

Iranians who joined the Arab armies were probably motivated by their own personal interests and beliefs, especially when considering that the Sassanid authority at the time was in tatters. As the Arabs completed the conquest of the Sassanid lands, it is believed that about a fourth of the army was composed of Iranian recruits, with most of them having converted to Islam.

Unlike most of the other lands the Arabs eventually conquered, the Islamification of Iran was far more difficult and far more fragmented, mainly because of the many regional differences that existed in the different provinces of Persia at that time. In some places, like the eastern province of Khorasan, the spread of Islam was peaceful and effective. The towns of the remote Iranian province had largely given up without any fighting, establishing a relatively stable relationship with the Arabs early on.

In addition, the Khorasan residents and the Arabs, who were now their suzerains, had common interests: to defend their lands from the Turkic and Hunnic incursions from the plains of Central Asia, something that had historically plagued Khorasan. Arab garrisons were stationed in Khorasan at all times. This constant presence certainly contributed to the conversion of many subjects, who were also encouraged to do so because of the heavy taxation the Arabs implemented on non-Muslim residents. The tax levied on non-Muslim subjects of the caliphate was called the jizya. Non-Muslims had to pay this tax in addition to the already existing taxes they had to pay to their administrative heads. Due to the high rates of the jizya and the intolerance of the Arabs toward those who refused to pay it, many non-Muslims were forcefully converted to Islam, among them Zoroastrians, who famously migrated in masses eastward to India.

After the Arab conquest of Persia, the Muslim world briefly found itself in an all-out civil war called the First Fitna, which eventually led to the end of the Rashidun Caliphate and the formation of its successor, the Umayyad Caliphate, in 661. Founded by a former Rashidun commander, Mu'awiya, who led the insurgents during the five-year civil war, the Umayyads imposed an even harsher rule on Iran and heavily discriminated against all the non-Arab subjects of the empire. The Umayyads would become the main dynasty of the Muslim world for nearly one hundred years and would conquer much of the North African coast and southern Iberia.

However, by the 740s, a growing sentiment against their harsh rule led to a rebellion in Khorasan. By that time, the notion of legitimacy for the ruler of the caliphate had become increasingly important in the Muslim world. Many protesters believed the Umayyads were not the legitimate rulers of the empire since they were not the descendants of Prophet Muhammad or his family. Therefore, they had no right to be in charge of the Muslims.

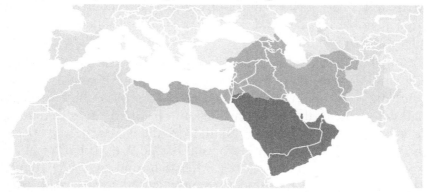

The growth of the Arab caliphate: Dark Brown indicates the Muslim world during the lifetime of Prophet Muhammad. Light Brown indicates the Muslim world during the Rashidun Caliphate. Yellow indicates the Muslim world during the Umayyad Caliphate.
https://commons.wikimedia.org/wiki/File:Map_of_expansion_of_Caliphate.svg

Eventually, in 747, the non-Arabs of the province united together in a revolution against the Umayyad Caliphate. Led by an Iranian Muslim general named Abu Muslim, the non-Arabs gained more and more support as they marched westward, eventually reaching Mesopotamia, where most of the Umayyad power was centralized. The rebels managed to overthrow the Umayyads in 750 and installed As-Saffah as the new caliph. As-Saffah was the descendant of Abbas ibn Abd al-Muttalib, an uncle of Prophet Muhammad, which gave the new ruler a sense of legitimacy, at least to a higher degree than the "usurper" Umayyads had held. The Abbasid Caliphate was born. It was the third Islamic caliphate that succeeded Prophet Muhammad and marked the beginning of a new Islamic era.

The establishment of the Abbasid Caliphate is especially important through the lens of Iranian history because the Iranians heavily influence the caliphate throughout its existence, primarily in the early decades. First of all, it has to be underlined once again that the Abbasids were far more tolerant than their predecessors toward the minorities in the realm. Even so, many revolts broke out in the Iranian provinces, but these revolts were not primarily seeking to gain more religious freedoms, although an anti-Arab conspiracy to restore the might of Zoroastrianism has been suggested as one of the causes. Instead, the rebellions throughout the 8th century in Herat, Azerbaijan, and Zarafshan were politically motivated. The local populations were discontented since the Iranian noble families had a lot of privileges stripped from them after the caliphate took over.

On the whole, however, it should not be that surprising that Iranians, in general, played a big role in the Abbasid Caliphate since the revolution that had taken place to replace the Umayyads had its origins in the Khorasan region. Historians have called this process the "Persianization" of the caliphate, which truly began during the reign of Caliph Haroun al-Rashid, who ruled for about seventeen years beginning in 786. Many Sassanid and older Iranian ideas, concepts, and institutions slowly started to fuse with their Arabic counterparts, which had their foundations in Islam, which was still relatively young. Persian literature was translated into Arabic and modified to better convey Islamic principles. Iranian recruits also composed a large portion of the Abbasid army.

The Arabs implemented different structures and offices that were primarily of Iranian origin in their administrative systems. For example, Arab rulers started employing viziers, which are the modern-day equivalent of ministers. They were responsible for different administrative functions. The Arabs adopted Persian coinage and taxation systems. Many Arabs started wearing attire that was traditionally Persian; even Islamic architecture started borrowing a lot from ancient Iranian styles. The influence of Iranian culture and the presence of many other distinct cultures under Abbasid rule contributed to the transformation of the caliphate from a primarily Arabic empire to one that was more focused on Islam rather than the ethnic or cultural differences between the people.

The introduction of Islam to Iran also had massive consequences. The Iranian way of Islamic practice developed separately from the rest of the Muslim world. Eventually, this version of Islam would be introduced to the migrating Central Asian Turkic peoples, who increasingly moved westward in the late 8th century. The Mongols and the Turks would ultimately become the masters of the Near East and gave rise to the Seljuk Empire and, later, the Ottoman Empire. However, they would first be introduced to Islamic practices and traditions once they crossed the Iranian Plateau. As they took over the territories previously held by the Byzantines, the Arab caliphates, and the Persian dynasties, they would emerge as stalwart defenders of the Islamic faith, spreading the version of Islamic life that had been born through Iranian culture on three continents, from North Africa to eastern Europe.

Chapter 5: Turco-Mongolic Iran

The Iranian Intermezzo

By the late 9th century, the Abbasid rulers would designate old Iranian noble families to rule over the different Persian provinces of the empire. This practice would last until the mass migration and eventual conquest of Iran by the Turkic peoples of Central Asia. This period would be dominated by a sort of revival of Iranian culture and statecraft and has come to be referred to as the Iranian Intermezzo. It starts with the founding of the Tahirid dynasty by an Iranian general named Taher, who, due to his achievements on the battlefield for the Abbasids, would be granted control of Khorasan in 821. Unlike the original province during the Achaemenid, Parthian, and Sassanid eras, Khorasan now included lands far to the west. Control over such a vast piece of territory and resources meant the Tahirids were essentially rulers of their own kingdom. Over time, they evolved a special relationship with the Abbasid caliphs, exercising a huge degree of autonomy over the lands they governed.

Several other Iranian dynasties emerged throughout the next hundred years that would take over the historical Persian territories and be assigned their governorship by their Arab suzerains. These dynasties produced a special blend of Perso-Islamic civilization since they were ethnically and culturally Iranian in all regards but were also bound to their Muslim brothers through their new religion.

In addition to the Tahirids, a powerful Iranian dynasty also emerged in Sistan, the most remote southeastern region of the caliphate. Sistan had proved to be very difficult to govern for the Abbasids due to its distance from the center of Arab civilization in the Levant. The Saffarids became the rulers of Sistan but, unlike the Tahirids, adopted far more aggressive policies toward their neighbors, including the Abbasid crown, to whose rule they were technically subject.

Founded by a man named Ya'qub ibn al-Layth al-Saffar, the Saffarids first waged wars on the non-Muslims who inhabited the bordering lands before turning their attention to the Abbasid vassals. They even took out the Tahirids in 873. Three years later, the Saffarids continued their efforts, invading the Persian provinces of Fars and Kerman and almost reaching Baghdad to overthrow the Abbasids. However, they were eventually defeated in 876 by the Arab forces and driven back to Sistan, where they remained as regional lords for years to come. The Saffarid dynasty holds a significant part in the history of early Islamic Iran, as it was the first to challenge Abbasid suzerainty and strive toward restoring a proto-national Persian state that would still remain Islamic.

The dynasty that would take control of Baghdad and succeed in undermining the Abbasids was the Buyid (Buwayhid) dynasty. It would rise up as a major Iranian power in the Daylam region, just south of the Caspian Sea. Led by Ali Buyeh (Buya) and his brothers, the Buyids quickly raised a capable army that conquered the territories in central and southern Persia, including the city of Shiraz and the rest of the Fars region. They eventually advanced into Khuzestan and Iraq in 945.

By this time, the Abbasid Caliphate was in a very unstable situation, fighting multiple foreign wars and domestic rebellions at the same time, which made it relatively easy for the Iranians to take control of Baghdad and essentially overthrow the caliph. The Buyids installed a puppet monarch, Moti, in his place and took over the political power from the Abbasids. For the next few decades, the Buyids were one of the most powerful Iranian dynasties to exist, along with the Saffarids in the southeast, with whom they generally maintained neutral relations.

The Buyids were supporters of the Shi'a branch of Islam, emphasizing the importance of Prophet Muhammad's blood while also underlining their royal history and ancestry from pre-Islamic Iran. Thus, they did not only contribute heavily to the spread of Shi'ite practices and rituals, but they also crucially adopted the title of *shahanshah*—the king of kings—from the Sassanid monarchs.

Another important Iranian regional dynasty that came to dominate the Persian territories of the Abbasid Caliphate was the Samanid dynasty. The Samanids were of noble *dehqan* descent and came from the far eastern part of Iran. They would eventually become the masters of the province of Khorasan and the Transoxiana region in Central Asia. The Samanids were perhaps the most successful dynasty of this period. They were first granted the governorship of Transoxiana by the caliphs in Baghdad, where they distinguished themselves by fighting and defeating the Turkic nomadic tribes that had been a thorn in the side of the Islamic communities formally under Abbasid control. From then on, the Samanids gradually advanced to the west after the conquest of the Tahirids by the Saffarids, challenging them in the Khorasan region and eventually defeating them by the early 10th century.

The Samanids controlled most of the Central Asian territories and remained loyal to the Abbasid caliphs even after the conquest of Baghdad by the Buyids. They increasingly employed the captured Turkic slaves in their armies instead of using the traditional Persian *dehqan* corps; this practice would quickly spread throughout all of Iran and Arabia.

Despite this, the Samanids also played a big role in the revival of the Persian culture, emphasizing their Persian ancestry and speaking a new version of the Pahlavi language, using the Arabic script to write it. The Samanids promoted the translation of important Arabic texts into Persian and also developed Persian literature and art. The most well-known national Iranian epic, the *Shahnameh* ("The Book of Kings"), was made during this time. The Samanid dynasty was a unique successor of the Persian civilization, as it respected its Arab suzerains and the Islamic religion it had adopted from them and contributed greatly to the spread of Islam and Persian culture to Central Asia.

Although we shall not cover the developments of each of these dynasties during the Iranian Intermezzo, it is important to understand that this period was a transitory stage from the Arab-dominated years after the collapse of the Sassanids to the Turkish conquests of Persia and the rest of the Middle East. Throughout this time, the Islamic Iranian dynasties held a special relationship with the Abbasid caliphs in Baghdad, essentially acting as independent kingdoms but also respecting the Arab lords to varying degrees. This division and the Abbasids' inability to maintain their control over Iran demonstrated the underlying difficulty of controlling Iran. Part of the problem stemmed from the extremely harsh terrain and the lack of connectivity between the most remote Persian regions. That is why regional dynastic rulership is considered to be one of the most prosperous times for Iran since the height of Sassanid rule, as it allowed for a more cohesive development of a new Perso-Islamic culture and statecraft, which ultimately would be composed of Central Asian elements, thus resulting in a unique and memorable part of Iranian history.

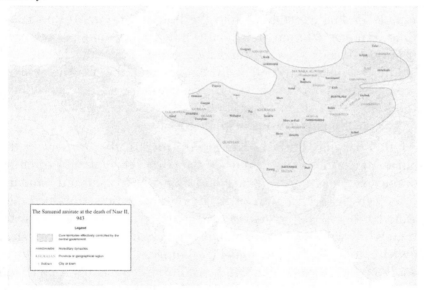

The Sasanid Caliphate in the mid-10ᵗʰ century before the arrival of the Turks.
Ro4444, edited by me, CC BY-SA 4.0 <https://creativecommons.org/licenses/by-sa/4.0>, via Wikimedia Commons;
https://commons.wikimedia.org/wiki/File:Map_of_the_Samanid_amirate_at_the_death_o f_Nasr_II,_943.svg

Turkic Iran

By the late 10th century, the Samanid dynastic rule started to show its problems, which mainly lay in the poor administration of the lands it controlled, something that was not unique to this part of the world. In addition, due to the increasing use of Central Asian mercenaries and slaves in their armies, as well as the Islamification of the bordering Turkic peoples, the Samanid dynasty would eventually be faced with a big challenge, something that ultimately resulted in massive changes to the overall political landscape of the region.

Sometime in the mid-10th century, a Samanid commander of Turkish origin named Alp-Tegin led his troops to take the city of Ghazna in modern-day southern Afghanistan. Ghazna was technically under Samanid suzerainty, but the lack of connectivity to the center of the dynasty's lands, where most of the power was concentrated, eventually resulted in the formation of a completely new state and dynasty independent from Samanid rule. The Ghaznavids, as they would come to be known in history, would last for about two hundred years. Throughout this time, they launched multiple raiding expeditions into the bordering non-Muslim lands of modern-day Pakistan and India. These raids would be organized on purely religious grounds and increasingly target the Hindu and Buddhist population centers in Punjab and the Ganges Valley, earning the Ghaznavids their reputation of being ruthless plunderers since they never bothered to seize control of these lands, instead being satisfied with the booty.

Other Islamic Turkish dynasties formed at the borders of the Iranian territories and would slowly consolidate their power by conquering neighboring lands and nomadic tribes and unifying under one leader, a warrior-king, in most cases. For example, located north of the Ghaznavids, the Kara-Khanid Khanate emerged, which would eventually conquer the Samanid capital of Bukhara in 999. By the mid-11th century, they would take over most of the former Samanid territories in Transoxiana and constantly engage in wars with the neighboring Turkoman chiefdoms. After their conquest of the Samanids, the Turkic peoples of Central Asia slowly migrated westward to occupy the former Persian lands and get acquainted with their way of life.

The Seljuk Invasion

In the early 11ᵗʰ century, another major Turkoman dynasty emerged that would forever change the course of Iranian and Islamic history. Founded by their original clan leader, a man by the name of Seljuk, the Seljuk Turks would first break away from the Khazars who inhabited the Eurasian Steppe north and northeast of the Caspian Sea and settled near the Aral Sea. The Seljuks would come to be known as great warriors, sometimes even offering their services to the neighboring Turkoman chiefdoms.

Under the leadership of two brothers, Tughril and Chaghri, the Seljuks started their expansion, crossing the deserts of modern-day Turkmenistan and invading the region of Khorasan, where they clashed with the Ghaznavids. In 1038, the Seljuks captured the city of Nishapur in eastern Iran, which would serve as their capital, and proclaimed a new independent Islamic sultanate. Then, two years later, they followed it up with another victory against the Ghaznavids at the crucial Battle of Dandanaqan, after which they took over most of the western Ghazvnavid territories and continued their expansion into the heart of the Iranian Plateau.

The Seljuks were ruthless, experienced warriors who were especially good on horseback, being able to easily run over any resistance they met on their westward expansion. Led by Tughril, they quickly subjugated the Persian lords before eventually reaching and capturing Baghdad in 1055, putting an end to the Buyid dynasty. In the following decades, the successor Seljuk sultans conquered even more lands in the west and in the north, challenging and largely defeating the Byzantines in Armenia, Georgia, and eastern Anatolia. Believing to be the holy *ghazi* warriors who fought in the name of Islam, the Seljuks quickly emerged as the most powerful political entity in the Middle East and greatly reduced the Byzantine Empire's influence in the contested regions.

The Seljuks were largely nomadic tribes led by warrior chiefs. Since they were only experienced in combat, they had no real ability to govern and administer the lands they conquered. Upon the death of Malik Shah I in 1092, the Seljuk Empire reached its greatest extent, occupying the regions of Outremer, Anatolia, the Caucasus, Mesopotamia, Persia, and Transoxiana—a vast territory that required a cohesive administrative system. Thus, the Seljuks adopted the government systems of the Persian dynasties they conquered, especially the Samanids. The Seljuk rulers employed Persian viziers, bureaucrats, and advisors, entrusting them with the administration of the realm and taking over the military matters themselves.

Perhaps the most distinguished Persian statesmen would be Nizam-al-Mulk, who would serve as the main vizier and advisor to both Alp Arslan and Malik Shah and eventually compile all the practices and theories of Iranian rulership values into an administrative handbook called the *Siyasatnama*. The *Siyasatnama* became a guide for the Seljuk rulers, influencing them with Persian concepts of governance until the collapse of the sultanate in the 12th century.

Although the Seljuks were ethnically of Turkic origin, their domination of Iran did not mean the domination of the Turkic culture over the Iranian culture. All aspects of Seljuk life, perhaps except for warfare, bore heavy Samanid or Perso-Islamic influences. Culture flourished in the realm by the time the Seljuk Empire reached its greatest extent. Art, especially poetry, was heavily promoted, and the Seljuk era produced some of the most famous Middle Eastern poets of all time, like Omar Khayyam. New advancements were also made in the field of science and history.

Most importantly, however, the Seljuks are responsible for the further development and strengthening of Sunni Islam, which the Turkic peoples had adopted increasingly since the late 9th century. By the time the Seljuks came to dominate the Middle East, the Fatimid Caliphate of Egypt was the other major Islamic power of the world but was a stalwart promoter of Shi'a Islam, presenting itself as a natural rival to the Seljuk Sultanate. Thus, the onus was on the Seljuks to promote and defend Sunni Islam as the true branch of Islam, something the Turks accomplished extremely well. Namely, they encouraged the establishment and spread of the madrasas, which were the first educational institutions that taught students the principles of Sunni Islam and its laws. The madrasas would slowly be established all around the Seljuk territories and maintained their special educational status for many centuries.

Islamic scholarship was promoted to such a high level that it eventually resulted in the emergence of Sufism, a new and unique form of Sunni Islam that put a greater emphasis on a more personal and emotional practice of religion. Sufism combined the elements of ritualistic mysticism and the more traditional ascetic Muslim way of life to produce a compelling version of Sunni Islam that quickly became widespread throughout the Seljuk Empire. It even became institutionalized by the mid-12th century and further demonstrated the fact that the Seljuk era was characterized by the blossoming of Perso-Islamic culture, despite being under the suzerainty of Turkic rulers.

The Mongols and the Timurids

Despite the Seljuk Empire's great achievements, it did not manage to last for a long time. In the mid-12th century, after the death of some of the most powerful and influential sultans, it started to enter a period of rapid decline. After the assassination of Nizam al-Mulk in 1092, the Seljuk princes started fighting over the throne. When no clear favorite seemed to emerge, the princes decided to abandon the centralized sultanate and start their own dynasties in various parts of the realm. This spelled the end of the sultanate, but it did not necessarily result in the reemergence of Iranian dynasties in the Persian territories.

In the early 13th century, Iran was exposed to the emerging Mongol threat, a new warring empire from the Asian steppes that had rolled over the opposition and conquered all the bordering tribes and realms. Led by the legendary Genghis Khan, the Mongols reached eastern Iran in 1219, decimating the local rulers and laying waste to much of Khorasan. The Mongols completely destroyed cities like Nishapur and Balkh. Unlike the Turks, who had invaded and conquered Iran a couple of centuries earlier, the Mongols were not Muslims, and their invasions were not religious wars. Instead, the Mongol tribes, which had been united by Genghis Khan, had been forged in warfare and became the most dangerous war machine of its time, easily defeating anyone on its way to conquest.

The Mongol invasions briefly ceased in 1223 but continued in 1255 under Hulagu Khan, Genghis's grandson. In the period from 1255 to 1260, the Mongol armies, which were mightier and more experienced than anything the disunified Islamic realm could muster, managed to plunder all of the Middle East, sweeping across not only Iran but also Mesopotamia, Syria, Armenia, and the Caucasus. In 1258, the Mongols captured and sacked Baghdad, killing the Abbasid caliph, who, despite all the years of turmoil, still retained its symbolic status, even if he held no actual political power over his "subjects." For the next three hundred years, the Mongols would be the masters of Iran.

It is important to understand that the Mongols' conquests would be divided by Genghis's successors upon his death; the empire was just too vast to be ruled efficiently by one leader. Thus, Hulagu Khan established his own Mongol state in western Asia, controlling the Iranian regions, northern Mesopotamia, eastern Anatolia, and the South Caucasus. His realm would come to be known as the Ilkhanate, and it became a powerful state alongside the Golden Horde, another Mongol state, which possessed territories from north of the Caspian Sea all the way to Russia.

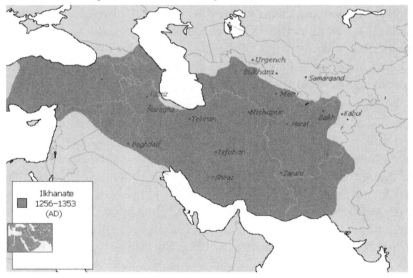

The Ilkhanate from 1256 to 1353.
https://commons.wikimedia.org/wiki/File:Ilkhanate_in_1256%E2%80%931353.PNG

A crucial development in the Ilkhanate's history would be its conversion to Islam under Ghazan Khan, who ruled from 1295 to 1304. Ghazan Khan was a rare Mongol ruler, as he cared quite a bit about the culture of his realm and people. Perhaps influenced by his Iranian vizier, Rashid-al-Din, he implemented a series of social and administrative reforms in the Ilkhanate, including, of course, his decision to adopt a new religion. Still, the Ilkhanate would experience a relatively short lifespan, disintegrating into smaller warring chiefdoms under different Mongol generals by 1335.

The latter half of the 14th century in Iran saw the coming of yet another Central Asian conqueror who, in true Mongol fashion, managed to subjugate all of Iran and the rest of the Middle East by the end of the century. Iran first received the wrath of Tamerlane (Timur Lang) around the year 1380 after the legendary conqueror of Mongol ancestry, perhaps even related to Genghis Khan himself, had already consolidated his power in Central Asia. Essentially, Tamerlane repeated his ancestors' path of conquest but also managed to achieve much more.

Persia was fragmented by the time of Tamerlane's arrival, as it had been divided by the successor dynasties of the Ilkhanate, which made it even easier for Tamerlane to seize Iranian lands. All of Iran, Mesopotamia, and most of Anatolia fell to the war chief, and he also invaded the lands of the Golden Horde in the north and the Mamluk Egyptian holdings in the Holy Land. He even ventured into India. In the span of half a century, Tamerlane emerged as the most powerful and feared man in the world, with his empire reaching an immense size.

Iran would once again be united under the Timurid dynasty. Although the Mongol yoke was difficult, the Iranian people quickly adapted to their new suzerains. After the actual invasion, the situation quietened down and became more stable. During this relative peace, which was guaranteed by the strength of the Mongols and the Timurids, the Iranian culture once again thrived. For example, under Mongol suzerainty, Iran would see perhaps its most fabled lyric poet, Hafez, who was so famous that he is said to have met the great Tamerlane himself, as he enjoyed the poet's works. Developments were also made in the study of history and geography.

Despite this, Iran never had the prospect of emerging as a nation-state under Mongol dominance. It would take the Iranians a couple of centuries to finally drive out the conquerors from their lands and reclaim them as their own.

Chapter 6: The Safavids

From an Order to a Dynasty

After Tamerlane, the Timurid lands broke off into several dynasties between his successors, although they continued to be regional powerhouses and retained control over the conquered territories. Eventually, an Iranian Islamic dynasty emerged in these lands, transforming from a religious order into a sovereign Iranian nation-state, a nation-state that would, after several stages of development, become the modern Islamic Republic of Iran. For a period of nearly three centuries, the Safavid dynasty, which was established after decades of struggle and political maneuvering in the time of Timurid control of Iran, rose up to form one of the most powerful Iranian states since the Arab conquest of the 7th century.

However, a mighty dynasty is only the latter half of Safavid history. Before becoming a full-fledged royal family that ruled over millions, the Safavid order had to be founded. It was created by a Sufi believer named Sheikh Safi al-Din in the southwestern Caspian province of Gilan in the 13th century. By 1301, he had moved the religious order northwest to the city of Ardabil. He and his followers helped the citizens of the town and organized the khanqah, a Sufi spiritual center where they sheltered the poor and provided them with food. Eventually, the khanqah in Ardabil became a prominent site for Sufi pilgrims and even gained recognition from Tamerlane himself, under whom the Safavids were bestowed more privileges, such as the ability to collect taxes.

The Safavid order developed for more than a hundred years until its fourth leader and a descendant of Safi al-Din, Sheikh Jonayd (Junayd), started to increasingly militarize the order, recruiting many followers as *ghazis* and launching attacks on bordering non-Muslim territories, especially in the Caucasus. By that time, the former Timurid conquests in the Middle East had been divided between the two major monarchies: Qara Qoyunlu (Black Sheep), which controlled the territories in northwestern Iran, Iraq, Azerbaijan, and the South Caucasus, and Aq Qoyunlu (White Sheep), which mainly ruled over eastern Anatolia.

After gaining much influence in the region, the ruler of Qara Qoyunlu, Jahan Shah, grew suspicious of the Safavids and forced Jonayd to leave the realm. The Safavid leader emigrated to the Aq Qoyunlu lands, seeking shelter from a powerful White Sheep monarch named Uzun Hasan. He gained a lot of respect from Uzun Hasan, even marrying his sister before eventually trying to return to Ardabil in 1459. However, this daring move would lead to his demise.

Sheikh Jonayd's young son, Haydar, would remain under Uzun Hasan's protection before he came of age and eventually married one of Hasan's daughters. After growing up, Haydar succeeded his father as the leader of the Safavid order and continued the endeavors started by his father, which ultimately resulted in the Safavids becoming a full-fledged political movement. Under Haydar's leadership, the Safavid order would invent and start using the iconic twelve-pleated red hats, symbolizing the order's support for what's known as the Twelver branch of Shi'a Islam, which puts an emphasis on the twelve divine imams, who are the spiritual successors of Prophet Muhammad. This distinct attire would be prominent in the Turkish tribal followers of the Safavid Order, earning them the nickname of Qizilbash ("red head"). Over time, the Qizilbash became some of the most ardent supporters of the Safavids, comprising a large portion of their armies.

As for Haydar, the Safavid sheikh tried to avenge his father, who was killed in an ambush by the Aq Qoyunlu forces, by launching a military expedition in the province of Shirvan in the East Caucasus, modern-day Azerbaijan. However, despite managing to raid and plunder the Shirvan lands, Haydar would be confronted by Prince Yaqub (Ya'qub) of the White Sheep, who defeated the Safavid leader with four thousand men in 1488.

Sheikh Haydar's eldest son would be captured and murdered in 1494 by the Aq Qoyunlu elite, perhaps fearing that a strong Safavid order posed a threat to the realm's unity, especially since the realm had been engulfed in turmoil after the passing of Prince Yaqub in 1490. Haydar's other two sons were forced into exile and fled to the province of Gilan, where they grew up under the protection of loyal Shi'ites. The youngest of Haydar's sons, Prince Ismail, would assume the leadership of the order.

Under Ismail, the Safavid order would see its reemergence among the Shi'a population, something that was likely a result of extensive propaganda. Ismail was no longer considered just a Sufi imam (a Muslim religious leader) by his religious followers or as a war chief by his *ghazi*. Instead, Ismail attracted new followers by claiming that he was a descendant of Prophet Muhammad through Imam Mousa al-Kazem, as well as by declaring himself as the promised "Hidden Imam," a messianic figure in Twelverism who is said to appear during a time of turmoil and restore peace and justice to the Islamic world. This elevated Ismail to another level, with a vast majority of his tribal Qizilbash followers buying into this idea and almost worshiping him as a divine deity.

Of course, historians have identified that this curious development could not easily happen, especially due to the fact that when Ismail emerged as the new leader of the Qizilbash and started to journey to reclaim the lost Safavid territories in 1499, he was only twelve years old. Most scholars believe that this narrative of Ismail being the Hidden Imam was a carefully propagated idea by the Shi'ite elite of Gilan and the more experienced Safavid disciples, perhaps to attract more followers and regain power.

Portrait of Ismail I Shah.

Nevertheless, Sheikh Ismail managed to conveniently gain a lot of traction when the Shi'a world apparently needed it the most. His astronomic rise to power coincided with the disintegration of Aq Qoyunlu into multiple rival dynasties in different parts of the Middle East, including in the province of Gilan, which was ruled by the Kar-Kiya dynasty. In 1500, with about seven thousand Qizilbash troops from the eastern Anatolian region of Erzincan, Ismail was ready to take back Ardabil and avenge his father and grandfather. Supposedly, Ismail's much smaller force was able to crush the army of Shirvanshah Farrukh Yasar and subsequently conquered all of Shirvan in the following years, taking Baku and Tabriz by 1503. During the next ten years, Ismail, who assumed the traditionally Persian title of shah, swept up most of the rest of the Iranian provinces, taking Fars, Hamadan, and Gorgan. He largely reunited Iran by 1508. Ismail also forced Safavid suzerainty over his subjects in the Caucasus, Khuzestan, and Kurdistan, essentially gaining control of key cities like Tbilisi and Baghdad.

Shah Ismail's impressive military endeavors earned him an illustrious reputation in the Muslim world. After years of expansion, the Safavid ruler was confronted by two of the realm's future enemies: the Ottoman Empire in the west and the Uzbek Khanates in the east. Both of these states were Sunni states, making them natural rivals of the Safavids. In fact, Ismail campaigned in the east and defeated the invading Uzbek armies in Khorasan at the Battle of Merv, killing their leader, Muhammad Shaybani Khan, and sending his severed head to the Ottoman sultan as a gift. In time, the Safavid-Ottoman rivalry proved to be very costly for both sides, and the two empires constantly engaged in some form of military activity.

Despite the fact that Ismail continued to tease and insult the Sunni Ottomans time and time again, the first time the two sides would meet in battle would not end well for the Safavids. After the accession of Selim the Grim to the Ottoman throne, the new ruler realized the danger posed by the Safavid Empire and its supporters and adherents in Anatolia. He suppressed tens of thousands of Shi'a Qizilbash in Ottoman Anatolia and forced them to migrate east. Shah Ismail was forced to act as the de facto defender of all Shi'ites in the Muslim world and assembled about forty thousand men. They marched west into the Ottoman lands.

The Ottomans and the Safavids met in western Turkey at the Battle of Chaldiran in August 1514. Relying heavily on his Qizilbash riders to overwhelm the enemy, Ismail found himself disappointed, as the Ottomans formed a defensive position to avoid cavalry charges from the enemy, utilizing their technological superiority and ruthlessly cutting down the Safavids with cannons and muskets. The Ottomans also outnumbered the Safavids, something that swung the tide of battle in their favor even more. Eventually, the might of Ottoman gunpowder forced the more traditional Safavid army to retreat, with Ismail being wounded and forced to flee the battle.

It was Shah Ismail's first major defeat and came as a shock to the Safavid monarch. Chaldiran also had massive symbolic importance, as the Ottomans were able to demonstrate their military superiority over their rivals and triumphed in the name of Sunni Islam over Shi'a Islam. The Safavids were ultimately forced out of some of their westernmost lands, including Tabriz, which was briefly occupied by Selim the Grim. However, the Ottoman sultan decided not to pursue his campaign against the Safavids after 1515.

Cavalier Ghezelbach. Epoque Séfévide
Qezelbash cavalryman, Safavid period

A typical Qizilbash soldier in early Safavid Persia.
https://commons.wikimedia.org/wiki/File:QIZILBASH.jpg

Safavid Shi'ism and Tahmasp I

The defeat at Chaldiran had a disastrous effect on the Safavid state and especially on Shah Ismail himself, who never again dared to lead his armies in battle. It was as if the shah had lost the will to assume responsibility. Up until his death in 1524, he isolated himself from all state activities and drank heavily. As for the realm, new borders of Safavid influence emerged, with the Turks becoming more prominent in eastern Anatolia and Mesopotamia. The Uzbeks also retaliated in the east and challenged the Safavids over the province of Khorasan, the historically Persian region that was always at the doorstep for Central Asian attacks. In short, Chaldiran halted the empire's growth, forcing the Safavids to rethink their strategy and approach to expansion and establish more cohesive borders and administration in the lands they controlled.

Thus, due to different factors, the Safavid realm largely became confined to those lands that were historically inhabited by the Persian peoples and that had been the cradle for so many different powerful dynasties in the past. It is unsurprising that this had a crucial effect on the development of Safavid identity, which quickly adopted elements of Iranian culture and produced a new unique dynastic era.

Obviously, the biggest influence the Safavid era had on Iran would be the clear and firm establishment of Twelver Shi'a Islam as the official state religion. After Ismail's initial conquests, the idea of Shi'a extremism, something that had mostly attracted the tribal Qizilbash peoples, was largely backtracked, and a more traditional version of Twelver Islam was promoted. Still, it must be acknowledged that the process of spreading Shi'a Islam was relatively effective and unopposed, perhaps contrary to the popular belief that the Sunni-dominated Iranian provinces of the time resisted their conversion from one branch of Islam to the other.

In fact, although Sunni Islam was the more popular of the two branches in Iran by the time the Safavids gained power, many regions housed Shi'a communities, especially in western Iran. Popular culture always had a place for the Shi'ite idea that emphasized the importance of Muhammad's blood, so it was not particularly necessary to force it upon the Sunnis. The Sunni ulama—the religious elite of the lands who held a lot of authority and even judicial powers—were gradually replaced by Shi'ite imams, who assumed the same responsibilities and consequently led more people into becoming Shi'a Muslims. However, this process was gradual and largely happened over the span of several decades.

The political enemies of Safavid Iran were overwhelmingly Sunni factions. In fact, Sunni Islam was most adhered to in Central Asia and had been since the conversion of the Turkic peoples to Islam during the Iranian Intermezzo, many centuries before the Safavids came to power. Through the continuous domination of different Central Asian peoples of Iran and the rest of the Middle

East, Sunni Islam became prominent in these regions. Thus, the fact that the Uzbeks in the east and the Ottomans in the west (being of Central Asian Turkic origin) were the two bastions of Sunnism should not be surprising. It should also not be surprising that fighting these nations led to the development of Shi'ism's fight with Sunnism.

Eventually, the influence of the Shi'ite ulama would grow drastically in the Safavid Empire, resulting in the formation of a very defined social class that influenced the realm. Safavid rulers contributed to the development of a clerical society, which became hierarchical. The clerics were granted various privileges and endowed with lands previously under state ownership. Later on, members of the ulama would be allowed to collect taxes from the lands they controlled, which further contributed to their increase of power and emergence as a dominant stratum in the Safavid society. All of this eventually resulted in the elevation of their status, as more of them claimed to have ancestry to one of the twelve imams and thus were believed to have more legitimacy and authority over the others.

During the reign of Shah Tahmasp, who succeeded Ismail in 1524, the importance of the Shi'ite Muslim clergy dramatically increased in the Safavid Empire. The shah, who was a pious believer in Islam himself, often asked the imams for political advice, and they would oblige. From early on in his reign, the young shah had to confront the problem caused by many Qizilbash tribes, which had grown disappointed after Shah Ismail's defeat at Chaldiran. They had stopped viewing him as an invincible spiritual leader and tried to undermine the power of his successor. By 1533, the new shah had dealt with the Qizilbash after years of campaigning against them. He made them swear fealty to him and all the subsequent Safavid rulers. Ismail's defeat at Chaldiran and the subsequent disappointment of his followers might also be one of the reasons behind the Shi'ite clergy's increased power.

Tahmasp's reign was plagued by constant threats from the Ottomans, who were, at the time, undoubtedly far more powerful and mighty than the Safavids. This prompted the Safavid shah to move the capital of the realm from Tabriz to the city of Qazvin, northeast of modern-day Tehran. Then, to indirectly challenge Ottoman power, he successfully invaded and subjugated the

Caucasus, a Christian territory. Many Christian Caucasians were either forced to convert to Islam or were deported to Iran, where the Safavid rulers used them in their armies as a new corps of troops called the *ghilman* (much like what the *devshirme* was to the Ottomans). In 1555, Tahmasp signed a peace treaty with the Ottoman Empire, where he was forced to divide the ownership of the Caucasus region with the Ottomans. The Safavids also ceded control of most of Mesopotamia, including Baghdad, but were able to retain control of Tabriz, their historical capital.

Shah Abbas

Tahmasp's death was followed by twelve years of civil war in Safavid Iran. The shah had been confronted with the problem of naming one of his sons as his successor, and after his death, different factions that supported different candidates emerged as contenders to the throne. After more than a decade of political maneuvering, Abbas, the third son of Shah Mohammad Khodabanda (who was the firstborn of Tahmasp and the "official" shah of the realm during this period of chaos), emerged as the new shah in 1588. Shah Abbas was the most influential Safavid ruler and would rule for the next forty years. He led Safavid Persia into its most successful period.

Portrait of Shah Abbas I the Great.
https://commons.wikimedia.org/wiki/File:ShahAbbasPortraitFromItalianPainter.jpg

To consolidate his power, Shah Abbas embarked on a journey of regaining the favor of the Qizilbash people. Those who displayed loyalty to the shah were favored by him. He found a place for the Qizilbash in his armies as the Shahsevan (shah lovers), something that contributed to ending strict tribal divisions between the Qizilbash. The army was also greatly improved, with Shah Abbas realizing that the Safavids were lagging behind in military technology and tactics, which had been quickly adopted by the rival Ottomans. In a way, Shah Abbas sought to decentralize the Safavid army, which had previously been heavily reliant on the Qizilbash corps. To do this, the shah started increasingly recruiting trained Persian musketeers and artillery corps. He also created a completely new royal cavalry unit composed entirely of the *ghilman*.

These much-needed changes eventually led to a brief period of Safavid military dominance over its enemies, first in the east against the Uzbeks and later in the west against the Ottoman Turks. In 1598, the Uzbeks were finally driven out of Khorasan, with the city of Herat returning back to Safavid control. New borders were established between the two sides. Then, beginning in 1603, Shah Abbas personally led his men in multiple campaigns against the Ottomans, pushing them back from much of Iraq to the borders of eastern Anatolia. The Safavids would later defeat a huge Ottoman army under Ottoman Grand Vizier Khalil Pasha, luring him into a trap in Tabriz before surrounding them and achieving a decisive victory. By 1624, the Safavids had managed to regain Baghdad and emerged as a mighty regional superpower.

Shah Abbas was for the Safavid Empire what Peter the Great was for Russia or what Sultan Suleyman (Suleiman) the Magnificent was for the Ottoman Empire: an influential, charismatic absolutist monarch who quickly managed to transform the political landscape of the time through his brilliant governance. Just like the rest of these successful absolutist monarchs, Shah Abbas's merits did not solely end with his military triumphs over his enemies. They were apparent in other fields as well, such as foreign policy. The Safavid shah sought to ameliorate diplomatic relations with potential partners, especially since they might be useful later on against his two main foes: the Uzbeks and the Ottomans. He sent emissaries to the Mughal Empire in northwestern India and gained a friendly relationship with an empire that had strategic interests in the region. In the west, Shah Abbas dispersed his dignitaries to different European realms with the similar objective of gaining support against the Ottoman Empire.

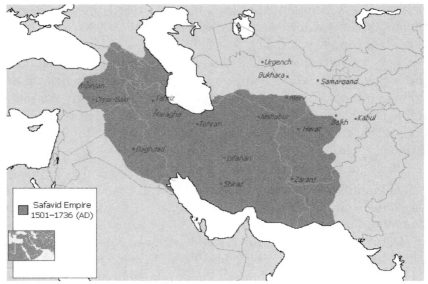

Safavid Persia at its greatest extent under Shah Abbas I.
https://commons.wikimedia.org/wiki/File:The_maximum_extent_of_the_Safavid_Empire_under_Shah_Abbas_I.png

Shah Abbas's reign coincided with the beginning stages of the Age of Exploration. The European powers had recently discovered a safe naval route to India around the Cape of Good Hope in South Africa and were slowly flocking there to interfere in trade in the region. The Portuguese, for example, had gained a few footholds in the Gulf of Hormuz by 1515, something that alarmed the shah, who sought to drive the colonizers out to regain the hegemony over the Indo-European trade routes. To achieve this goal, Shah Abbas got help from the Dutch and English trading companies, which were planning to pursue similar interests in the region. Thanks to their help in exchange for trade privileges, the shah was able to reclaim Hormuz Island from the Portuguese in 1622 and continued to maintain open relations with the Europeans for the rest of his reign—a factor that further elevated the status of the Safavids in their eyes.

Shah Abbas's reign is also remembered for a Persian cultural renaissance, which is an indicator of a prosperous and peaceful period. An advocate of the arts and literature, Shah Abbas promoted the creation of new works during his time as the ruler of the Safavids. He was also responsible for moving the capital from the city of Qazvin back to Isfahan in the center of the Iranian Plateau, a site favored by many different rulers, especially the Seljuks. The amazing growth and development of Isfahan from a forgotten city into one of the most attractive cultural and social centers in the world is truly remarkable. With advanced urban planning (at least for the time) and the excellent architectural style of 17th-century Safavid Iran, which borrowed heavily from the classical Persian periods, Isfahan became a crown jewel of the Safavid Empire and perhaps the best symbol of Shah Abbas's prosperous reign.

Although Shah Abbas is responsible for making the Safavid Empire a true powerhouse by modernizing and expanding its army, building diplomatic relationships with different powers of the world, and implementing administrative and social changes to better govern his people, his reign certainly contained several flaws that would become a thorn in the side of the Safavid rulers after him. For instance, the shah was reluctant to have his sons gain experience in administration and governance, forbidding them from becoming regional rulers, which would have been a great help considering they were one day bound to be his successors. Instead, he had them confined to the royal harem, which gained quite a lot of influence in the shah's court and often operated from behind the scenes, intervening in state affairs. Over time, the harem's influence would have detrimental effects on the Safavid political systems, as the future shahs would find themselves struggling among different factions that had arisen in their courts. In this aspect, the Safavids are quite similar to their Ottoman neighbors to the west.

Some of the administrative reforms implemented by the shah also had grave long-term consequences for the realm. State bureaucracy was increased, and several new institutions were established to help better govern the Safavid lands in different areas of life, but the sheer vastness of the Safavid realm and the lack of connectivity between the central government and the local bureaucrats quickly turned the latter to corruption. Shah Abbas sought to centralize his power, and although he managed to largely achieve that, a highly centralized empire always requires a powerful leader at its head, something the Safavids would come to learn the hard way. To revamp the taxation system, many "state lands" were seized and converted into special "crown lands." Although the royal treasury saw increased revenue at first, it ultimately made the shah more directly responsible for defending his territories. Before this change, the local landowners paid fewer taxes but raised their own armies to serve under the shah.

All in all, Shah Abbas was an instrumental figure in the history of Iran, helping transform the Safavid Empire into a regional powerhouse. His illustrious reputation as a pious man, brave warrior, and great administrator resulted in the elevation of Safavid Iran's status in the eyes of other world superpowers. For his merits, the shah will forever be remembered in Iranian history. However, some of the problems spawning during his reign also had negative effects on the Safavids in the following decades.

The Shi'a Ulama Takeover

It is not difficult to notice that the Safavids started to enter a period of slow decline after the death of Shah Abbas in 1629. Many reasons contributed to this, all of which stemmed from the monarch's declining influence and the increased role of the Muslim ulama in state affairs and politics. The religious elite also saw their status greatly improve during the reign of Shah Abbas, who was a famously god-fearing person and greatly respected the Islamic tradition of the Safavid state, seeing it as one of its main pillars. Indeed, Shah Abbas is responsible for funding the construction of some of the most amazing mosques in the Muslim world. Masjed-e Shah, or Shah Mosque (now called Majed-e Emam, or Persian Mosque), is an impressive piece of Islamic architecture that still dazzles visitors today with its colorful tiles and complex ornaments. The shah also visited various Muslim landmarks in Iran, like the famous Imam Reza shrine in the northeast, to personally pay his respects and pray there. Not only that, but Shah Abbas, on many occasions, directly endowed the religious elite with lands and funds and even implemented special laws that increased the income of the ulama.

During Shah Abbas's reign, the ulama started to regard themselves as increasingly more powerful and influential, even more so than the ruler. The status they achieved was certainly impressive, but they eventually started to use it to gain more power in a society that already deeply respected them. It is important here to remember that the Safavid state was heavily based on the idea of the leader possessing the divine right to rule; his religious status was instrumental to his legitimacy. The shah was supposed to be a representative of the Hidden Imam, a concept that held a crucial role in Shi'a Islam. However, with the growing influence of the clergy, the role played by the monarch started to diminish, as it was heavily undermined by the ulama, who overenjoyed their privileges. Slowly, the religious elite of the Safavids would unofficially deprive the Safavid monarchs of their legitimacy by asserting and reinforcing the idea that the ulama was the true representative of the Hidden Imam and that, therefore, the people should follow them. The shahs were supposed to respect them as their superiors.

The growing influence of the ulama especially became prominent during the troubled reign of Shah Soltan Hoseyn, who ascended the throne in 1694. He was already quite unfamiliar with state affairs since he had been raised in the royal harem, so it is surprising that the shah was easily swayed by powerful political actors when he assumed power. He was famously superstitious and lacked a resilient personality, which made him prone to bending to the religious elite. Notably, Mohammad-Baqer Majlesi, a Shi'ite scholar and jurist, would come to greatly influence the shah and manipulate him with his visions.

Majlesi was one of the leading religious figures of the time who strived to reduce the influence of Sufism in the realm—something that is ironic since Sufi ideology had been the main part of the original Safavid order and, therefore, a founding principle of the state. Under Majlesi, the Shi'a branch of Islam as we know it today would be heavily separated from all forms of Sufism, and the hostile attitude between the Shi'a and Sunni Muslims would be refueled. The Shi'a imam directly influenced the shah, making him exile or execute many non-Muslims and Muslims he personally believed to be a threat to the realm and his status.

The problems during Shah Soltan Hoseyn's reign did not only end there. Oblivious to what was going on in his empire and unwilling to take part in any political activities, the shah led the Safavids into a period of turmoil and instability, as foreign actors struck the realm from all sides. In the east, the fanatical Sunni Afghani tribes united under the Ghilzai tribe, whose leader, Mir Mahmud, quickly managed to gather his supporters and launch raids into the Persian territories in the early years of the 1710s. Seeing that the Safavids were preoccupied with the Russians over their disputes in the Caucasus and realizing that Soltan Hoseyn was not a capable leader, Mir Mahmud ventured deeper and deeper into Safavid territories, capturing Kerman in eastern Iran in 1719. Two years later, he launched an all-out invasion of Iran, reaching Isfahan and besieging the Safavid capital in 1722. The Ottomans also used the opportunity to renew their skirmishes in the west, further weakening the Safavids. After six months of the siege, the shah was forced to abdicate, surrendering to the Afghans and suffering a humiliating defeat.

The Last Safavids and Nader Shah

The Afghan conquest completely threw the Safavids off-guard and brought further instability to the realm, which had already been regressing quite substantially. The Hotak dynasty of Mir Mahmud continued to rule parts of southeastern and central Iran for the next few years. However, despite their capture of Isfahan, the Ghilzai were still largely a primitive society and could not maintain control of such well-developed territories. Although the Safavid power had been greatly reduced and the centralized state was basically destroyed, the Persians would be able to retaliate.

In 1727, the Qizilbash peoples of the realm would find their savior in Tahmasp II, son of Shah Soltan Hoseyn, who had fled to Tabriz during the siege of Isfahan. Tahmasp II sought to reclaim the lost throne and granted the command of the local Qajar and Afshar tribes to a man by the name of Nader Khan, who would eventually emerge as one of the most remarkable generals in Iranian history. Nader Khan led the loyalist troops in Khorasan, defeating a much larger Ghilzai force in 1729 at the Battle of Damghan. By late November, Nader had recaptured Isfahan and ceremoniously led the shah back into the capital. Then, one year later, he ventured out to the west, starting a campaign against the

Ottomans who had been running over the western Safavid territories for a long time. In 1732, Nader Khan was forced to abandon his offensive in the Ottoman territories, instead returning to the east and recapturing the city of Herat from the Afghans.

Despite his merits in defeating the Safavid enemies, by 1733, Nader Khan appeared to have made little progress. This was mainly due to the fact that Tahmasp II had decided to launch his own campaign into the Caucasus, a heavily contested region between the Safavids, Russians, and Ottomans. He suffered a humiliating defeat, forcing him to give up land. The reason behind Tahmasp's decision to invade the Caucasus is unclear, but it turned out disastrously for him. By the time Tahmasp returned from his campaign, Nader Khan had gained a lot of influence among the Safavid loyalists. Acting either for his own personal motives or for the good of the realm, Nader Khan persuaded members of the elite to overthrow the shah.

Thus, Tahmasp II, afraid and powerless in front of his most popular general, abdicated the Safavid throne in 1732 in favor of his young son, Shah Abbas III. For the next three years, Nader Khan continued to fight the Ottomans and managed to recoup some of the losses made by Tahmasp. In 1735, the Safavids signed the Treaty of Ganja with Russia, which ended their rivalry in the North and South Caucasus. The treaty clearly defined the borders and made the two nations allies against the Ottoman Empire.

Then, in 1736, affairs took an interesting turn, as Nader called for a large assembly of notables at Moghan Plain in southern Azerbaijan. Many historians speculate that from the nature of the assembly and the order in which developments transpired, everything had already been planned by Nader and his most trusted allies. Nader Khan announced that he was planning to retire from being a military commander and conveniently suggested that the assembly elect a new ruler of the Safavid Empire. This was a logical suggestion, as Abbas III was only four years old, having been crowned as an infant after his father's abdication. Abbas III was nominally been in charge of the empire, as Nader Khan was truly its ruler.

It is unsurprising that instead of searching for a new man to become the ruler, the assembly wholeheartedly decided to elect

Nader as the new shah. Nader obliged and was crowned as shah on March 8th, 1736, in front of the realm's notables and putting an end to the Safavid dynasty.

Nader Shah would be remembered in history as one of the most successful Iranian commanders to ever live, and his military achievements are certainly noteworthy. However, Nader Shah is also responsible for one of the most compelling cultural developments in Iranian history. Soon after becoming shah, Nader pursued an interesting religious policy; he declared that Shi'ism would no longer be the official state religion of Safavid Iran. This was a shocking move since the Safavid state had been entirely built on a concrete Shi'a identity, distinguishing it from other major Muslim powers, which were predominantly Sunni.

The reason behind this decision might have been twofold. Firstly, the shah, although having been brought up as a Shi'a himself, had always had a soft spot for Sunni Islam in his heart and did not view the Sunnis as inherent enemies. Secondly, the decision to strip Shi'ism of its official state religion status might have been strategical, as it would allow the realm to appear friendlier toward the Ottoman Empire and put an end to centuries of fighting.

The second reason sounds more probable when we take into consideration the fact that a certain Ottoman emissary was present at the assembly that elected Nader as the new shah and could hear firsthand the shah's new proposal. All in all, the relationship between the Ottomans and Iran stabilized, even to the point where Iranian pilgrims were able to freely travel to Muslim holy sites (then under the control of the Ottoman Empire) to freely practice their religion there.

Nader Shah declared that Shi'ism could still be freely practiced in the realm but was to drop its derogatory attitude toward the Sunnis, including the offensive practices that firm Shi'a followers pursued toward the Sunnis, whom they considered to be inferior. In addition, since the Safavid dynasty was closely associated with Shi'a Islam, the decision to reduce Shi'ism in importance also served the purpose of reducing the importance and legitimacy of the Safavid dynasty, which had just been replaced by Nader Shah of the Afsharid dynasty.

Portrait of Nader Shah.

https://commons.wikimedia.org/wiki/File:Painting,_portrait_of_Nader_Shah_seated_on_a_carpet,_oil_on_canvas,_probably_Tehran,_1780s_or_1790s_(cropped).jpg

Stabilizing relations with the Ottoman Empire through the means of appeasement and the establishment of a similar religious identity paid dividends for Nader Shah, who could turn his armies from the west, where the war had died out, to the east. In 1738, the shah was able to launch a campaign and finally defeat the Afghan Hotak dynasty, capturing the city of Qandahar. After his victory against the Afghans, Nader Shah found a justification to attack the Muslim Mughal Empire in western India, which was a weakened but rich state. Nader Shah justified his invasion of India by claiming that the rebel Afghans were being hidden by the Mughal emperor, Mirza Muhammad Shah. After winning several small-scale skirmishes, Nader Shah crossed the Indus River and was confronted by a massive Mughal army at the Battle of Karnal in February 1739. Despite being outnumbered, Nader Shah once again proved his military genius by decisively defeating the Indians, following up his victory by occupying and sacking the capital city of Delhi. This was arguably the farthest any Iranian leader had campaigned in the Indus Valley.

After capturing Delhi, Nader Shah arranged a marriage between one of his sons and a Mughal princess, which guaranteed him even more wealth and power. He also seized all Mughal lands west of the Indus. By the end of 1740, Nader had campaigned in the north and defeated the Uzbeks, establishing new borders along the Oxus River and fully consolidating the eastern borders of Iran.

Although Nader Shah was a remarkable commander, he lacked other characteristics that are crucial for a ruler of such a huge empire. Throughout his reign, he acted almost completely alone, which resulted in him being unable to properly administer the lands under his control. It didn't help that he was a ruthless monarch. He did not refrain from executing, flaying, or blinding those he suspected of treason, including his own kin. This, when paired with his inability to create a cohesive, more modern administrative system that would address the needs of the population, eventually caused his demise. Iran had an old-fashioned structure. It was not as financially strong as it had once been, and the spoils of war could only fund the shah's endeavors for so long. Although the conquest of western India and the campaigns against the Uzbeks and the Afghans were followed up by the efforts to build a capable navy to challenge the growing sea power of European and Asian nations, something that eventually led to his conquest of Oman in 1743, it was not enough to keep the empire up and running.

The truth of the matter is that no empire can solely be built upon the premise of expansion through warfare, something that Nader Shah failed to realize or simply did not want to accept. His efforts to further reform the religion also caused discontent among his subjects, and he was a target of several failed assassinations during his lifetime. In the end, the conspirators, perhaps motivated by the Shi'a religious elite and the sympathizers of the faith, did get to him. His generals led the charge. Nader Shah was murdered in 1747 while he was sleeping in his tent. His successors of the Afsharid dynasty, who would rule parts of Persia for another fifty years, failed to make a significant impact on Iranian history. None of them were able to assert Iran's dominance over its enemies, losing multiple small wars and being undermined by domestic issues.

Chapter 7: Early Modern Iran

Karim Khan Zand

Persia would once again descend into chaos after the death of Nader Shah. Several new actors emerged on the political scene as contenders to the throne, aiming to seize the opportunity when the power in Iran was decentralized. One such contender was Karim Beg, leader of the Kurdish-Iraqi Zand tribe. The Zand had returned to their historic homeland of the Zagros region after being briefly moved to Khorasan by Nader Shah. They soon started to assert their dominance over the neighboring lands. Allying with the local Bakhtiari tribe, Karim Beg, who would later assume the title of khan, soon became a dominant actor in western and central Iran, proclaiming the city of Shiraz as his seat of power. He also placed Ismail III, the grandson of Shah Soltan Hoseyn, as the new Safavid shah in Isfahan in 1751. Although Ismail was nominally the new shah, he was simply a puppet of Karim Khan Zand, who was really in charge.

After assuming a lot of power, Karim Khan Zand proceeded to eliminate his ally and the leader of the Bakhtiari tribe, Ali Mardan. He thus became the sole regent of the young shah in Isfahan and essentially had complete freedom over Iranian politics. In the following years, Karim Khan asserted his dominance over almost all of central and western Iran, only missing the province of Khorasan, which still remained outside of his grasp. It was ruled by Nader Shah's successor Afsharids.

Karim Khan continued to rule until his death in 1779. He was largely unopposed, at least internally. The one rival that was a thorn in the side of Karim Khan was the Qajars, a Qizilbash clan that dwelled in northwestern Persia in the area that is now Armenia and Azerbaijan. The Qajars had struggled against Karim Khan after he appointed Ismail III as the new shah, as they wished to regain the important status they had held during the Safavid era and throughout the reign of Nader Shah. Karim Khan Zand managed to suppress the Qajars by early 1763, taking the tribe's leader's sons as hostages to ensure the Qajars would never again rise up against him.

Although Karim Khan's dynasty would only last for a short time, he managed to affect Iran quite substantially when it came to foreign policy. His accession to power coincided with an increased presence of European colonizers in the Indian Ocean, something the Zand ruler realized early on in his reign. For example, in 1763, he opened up the port city of Bushehr in southern Iran to the British East India Company. There, the British organized their base of operations and pursued trade in the region. To further monopolize Iranian control over the seas, Karim Khan Zand also waged a brief war against the Ottomans, managing to take control of the port city of Basra by 1776.

Although Karim Khan had risen to power in an untraditional and cunning way, he was a surprisingly good ruler who contributed quite a lot to the stabilization of the country after the assassination of Nader Shah. He never became the shah, sticking with his title of *Vakil al-Raaya* ("the regent for the people"). He assumed responsibility for the Safavid shah in Isfahan and emerged as a noble ruler himself.

The Zand ruler was relatively modest and calm, and his domestic policies were certainly helpful to Iranian society, which had been overtaxed and deprived of its traditional religion by Nader Shah. Compared to Nader Shah, as well as some of his predecessors and the shahs that ruled after him, Karim Khan might be remembered somewhat positively by history due to the fact that he was not solely concerned with warfare, although the Zand leader was quite successful in war.

The Rise of the Qajar Dynasty

One man would dominate Iranian history in the late 18th century: the infamous Agha Mohammad Khan Qajar, who emerged as the ruler of Iran during the chaotic period following the death of Karim Khan in 1779. Agha (Aqa) Mohammad Khan had been taken as one of the hostages from the Qajars by Karim Khan Zand when he quelled the Qajar rebellion in the 1750s. Being the eldest son of the Qajar tribal chief, Mohammad Hassan Khan Qajar, he had first been captured and castrated by the Afsharids after the death of Nader Shah in 1747, granting him the nickname *aqa*, a term used to refer to eunuchs and roughly translates to "chief eunuch." Later on, Agha Mohammad Khan was captured by Karim Khan and brought as a hostage to Shiraz, but the Zand leader treated him very kindly, respecting his status. After the death of Karim Khan, Agha Mohammad Khan escaped Shiraz and fled to Tehran, where he started to assemble supporters who would fight for the ambitious Qajar prince.

Emerging as the new leader of the Qajar clan, Agha Mohammad Khan found a lot of support in Tehran, which allowed him to conquer the province of Mazandaran on the southern coast of the Caspian Sea. Further consolidating his power by attracting supporters from other tribal chiefs, Agha Mohammad Khan then launched raids into the neighboring region of Gilan while the Zand princes were fighting among themselves to assert their dominance after Karim Khan's death. In 1784, he returned to Mazandaran, defending the province from a Zand invasion. He followed up his victory by capturing Isfahan and Tehran a year later. By 1786, Agha Mohammad Khan had unified parts of central and northern Iran along the Elburz Mountains and had emerged as a force to be reckoned with.

Agha Mohammad Khan Qajar.
https://commons.wikimedia.org/wiki/File:MohammadKhanQajari.jpg

It took Agha Mohammad Khan a couple of years to unite the rest of the Persian territories after he captured Tehran. Slowly, he defeated his main opponent, Lotf-Ali Khan of the Zand dynasty. Agha Mohammad routed his armies on a couple of occasions and ruthlessly pursued his fleeing enemies. Shiraz and Kerman fell one by one, as the Zand army was chased down and brutally massacred. The Qajar ruler decapitated his prisoners of war and ordered a pyramid to be built with their heads to make sure that everyone knew he would stand unopposed as the one true ruler of Iran. Not only that, but after Lotf-Ali Khan's brief escape to the city of Bam in northern Kerman, Agha Mohammad Khan had the city inhabitants tortured before they revealed to him where his enemy was hiding.

By 1795, Agha Mohammad Khan had eliminated Lotf-Ali Khan and put an end to the Zand dynasty. After that, he campaigned in Georgia, demanding that King Heraclius II swear fealty, completely running over the country and bringing never-before-seen levels of destruction to the Georgian lands. It was only after his conquest of Georgia that Agha Mohammad Khan was finally crowned in March 1796 as the king of Iran. He then set out on yet another military campaign, this time to the east, to capture the region of Khorasan, which was still held by the Afsharid successors of Nader Shah. Agha Mohammad Khan tortured the last Afsharid ruler, Shahrokh, effectively uniting almost all of Iran to the same borders as under Nader Shah. He was one of the more successful kings who had achieved this feat.

However, just like Nader Shah, Agha Mohammad Khan met his demise via his own servants, who assassinated the brutal Iranian ruler in his sleep. because he had promised to have them executed after they irritated the shah. And just like that, on a seamlessly calm summer night in 1797, one of Iran's most ruthless and successful monarchs had been murdered. Since he had already designated his nephew, Fath-Ali Khan, as his heir, avoiding the total collapse of the country. The Qajar dynasty persisted through Fath-Ali Khan, although the new shah experienced an array of problems that would plague his reign.

Iran and Imperialist Europe

Although Agha Mohammad Khan had chosen an heir during his lifetime and had thus avoided a major succession crisis that would have likely broken out in the realm after his death, the new shah did not exactly have all the support in the world from his subjects. Fath-Ali Shah was not completely unopposed, as pretenders from former ruling dynasties tried to rise up against him, such as Agha Mohammad Khan's brother, Ali-Qoli Khan. There was also a Kurdish war chief named Sadeq Khan; he was the leader of the Shaqaqi (Shekak) tribe, and he also tried to besiege Tehran with a small army. However, all of these pretenders were swiftly dealt with by the year 1803, thanks to the shah's much larger force.

Fath-Ali did not prove to be quite as capable of a commander or ruler as his late uncle. To start with, one of the new shah's first decisions was to remove Hajji Ebrahim Shirazi, the *kalantar*, or governor of Shiraz, and the grand vizier, from office. During Agha Mohammad Khan's reign, Hajji Ebrahim was an instrumental figure, dealing with most of the administrative problems of the realm and emerging as one of the shah's primary advisors. He crowned Agha Mohammad Khan in 1796 and later supported Fath-Ali Shah at the beginning of his reign. Still, the *kalantar* was dismissed from his position in 1801 after Fath-Ali Shah had basically guaranteed the safety of Iran from domestic threats. Hajji Ebrahim was eventually tortured and executed, likely because he was such a powerful figure.

The decision to remove such an experienced and seasoned politician from the court proved to be costly for Fath-Ali Shah in the long run, as he mostly spent his time as shah doing everything other than properly administering. He held excessive ceremonies and obsessed over art. He did use his authority to its fullest extent and spent the royal treasury lavishly. This became costly for the shah, whose reign would be challenged by European interests in the Middle East, which saw old-fashioned Iran as a weak nation in every aspect and sought to exploit its weaknesses.

The beginning of the 19th century saw Europe engulfed in the Napoleonic Wars, but the wars between Napoleon Bonaparte's France and the rest of the European powers were not solely confined to continental Europe. Instead, direct and indirect struggles took place all around the world, including Iran, where ambassadors flocked in from both sides of the conflict. What complicated these European diplomatic missions was the ongoing war between Persia and Russia, which started over the disputed Caucasian territories in 1804. Since Russia was also at war with France in Europe, the French sent a diplomatic mission under Claude Matthieu de Gardanne to Tehran with the hopes of increased Persian support against the Russians on the Caucasian front in early 1807. However, in May, the French and Russians signed the Treaty of Tilsit, ending their conflict and rendering the negotiations with Iran useless. It also opened up new opportunities for other European powers.

Great Britain was particularly interested in Persian foreign policy, as the British East India Company had come to dominate the Indian subcontinent through its increased efforts over the past few decades. The British mainly wanted Iranian support in Afghanistan and also sought to secure favorable trade agreements to dominate the cheap Persian market. In 1809, the two sides concluded a treaty, according to which Britain promised Persia aid against Russia in the Caucasus in exchange for their demands. But in 1812, the treaty was effectively annulled when Russia and Britain entered a new alliance against Napoleon in Europe. All of this diplomatic maneuvering went on while the Persian forces were being dominated by the Russians on the front lines, eventually resulting in the Treaty of Gulistan in 1813. Fath-Ali Shah was forced to accept his defeat in the war. Iran ceded control of what is essentially modern-day Armenia, Azerbaijan, and Georgia to the Russians, which was humiliating since they had been fighting for nearly a decade. In addition, Russia forced Iran to give up its naval presence in the Caspian Sea, which further weakened Persian aspirations in the region.

This treaty was followed up by another agreement in 1814, this time between Persia and Great Britain. The new treaty compelled the British to come to the aid of Persia if it was attacked by another European power and asserted that Persia should, in turn, provide support in Afghanistan if the British decided to attack. This point did not go both ways, as the British retained the right to declare neutrality if Persia and the Afghan Emirate went to war. Not only that, but Persia also had to intervene against any forces that wished to get to British India through its territories. In exchange, Britain provided commanders to train old Iranian military contingents.

Still, it was apparent that Persia was actively being exploited by stronger powers, something that angered the local population and negatively affected the shah. In 1826, Abbas Mirza, the crown prince, launched an attack on Russia somewhat independently. What "officially" prompted Abbas Mirza to reignite the war against the Russians was the increased levels of discontent and immigration of Muslim subjects to Iranian-controlled regions from the lost Caucasian territories, which were being forcefully converted to Christianity by Orthodox Russia. Tsar Alexander I had also decided to move his forces into the Armenian territories, which were still under Iranian control. The Persian crown prince had an unfulfilled desire to distinguish himself from his brothers, as he had failed to make any progress in the previous war against Russia and felt humiliated after the defeat.

This time, an unexpected invasion in June 1826 saw the Persians make initial progress, but the might of the Russian army proved too difficult to surmount. The tsar's forces soon launched a counteroffensive, pushing Abbas Mirza back. Meanwhile, Fath-Ali Shah was reluctant to provide assistance to the crown prince. In the Treaty of Turkmenchay, which the two sides would sign in February 1828, Persia was forced to pay war reparations up to twenty million rubles—an amount that was an added burden to the country, which was already in quite a bad situation financially.

After the end of the war, Russia became increasingly involved in Iran's domestic politics, which eventually led to one of the most infamous episodes that perhaps first sparked Iranians' sense of discontent and distrust toward foreign powers meddling in the internal affairs of the country. The episode transpired after the new Russian ambassador, Alexander Griboyedov, who was notorious for his dislike toward Middle Eastern and Asian people, arrived in Tehran in February 1829. Griboyedov was received by the shah and his court, but he was met with Persian crowds that protested his arrival outside the Russian embassy in Tehran. What triggered the escalation of these hostile attitudes was an incident involving two escaped Armenian women and a eunuch from Fath-Ali Shah's harem, who, for some reason, had sought refuge in the embassy.

The shah demanded that they be handed over. The request was denied by Griboyedov. According to one of the terms of the Treaty of Turkmenchay, the Georgian and Armenian subjects of Persia had the right to return to their homeland, and the Russian ambassador was going to take them with him. This caused the mob outside the embassy, which was already full of anti-Russian sentiment, to break into the embassy and overwhelm the Russian staff, killing everyone, including Griboyedov. His body was thrown out of the window and mutilated by the crowd.

Despite such an extreme violation and poor treatment of diplomats, which was enough reason for Russia to go to war with Persia again, the tsar was forced to reluctantly accept Fath-Ali Shah's apologies since he was already engaged in a conflict with the Ottomans and could not risk opening another front. Still, the murder of Griboyedov and the rest of the Russian delegation would be one of the first instances of a violent manifestation of Iranian anti-foreign sentiments.

Throughout the rest of the century, Great Britain and Russia continued to interfere in Persian domestic affairs, influencing the country on several different occasions. For example, from 1833 to 1834, after both the crown prince (Abbas Mirza) and Fath-Ali Shah had passed away, the British and Russians interfered, making sure that Persia did not descend into a dynastic succession war once again. They supported the son of Abbas Mirza, Muhammad Mirza, who became the shah over his uncle, who had also been one of the contenders.

The Europeans found it much more difficult to manipulate Muhammad Shah, who was instead very reliant on his grand vizier, Haji Mirza Aqasi. The new Qajar shah waged a military campaign against Herat, besieging the city with about forty thousand men in 1837. The British were well aware of the situation and viewed Persian expansion into Herat as a threat to their interests in the region. They sent one of their officers to organize the defense of the city while also advising the shah not to proceed with an assault on the city. When Muhammad Shah did not back down, the British occupied Kharg Island in the Persian Gulf and threatened to launch an invasion of Iran, which finally prompted the shah to give up his offensive and retreat.

The Europeans also played a prominent role in the following years, helping mediate conflicts between Persia and the Ottoman Empire. After years of negotiation, the two sides agreed on the Treaty of Erzurum in 1847, which addressed the border disputes between the two Muslim powers.

All in all, however, the increased involvement of Russia and Great Britain in Persian affairs suffocated the country, and the Qajar monarchs had less room to maneuver their way around the political pressure exerted by the Europeans. The truth of the matter was that Iran was slowly becoming a victim of European colonial imperialism, as the British and Russians wished to exploit the relative "backwardness" of Persia for their own good. Persia was less industrialized and thus heavily dependent on the export of raw materials rather than domestic production or manufacturing. This made it an easy target for more technologically advanced powers, which were quick to capitalize on Iran's weaknesses and led to one of the most ambiguous periods in Iranian history.

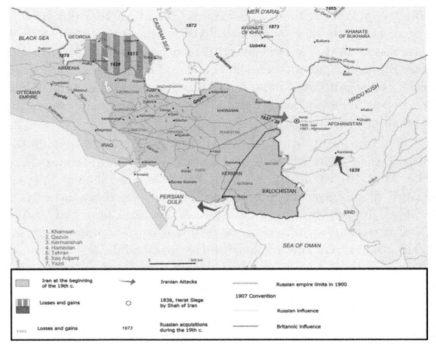

Map of Qajar Iran.

Amir Kabir's Reforms

Naser al-Din Shah would become the new monarch of Persia after the death of Muhammad Shah in September 1848. The accession of the ambitious sixteen-year-old marks the beginning of the first attempts at reform in Qajar Persia. Before Naser al-Din, Persia, much like its Muslim neighbor, the Ottoman Empire, was quite old-fashioned by European standards. Education levels were low, and members of society enjoyed limited freedoms that were only compatible with Shi'ite laws. The two nations lacked a strong industrial core, and its army, although traditionally strong and numerous, was not modernized.

Some steps had been taken to address a few of these issues, but they had only partially worked. Under Abbas Mirza, for example, the Persians had imported British officers to train the military and increased its funding, but ultimately, due to the lack of sufficient technology, they would be crushed by the Russians, who, by no means, possessed a highly disciplined army themselves. When it came to education, efforts had been made to send several students abroad to receive education in Great Britain and France, which had a more positive effect. Returning Oxford alumnus Mirza Saleh founded the first Iranian newspaper in 1837 and contributed greatly to the spread of general knowledge he had acquired during his time in Europe.

However, under Naser al-Din Shah, the reformation of Persia really took off. The shah put all of his trust into his mentor and grand vizier, Mirza Taghi Khan, who had assumed the role of regent and is known as Amir Kabir. Amir Kabir had already proven himself as a political figure, having ascended the governmental ranks after taking part in some of the most important developments in the country. For instance, he had been part of a delegation that visited Tsar Nicholas I in St. Petersburg to formally apologize for the murder of the Russian diplomats in 1829. In Russia, Amir Kabir became acquainted with the more modern Russian style of government and administration, society, industry, and cultural life. Amir Kabir also participated in the drafting of the Treaty of Erzurum with the Ottomans Empire. All in all, he had developed a more modern vision for the country's development and was perhaps the right man to lead the reforms.

Amir Kabir had been aware of the country's military needs even before his appointment as prime minister. During his time as a military commander in Azerbaijan, he oversaw the administrative matters of the Persian army contingents that were stationed there. One of his primary initiatives was to help retrain the core of the Persian army, which still consisted of units from different tribes. To do this, Amir Kabir implemented a new conscription system and paid the soldiers more directly instead of trusting the officers with their wages. To diversify the training of the troops and reduce Persia's reliance on Britain and Russia, Amir Kabir invited new veteran officers from Austria and Italy to come and share their expertise with his officers. Ultimately, he sought to create a strong arms industry in Persia, which he believed was essential for maintaining a capable army.

Amir Kabir implemented more radical changes when it came to the financial and administrative systems of Persia. Corruption had spread to the point that it had almost killed the effectiveness of the country's institutions. To guarantee more funds in the royal treasury, the prime minister heavily reduced the number of state officials and also cut the wages of those who remained. This was followed by the reduction of state pensions to people who contributed little to the government, including restricting the royal harem's access to the state funds—a move that was extremely unpopular with the higher-standing individuals in the shah's court.

Amir Kabir also pursued an interventionist policy in the state's economy, regulating customs tariffs (which the government now collected instead of individual merchants), subsidizing cash crops, such as sugarcane and cotton, and overhauling the taxation system. The landowners were now taxed according to their productivity, not just by the size of their properties. These changes encouraged more people to pursue agriculture, greatly developing the field and ultimately benefiting the middle and lower-middle classes in the country. The prime minister's reforms also increased the local production of goods, resulting in the building of new factories and the implementation of new techniques for manufacturing different products.

To make sure the people of the realm were up to date with the new government changes, Amir Kabir issued a state gazette, which was widely distributed. The newspaper talked about the new regulations and local and foreign developments. Amir Kabir encouraged the creation and publication of new literary pieces by Persian authors.

The crown jewel of Amir Kabir's achievements was the founding of Dar ul-Funun, the very first institute for higher education in Iran, which would be opened in 1851. Being completely sponsored by the government, the military and technical college was located in Persia and specialized in teaching different disciplines to young, upper-class male Persians who had already completed their primary education. The lessons were mostly taught by foreign instructors, who educated the boys in French and Persian. Dar ul-Funun educated the youth in military, medicinal, engineering, historical, mathematical, linguistic, and many more matters. It was a revolutionary institution that greatly contributed to Persia's modernization. One of its side effects was the creation of more higher education institutions throughout the country in the following decades.

Amir Kabir would meet his greatest obstacle and the cause of his ultimate demise when he tried to crack down on the ulama and the legal system of the country, which was filled with corrupt religious *mujtahids*—Shi'a imam-jurists who held the main power in the courts. The ulama had already been quite reluctant to declare their full support to the Qajar dynasty, seeing themselves as possessing the divine right to rule Persia, a sentiment that had been present for quite some time and alarmed Amir Kabir. Thus, he tried to exert his influence over the judiciary system, removing and punishing the corrupt judges and personally appointing those he trusted to higher-level positions in the Muslim court. In short, Amir Kabir made it so that it was impossible for important legal decisions to be made by the *mujtahids* without his indirect approval. This was also followed by prohibiting the ulama from granting the *bast*—a process the religious officials used to "save" convicted criminals by sending them to sanctuaries in mosques and religious shrines. This decision further served to root out corruption at all levels of the judiciary system.

However, Amir Kabir's ambitious but productive policies were not enough for him to last in office for a long time. Since the young, inexperienced shah was not ready to rule on his own, the prime minister had a free hand when implementing reforms, many of which were perceived as radical by the more traditionalist types within the country. Eventually, his effective crackdown on the high-ranking bureaucrats, members of the royal court, and the ulama led to the creation of a faction that ultimately got rid of the prime minister.

In November 1851, only about three years after becoming the grand vizier, Naser al-Din Shah, influenced by the queen mother and other members of anti-Amir Kabir factions, dismissed the minister, whose reforms had actually set Persia on a course toward much-needed modernization and development. Naser al-Din Shah demoted the former prime minister to an army chief before sending him to Kashan, where he would be detained by his troops. This decision came as a shock to the Russian ambassador, who especially became alarmed by the new prime minister, Mirza Aqa Khan Nuri, whom they suspected of being too pro-British. This turned out to sign Amir Kabir's death warrant, as the young shah was informed that the Russians were planning to send a small contingent of troops to put the former prime minister under their protection. In January 1852, Amir Kabir, the man who had attempted to reform Iran, was executed on the shah's orders.

Reaction to Reform

Mirza Aqa Khan Nuri succeeded Amir Kabir as the shah's new chief minister. He was one of the members of the faction who had worked hard to influence Naser al-Din Shah and end Amir Kabir's regime. Aqa Khan Nuri's time in office marked the beginning of a reactionary period to the reforms implemented by his predecessors. The new prime minister did not exactly demonstrate the same aptness as Amir Kabir when it came to politics. The first years of his time in office effectively led Persia into a critical period, as the nation was unable to maneuver its way to a more favorable position on the international stage.

The new prime minister, perhaps seeking to regain some of Iran's former western territories, was reluctant to declare neutrality in the Crimean War. He intended to invade the Ottomans while they were engaged in a conflict with Russia. In the end, Persia did not become involved in the war, which ended with Russia's defeat. But Aqa Khan Nuri's actions forever ruined relations with the British, who had supported the Ottoman Empire in the war. This was followed by a scandal that involved the British ambassador in Persia, resulting in the European power breaking off all diplomatic ties with the Middle Eastern country in late 1855.

Aqa Khan Nuri made the fateful decision to attack the Afghanis at Herat. This time around, the city was captured in October 1856. However, the British were not to be toyed with. As a response to the Persian government's actions, Britain declared war in November. It should come as no surprise that the British military easily overpowered the Persians and made them suffer several defeats. The British first occupied Kharg Island and then landed at Bushire in January 1857, where they crushed the Persian resistance and virtually gained free access to the heart of the country.

Naser al-Din was forced to sue for peace, which would be mediated by Napoleon III of France in April. Luckily for the defeated Persians, the British did not want to completely take advantage of their victory, fearing that this move might sway the Persians to join the Russians, which would hurt their interests in the region. Thus, Persia was only made to give up Herat and all of its claims on the Afghan territories; Persia did not have to pay any war reparations. After the peace was brokered, the British resumed diplomatic actions in Tehran.

Just like that, Aqa Khan Nuri started his time in office with a major setback. The shah, who believed that he had given the new prime minister enough time to do something worthwhile, dismissed him from office in early 1858. For a brief period of time after Aqa Khan Nuri's dismissal, Naser al-Din Shah became more involved in ruling his country, directly overseeing some of the important processes that took place during the 1860s. The most significant development of this period was the construction of the first Persian telegraph line, which linked Tehran to parts of southern Iran.

Unfortunately, however, the period was also plagued with unlucky developments for Persia, which proved to be difficult for the shah to surmount. Famine ravaged the country as its agricultural exports saw a decrease; drought and bad harvests also affected the situation. More importantly, Russia managed to make significant advancements in Central Asia, taking over territories that bordered Iran from the northeast by the late 1860s, which alarmed not only Persia but also Britain, whose position in the region was becoming increasingly challenged by the Russian presence.

In the 1870s, a new figure emerged on the Persian political scene who would try to push for more modernization. Mirza Hosein Khan Moshir od-Dowleh was a seasoned diplomat who accumulated a lot of experience during his time as a consul in Tbilisi and later as an ambassador to Istanbul—during the most successful period of the Tanzimat reformation of the Ottoman Empire. After experiencing the advancements the Ottomans had made over the past few years, Moshir od-Dowleh became an avid Westernizer and one of the biggest proponents of Iranian nationalism and modernization, which earned him a great reputation in the eyes of the like-minded intelligentsia of Persia. From his appointment as an ambassador to 1870, he maintained a close relationship with Naser al-Din Shah, sending him letters where he described the sociopolitical and economic developments that were taking place in the Ottoman Empire and praising the advancements the sultan's government had made by embracing

Western ideas. This eventually resulted in him accompanying the shah to Baghdad in late 1870, where Naser al-Din saw for himself the extent to which the Ottomans had been able to modernize. In the following years, the shah, excited by the same prospect and impressed by Moshir od-Dowleh, appointed him as the new prime minister.

Although the new prime minister was adamant about reforming the country and did make quite a few changes to the administrative and legal systems of the country, his time in office and the reforms he implemented differed significantly from Amir Kabir. The main difference was that Moshir od-Dowleh appeared to be a proponent of encouraging foreign involvement in Iranian affairs. For instance, the new prime minister wanted to improve the Persian economy but looked toward the British to help him achieve his goal. This attitude became most clear when Moshir od-Dowleh pushed for the so-called Reuter concession soon after assuming his position.

The concession, which was eventually signed in 1872 between Naser al-Din Shah and British Jewish businessman and banker Baron Julius de Reuter, granted the latter the exclusive right and, effectively, total control over the construction and development of Persian telegraphs, roads, mines, railways, dams, and other public works for the next seventy years. Although it had been proposed by the prime minister with good intentions of getting much-needed help in developing the country's infrastructure and industry, the Reuter concession was an outrageous exploitation of Persia's resources. The agreement was akin to what the British forced upon their colonized territories.

The Reuter concession turned out to be disastrous for Moshir od-Dowleh and greatly hurt the shah's status in the eyes of the Iranian people, who saw the decree as an infringement of their sovereignty. The prime minister probably had made the decision to push for the concession since he saw Great Britain as a potential protector of Persia from Russia, a notion he likely gathered after seeing the protectionary role of the British over the Ottomans during the Tanzimat era.

Unsurprisingly, the total public outrage, pressure from the Russians, and even the British government's reluctance to fund such a lavish endeavor of a private businessman rendered the

Reuter concession useless. Naser al-Din Shah canceled the contract a year after it was signed. However, the cancellation did not fix Persia's problems in any way whatsoever. Although it had produced a revival of anti-foreign sentiment, parts of the Iranian population increasingly supported Russian or British involvement in Persia's economy and politics, believing that it was the right path for the country to take.

The country was bankrupt, prone to further exploitation from outside actors, and had no ability to force changes that would impact it positively. It certainly did not help that Naser al-Din Shah made three visits to Europe after the Reuter concession, which further strained the country's treasury. The bureaucrats and the religious elite returned to their corrupt practices and contributed little to whatever potential Persia had of keeping on track.

By the 1890s, although Persia was not engaged in any external wars, it had become increasingly dependent on foreign involvement. The Russian Cossack Brigade was established in Tehran in 1879 and assumed great control over Persia's military system. It allowed Russian officers to become the most influential commanders in the army. Meanwhile, the rich Baron Reuter managed to exert his influence over the shah with the establishment of the Imperial Bank of Persia, which opened in 1889. The bank was a British-led and controlled institution. It served as a state bank and had exclusive rights to produce bank notes, effectively holding a monopoly when it came to Persia's financial services.

Chapter 8: The Birth of Modern Iran

The Tobacco Protest

The latter half of the 19th century was an extremely tumultuous period for Persia. The shah's power and legitimacy came under question for the first time in a long while. The economy was practically dead, as it was reliant on the export of raw materials for low prices. The country lagged behind in industrialization and still had infrastructural problems, which affected regional connectivity. And lastly, the European powers influenced Persian political and socioeconomic developments on a larger scale than before, exploiting the government and people in different ways. All in all, the future did not look promising. Still, an event would take place in Persia that is largely considered to be the first development that triggered the beginning of the modern nation-state of Iran we know today.

By the end of 1889, the Persian treasury had gone bankrupt, partly because of Naser al-Din Shah's third extravagant third visit to Europe, which had produced one of the most lucrative deals in Iranian history. It was nearly on the same scale as the Reuters concession, which had fallen through in the 1870s but had still manifested itself in some way through British control over the Persian banking system. In March 1890, the shah, not learning from his past mistake and desperately searching for funds to keep the economy running, agreed to sign a document that gave British Major Gerald Talbot a complete monopoly of Persian tobacco production, distribution, and export for fifty years. Thus, in exchange for 25 percent of all profits earned by Major Talbot, as well as a yearly set payment, the Imperial Tobacco Corporation was established, forever changing the course of Iranian history.

The concession of such exclusive rights to a British subject was, unsurprisingly, a big deal for the local population and the market since tobacco was one of the most used products. Once the negotiations were finalized and word of the concession spread, critics of the decision emerged from all social classes, ranging from ordinary consumers to richer tobacco traders to members of the intelligentsia. They viewed the Imperial Tobacco Corporation as another instance of unwanted foreign meddling in Persian life. In the spring of 1891, protests erupted throughout the Persian bazaars after the arrival of company employees. Local tobacco producers and traders refused to give up their work to a foreign business. The merchants were soon supported by the Shi'ite ulama, who believed they operated according to the country's true national interests, which were rooted in Islam and did not include foreign involvement on this scale. Not only that, but the new regulations directly clashed with Sharia law, taking away the rights of local merchants to pursue trade as they had done for centuries. The ulama was also outraged because the tobacco concessions would hurt them financially, as members of the religious elite had close ties with rich merchant families in the country; the ulama even allowed them to grow tobacco on clergy-owned lands. By late April, nearly all of Persia was protesting.

Big cities like Tehran and Shiraz became the centers for protests. Naser al-Din's government tried to suppress the revolts by arresting local leaders and forcing the merchants to reopen city bazaars. In the end, the outraged protesters placed their trust in the prominent Shi'a *mujtahid* by the name of Mirza Hasan Shirazi. Shirazi, who held a prestigious position, personally wrote a letter to Naser al-Din Shah, in which he expressed his views regarding the shah's decision, criticizing the tobacco concession and urging the shah to retract his decision. When his letter did not produce the desired effects, in December 1891, Shirazi and the anti-concession ulama issued a fatwa (a legal ruling concerning Islamic law), denouncing the shah's actions and declaring the use of tobacco as a crime for the followers of Twelver Shi'ism. They wished to discourage the people from using tobacco, thus rendering the newly acquired British monopoly useless.

The fatwa was widely distributed in the major cities of the country and played the biggest role in the people's fight against the tobacco concession. Not only did hundreds of thousands boycott the use of tobacco, including those closest to the shah in his harem and court, but many landowners who grew tobacco also burned their supplies to resist the British takeover. The truth of the matter was that the ulama was a very influential force in late-19th century Persia, so the people would respect a religious ban on anything, even tobacco, which had been considered essential. It was even smoked in mosques.

Seeing that there was no way to fight the majority of the population and realizing that he had made a stupid and desperate decision, Naser al-Din Shah agreed to cancel the contract in January 1892. He was under pressure from thousands of countrywide protests that grew in size every day. Obviously, backing out of the deal cost the monarch an excessive amount of money. He was forced to pay £500,000 to the British. He did not have that kind of money, so he had to loan it from Russian and British banks.

The Tobacco Protest clearly demonstrated the Iranian people's will to resist the imperialist desires of foreign powers. It also showed the religious elite's influence. Although the event is largely regarded as a proto-nationalistic development in the history of Iran, it has to be said that, in hindsight, the protests lacked the cohesion and unity of the latter movements that gave birth to the Iranian nation-state. Despite the majority of the population being against the implementation of the tobacco concession, there were still factions that either supported it or did not boycott the changes to the same extent. Naser al-Din, who was a weak and easily manipulated ruler, is thought to have had doubts about the concession but may have originally proceeded with its implementation not to anger the British. The people, on the other hand, were motivated to take to the streets because they despised foreign domination and were afraid that the British monopoly over tobacco would drive many of them into poverty. Thus, the protests weren't really a way for the people to demonstrate their nationalistic spirit, at least not in the full sense of the term.

Historians have also identified the role of the Russians in instigating and motivating the protesters, as St. Petersburg naturally viewed the concession as a threat to its own interests and wanted to oppose it before it could sufficiently manifest. Still, the Tobacco Protest had an effect on the Iranian people and their mindset regarding the presence of foreign powers in their lives.

Constitutional Revolution

The debacle over the tobacco concession had further detrimental effects on Persia when it came to its economy and society. The growing instability and Naser al-Din Shah's inability to find good solutions to the crises in his country resulted in increasing public hatred toward the Qajar monarchy. In May 1896, as the shah was on his way to celebrate the beginning of his fiftieth year as the leader of the country, Naser al-Din was shot and assassinated. His son, Crown Prince Mozaffar ad-Din, would emerge as the new ruler of Persia. Having already served as governor of Azerbaijan, Mozaffar ad-Din ascended the throne, hopeful to fix his father's mistakes. But during his thirty-five-year tenure as the governor, he had always heavily relied on his entourage. The new shah first tried to appoint his own prime minister instead of Mirza Ali Asghar Khan Amin al-Soltan, who had served during the later period of Naser al-Din's reign, but two years later, in 1898, Mozaffar ad-Din invited Amin al-Soltan back, as he had become disappointed with his candidate.

During the time that Amin al-Soltan had been dismissed from office, he had traveled to Japan, China, Russia, and Switzerland and had come across the different practices used in these countries. The new shah's main mission was to drag Persia out of the economic crisis it was in. So, upon Amin al-Soltan's return, the prime minister once again turned to Russia, where he had made some contacts. He borrowed considerable funds from St. Petersburg in 1900. This money was used to pay off loans from other countries and made Persia increasingly dependent on Russia financially.

To repay the borrowed money and to address some of Persia's economic problems, the prime minister invited a Belgian delegation under Joseph Naus and, together, implemented a new customs tariff system in the country. The new system increased the tariffs on imported products from Great Britain but lowered the duties on Russian goods. This decision alarmed the British, as it signaled to them that Persia was slowly becoming pro-Russian. The British also believed it would further dissuade any potential British investors from entering the Persian market, especially after what had happened during the Tobacco Protest.

A year later, Amin al-Soltan, realizing British concerns and wanting not to completely alienate the greatest power in the world from conducting business with Persia, brokered what turned out to be a shocking deal with William Knox D'Arcy, a British-Australian millionaire. According to the agreement, which would be signed in May 1901 and alter the course of Iranian history forever, D'Arcy gained exclusive rights to Persian gas and petroleum resources in almost all parts of the country for the next fifty years in exchange for £40,000 and 16 percent of the revenue, which were to be paid directly to the Persian government.

Now, at the time, although gas and oil were pretty valuable, not everyone was aware of the huge reserves that Iran possessed. For the first few years, the British investment yielded no significant results. However, on May 26th, 1908, D'Arcy's men struck oil, leading to the creation of the Anglo-Persian Oil Company a year later. In 1914, after expanding the industry and finding more and more oil sites in southern Iran, the British government became the majority shareholder of the company, which essentially meant that it held a total monopoly over the Iranian oilfields.

One of the first Iranian oil refineries.
https://commons.wikimedia.org/wiki/File:Aiocoil.jpg

Amin al-Soltan's efforts did not outright lead to a better economic situation. The projects started under the prime minister were supposed to have long-term benefits for the country, but the Persian population did not have that much time. A big factor that halted Persian economic development was the silver standard; most other nations of the world had already completed their move to the gold standard, making it difficult for Iran to adjust to global market price changes and causing high levels of inflation. However, amidst the social and financial hardships, the Persian people would find their saving grace, leading to one of the most fruitful and influential social reactionary movements during the first decade of the 20th century: the Constitutional Revolution.

The formation of increasingly liberal governments had indeed been the trend throughout the 19th century, as Europe and the rest of the world saw the gradual diminishing of monarchies and the rise of hybrid republics with constitutions that did not allow for the concentration of power in the hands of a single individual. In Persia, the movement that eventually led to the so-called Constitutional Revolution was a long process, starting primarily in 1904/1905. The sentiment for reformation had long existed in

Iran, and members of different social classes had different reasons for their discontent toward the central government in Tehran. After 1904, this sentiment led to the establishment of multiple secret and sociopolitical societies throughout the country. These parties were led by members of the intelligentsia and comprised of like-minded individuals who were united under the banner of wanting to reform the country at the expense of the Qajar regime. The societies substantially grew their ranks within the span of several months. They even managed to gain support from prominent members of the ulama, namely Mirza Sayyed Mohammad Tabatabai and Seyyed Abdollah Behbahani.

The revolutionaries gained even more followers and publicly spoke out against the regime after an incident in December 1905. Tehran's governor ordered the beating of two merchants for refusing to comply with new regulations. People took to the street, protesting the violence toward the merchants and causing Tehran's government to mobilize forces to suppress the riots. Mohammad Tabatabai "offered" some two thousand protesters to take the *bast*, meaning they were to find sanctuary at the Shah Abdol-Azim Shrine, giving them an opportunity to legally escape from the city police and regroup. The government simply could not violate the *bast*, so its forces were unable to storm into the religious establishment to arrest the protesters. More and more people took the *bast* and voiced their demands under the protection of the ulama. After about a month, in January 1906, the activists forced the shah to agree to dismiss his prime minister and create the "House of Justice," the first iteration of what would become the Iranian Parliament.

In the summer, the situation escalated when Tehran's police attempted to crack down on some of the protesters, arresting several leading activists. This caused Mohammad Tabatabai and Abdollah Behbahani to organize a new *bast*, first in Qom and later in the British Embassy, where more than thirteen thousand people gathered by the end of July 1906. There, the leaders of the protests addressed the gathered protesters, clearly laying out their demands and vision for Iran's future, which was supposed to be bright and prosperous. The protesters were especially motivated by similar successful demonstrations in Russia, which led to the revision of its constitution and the creation of the Russian duma in May 1906 at the expense of the tsar's autocratic power. The assembled activists in the British Embassy voiced similar concerns and demands, which forced the shah to agree to the establishment of the Majles, a national representative assembly, in August.

The first elections for the Majles would be held a month later after all male Iranian property-owning citizens over thirty were granted the right to vote, a decision that did not take the voters' religion into consideration. It also excluded peasant members of society who could not vote since they did not own anything. After holding the elections, the National Representative Assembly of Persia would assemble, for the first time, on October 7th, 1906. By the end of the year, it drafted a preliminary constitution called the Fundamental Laws, which proposed the creation of a senate and bicameral legislature. Although the shah was granted the right to elect many representatives in the Senate, the Majles, whose members were elected by popular vote every two years, technically held more power and had more responsibilities.

Mozaffar al-Din Shah signed the Fundamental Laws on December 30th, thus authorizing the first version of the Persian Constitution. The shah died soon after signing the laws, being replaced by Crown Prince Mohammad Ali Shah. The new shah, along with several other factions, emerged as the main opponents to the Constitution of 1906 and the liberal regime for which the Persian intelligentsia pushed.

Representatives of the First Majles.
https://commons.wikimedia.org/wiki/File:Representatives_of_the_First_Iranian_Parliame nt_WDL11288.png

Such quick progress toward the establishment of a modern, capable constitutional monarchy did not go unnoticed by the great powers, who still maintained their interests in Persia. This would become apparent after the Anglo-Russian Convention in August 1907, which took place not even a year after the creation of the Majles in Tehran. Great Britain and Russia had carefully watched the revolution unfold in Persia, with the British legation not only sheltering the protesters on the grounds of the embassy as a *bast* but also giving some advice to their leaders and helping the activists reach their goal. The Russians remained aware of the situation in Tehran thanks to their increased role in the Persian military and internal affairs due to the Cossack Brigade, which was stationed in the country at all times.

Still, the constitutionalist hopes of receiving any sort of aid after the formation of the Majles would be crushed after the Anglo-Russian Convention of 1907, as its primary goal was allying Europe against an emerging common enemy: Germany. In addition to this, Russia and Great Britain agreed to neutralize any prior conflicts they had in the Middle East by dividing Persia into two separate spheres of influence. Each power would have the right to freely pursue its political and socioeconomic interests without being afraid of the other's intervention.

Although the terms of the agreement bound both states to respect the territorial integrity and sovereignty of the Persian nation, this did not stop them from proceeding to form zones where each power would be more dominant. It has to be said that the divisions were not really that precise, but effectively, the northern part of Iran, including Tehran, Azerbaijan, Khorasan, and Gilan, with Isfahan as its southernmost point, became part of the Russian sphere of influence. The British got the southeastern Persian territories of Sistan and Kerman. This meant the newly formed Majles was essentially left with control over Fars and southwestern Persia, something that greatly hurt the government's status since it could not really do anything about the division of the country's lands.

Royalist Reaction and the End of the Revolution

In addition to foreign meddling and the shah's opposition, the Majles was driven into further disarray because of the divisions among the constitutionalists themselves. There were the more radical types who pushed for secularism and more liberal policies, and there was the conservative wing of the party that wished to assert the importance of Shi'a Islam and maintain the Arabic names for the new institutions instead of using European terminology like "parliament" or "congress." In the early days of the Majles, the liberals, although they held fewer seats in the assembly, were far better organized. They had clearly outlined their visions for the country's development and seemed to be gaining the upper hand over their conservative counterparts. The left-wing flank of the constitutionalists would push for the addition of the "Supplemental Laws" to the Constitution, which would eventually constitute the Constitutional Amendment of 1907.

Still, the amendment did not pass without encountering an array of problems from the conservative n of the Majles. Eventually, the conservatives pushed for their own demands to be considered and added to the liberals' proposal, an initiative that was supported by the new shah, whose goal was to undermine the constitutionalists. He might have suspected that they wanted to abolish the monarchy and thus diminish his power.

In October 1907, after months of negotiations, the shah and the conservatives agreed to pass the amendment, which still largely contained liberal points but also included the proposals supported by the conservatives, most notably the point that Twelver Shi'ism was to be the country's official religion. The declaration of the state religion was the first article of the amendment, followed by the assertion that all changes to the country's laws were to be approved by a special committee comprised of religious officials—another win for the conservative constitutionalists.

Despite a sort of successful cooperation between the two groups of the Majles, the shah still remained hostile toward the constitutionalists, who were slowly growing their power in the country and their reach over Persia's institutions. In fact, in December 1907, the relations between the monarch and the Majles had become so strained that the former attempted to take over the building of the National Assembly with the help of local royalist sympathizers. The attack on the Majles building was repelled by the radical constitutionalists inside, and the growing pressure from the British and Russian legations in the country caused the shah to back down, as he did not want to anger the great powers.

Mohammad Ali Shah would try once again to take power over the country and undermine the Majles in June 1908. By then, the radicals had managed to become the more prominent faction in the National Assembly, having defended themselves successfully from the royalist insurrectionists. The growing power of the Majles, as well as its demonstrated attempts to forge contacts with Germany, alarmed the British and Russians, who backed the shah in the coup of June 1908. Operating through the Russian Cossack Brigade, Mohammad Ali Shah demanded that prominent members of the liberal flank of the Majles be arrested, an ultimatum that was rejected by the Majles, whose members mobilized supporters to defend the building again. On June 23rd, the Cossack Brigade proceeded to shell the Majles building, killing many liberal constitutionalist leaders and arresting the rest, who were forced to surrender to the shah's troops. The Cossack Brigade then executed several prominent figures of the Majles, including Jahangir Khan, the founder of the most popular liberal magazine, *Sur-e Esrafil*, and Malek al-Motakallemin, one of the radical leaders. Other constitutionalists, like Tabatabai and Behbahani, who had been at the head of the movement since its inception three years earlier, were arrested.

With the constitutionalists defeated and the Majles building destroyed, it seemed as if the royalists and Mohammad Ali Shah had scored a victory over the opposition. However, the shelling of the Majles building and the arrest and execution of the movement's leaders were not enough to kill the drive for reform and modernization, as critiques of the shah's actions emerged in all parts of the country. Even members of the Shi'a ulama condemned the shah's actions and urged him to restore the Majles. While Persian constitutionalists who had managed to flee or lived abroad tried to sway the public opinion back in their favor in Europe, local revolutionaries also started to mobilize to take back the power from the shah. Persian resistance was concentrated in Azerbaijan, in the city of Tabriz, which housed thousands of pro-constitutionalist people who had come from different parts of Persia.

Having heard of the growth of the resistance in Tabriz, the shah ordered his troops to besiege the city and force the constitutionalists to surrender. The rebels rallied under Sattar Khan and were able to defend themselves against the shah's forces for nearly ten months. In February 1909, just as the revolutionaries had been completely surrounded by the royalist troops, Mohammad Ali Shah was forced to abandon the siege, as he was being pressured by the Russians. The exact motivations behind this decision are unclear. Perhaps Russia felt responsible and wary of the instability in what was effectively its Persian sphere of influence, or it may have wanted to remain on friendly terms with the British, who, after the shah's shelling of the Majles, were more pro-constitutionalist. In any case, in April of the same year, a contingent of the Russian army came to relieve the siege in Tabriz and saved the revolutionaries.

At the same time, constitutionalist supporters were growing in number in different parts of the country, most notably in the city of Rasht southeast of Tabriz. Led by Yeprem Khan, an experienced commander and public figure, the constitutionalist supporters gained enough men to take control of the city. In early May, they marched toward Qazvin, where they joined up with the relieved forces from Tabriz. Together, the constitutionalists marched toward Tehran, reaching the city in mid-July and taking control after a few days of fighting. Declaring themselves as the "special assembly," the revolutionaries deposed Mohammad Ali Shah, forcing him into exile in Russia, and placed his young son, Ahmad, on the throne. The revolutionaries also set up a provisional government until the Majles could reconvene in December. They arrested the prominent anti-constitutionalist conservatives throughout the country and established their firm control over Tehran with support from both the British and the Russians.

The Second Majles convened in December 1908, and constitutionalist rule was reinstated in the country. But despite seemingly defeating the royalists, subsequent developments did not yield good results for Iran. The reasons behind this unsuccessful period are multiple and include the hostile nature of the opposing parties of the Second Majles. The biggest mistake the Second Majles made was to assume that it now had a free hand in dealing with Persia's problems without consulting the Russians and British, who perceived the constitutionalists' actions as threats to their own positions in the region. For example, the Majles decided to reform the police, diminishing the importance of the Russian Cossack Brigade and establishing a Swiss-led Gendarmerie, something that angered St. Petersburg.

Most notably, the arrival of an American financial advisor named Morgan Shuster forever antagonized the relations between the Europeans and Tehran. Shuster was an experienced lawyer and a financial officer. He quickly realized that Persia lacked a cohesive, working taxation system and that the involvement of foreign powers in the country's domestic affairs had ultimately caused it to go bankrupt. Shuster was granted a lot of freedom by the Majles. He was indifferent toward the Russians and British and instead focused on Iran's development. He surprisingly managed to lay the foundations for different administrative institutions that would guarantee the growth of the Persian economy at the expense of Russian and British influence.

Shuster's reckless policies greatly angered St. Petersburg, which demanded, on many occasions, his dismissal from office, only to find its request rejected by the Majles in Tehran. In July 1911, when Mohammad Ali Shah attempted to return with a small royalist force to retake power, the Majles easily defeated him and demanded that his brother, Malek Mansur Mirza, who held a lot of rich lands, pay reparations to the government due to his brother's attempt to instigate a coup. Shuster was tasked with confiscating the Qajar prince's lavish properties, and the American obliged, having already made sure that other members of the Qajar royal family paid their taxes. This was the last straw for Russians, who had been constantly made fun of by the American financial advisor. Additionally, Shuster had tried to undermine Russia's control of northern Iran by appointing anti-Russian officials in various important offices.

The Russians sent another ultimatum to the Majles to remove Shuster, and after getting rejected once again, they moved in with their forces in Azerbaijan, occupying Tabriz and later Rasht. Then, they started to converge on Tehran, where part of the local population had come to increasingly criticize the Majles. Under pressure from foreign powers and wishing to avoid another political disaster, the young Ahmad Shah, who was still under the regency of his uncle, Ali-Reza Khan, made the decision to dissolve the Second Majles in late December 1911, marking the end of Iran's Constitutional Revolution.

A Post-Revolutionary Interlude

The Constitutional Revolution had been a failure, as the Majles was eventually overpowered by the shah's authority. The constitutionalists had also failed to produce a functioning constitutional monarchy with a bicameral legislature. Similar movements had also failed in Europe, but the difference between the European revolutions and the events in Persia was when they took place. The European nations had largely pushed for more liberalism about half a century earlier, resulting in the undermining of autocratic monarchies throughout the continent. By the beginning of World War I, most of Europe was in a prime political position. In Persia, on the other hand, the changes took place far later. Although many of the members of the Majles had acted with good intentions, they were unable to assert their authority in the country, which was once again preyed upon by foreign powers.

Despite the fact that Persia was technically a neutral country during World War I, fighting happened in the country. The Ottoman Empire joined the Central Powers, which eventually resulted in a part of the conflict taking place in Persian territories, something over which the shah, who had just come of age and been officially crowned, had no power whatsoever. Although the fighting between the Ottomans and the Russian and British allies took place on a relatively smaller scale (mostly in northwestern Iran), the shah and the Persian government were unable to have a proper say in the events, mainly because the army at their disposal was practically nonexistent, consisting mainly of the Cossack Brigade and the Gendarmerie and counting no more than twenty thousand men at best.

A crucial wartime development that greatly affected Persia was the Russian Revolution in 1917 and the subsequent creation of the Soviet Union. With the Treaty of Brest-Litovsk, the Russians, who were unable to continue fighting against the Central Powers due to the domestic chaos caused by the socialists, were forced out of the war. In the Caucasus and northwestern Iran, the fighting was completely taken over by the British, although by that time, the

Ottomans had exhausted their military strength and posed no real threat. Not only that, but the newly formed Soviet Union proceeded to formally declare the end to Russia's pursuit of interests in Persia, condemning it as a blatant imperialist approach of tsarist Russia. This meant the Russians were finally out of northern Persia and that Great Britain, which had just emerged victorious from the war and had taken over much of the Ottoman territories in the Levant, remained the only foreign power with a declared interest in Persia, which further complicated the political climate.

The British assumed a dominant role in the region and pursued a foreign policy that clearly underlined the fact they had become the only interested party in Persia. Russia's withdrawal also coincided with the presence of some of the most imperialist-minded individuals in British foreign affairs, like Foreign Secretary Nathaniel Curzon and British Minister to Iran Percy Cox, who viewed creating a British protectorate border state out of Persia to defend British holdings in India from expansionist and hostile powers such as Russia as necessary, even though the Russians had decided to officially abandon their endeavors in the region. This, when combined with the infamously pro-British cabinet of ministers that had been appointed by Ahmad Shah to take over the responsibilities of the Majles, led to the signing of yet another absurd agreement between the two countries.

The Anglo-Persian Agreement of August 1919, which was less of an "agreement" and more of a decree proclaimed by the British due to the influence they held over Persia's government, doubled down on Persia's reliance on Great Britain. The agreement asserted that Persia needed Great Britain to surmount the tough period it had experienced over the past few years and that only the British had enough presence in the region to provide the assistance and protection required for Persia to modernize and reorganize. In exchange for exclusive British access to *all* of Persia's oilfields, Britain would provide Persia with a loan of two million pounds for twenty years, send officers and equipment to restructure the Persian army, oversee the development of the country's infrastructure and communication networks, and assist Persian officials in revising the tariff system that had long been imposed on imported British goods. It was a good deal for the British and provoked criticism from France and the United States, which viewed the endeavor as another instance of Britain strengthening its position at the expense of a foreign, underdeveloped country.

The shah's ministers approved the agreement, although, according to the country's Constitution, it had to also be ratified by the Majles, which had still not been reassembled. However, as if it already was not clear enough, the Persian population soon realized the British were self-motivated and unwilling to commit to the scale they had proposed in the agreement. The news of another hurtful decision by the government sparked nationalist movements throughout the country, especially in the provinces of Gilan and Azerbaijan, which had led the activism movements a decade and a half earlier. People became suspicious of direct British control of the shah, believing that the Europeans may have bribed the monarch and the ministers employed by him.

A small Soviet army contingent landed in the Caspian port town of what is now Bandar-e Anzali, fearing that the British intended to support the White Russians, those who opposed the Bolsheviks and supported the tsar, by giving them refuge in Persia. They demanded that Britain remove its forces from the Persian territories, perceiving them as a threat to their security. This event again demonstrated that Britain was not prepared to defend Persia's sovereignty and interests in case of a concentrated foreign intervention. The disorganized nature of the Persian government, combined with the incident with the Soviets and the reluctance of British officials in London to support Curzon's endeavors, eventually forced Great Britain to evacuate all of its forces from Persia in April 1921, not two years after the agreement had been signed. The Anglo-Persian Agreement was effectively dead.

The Fall of the Qajar Dynasty

Seeing that Curzon's deal with Persia was dead and that pressure from the Soviets was mounting, the British soon changed their approach to Persia once again, this time favoring the formation of a capable Persian government that would not be attracted to the Russians and, at the same time, maintain stability in the country to the point that Britain's economic interests were still fulfilled. This change of policy led to the coup of February 21st, 1921, two months before the British withdrew from the country. A

Cossack Brigade force under Colonel Reza Khan marched from Qazvin to Tehran and took the city, taking control of the government and declaring martial law. Reza Khan and a prominent pro-British journalist named Sayyid Zia led the nationalist movement, which was most likely instigated secretly by British officials without Curzon's awareness. The details of how the coup actually came to be or how its leaders, who had limited political experience, managed to unite other nationalist-minded individuals under their banner are unclear. Still, the leadership of Sayyid Zia, who had previously been the editor of a pro-British newspaper in the country and was well known for his pro-British attitude, led many Iranians to believe that London stood behind the coup, organizing it for its own benefits.

Reza Shah Pahlavi in the 1930s.
https://commons.wikimedia.org/wiki/File:Reza_shah_uniform.jpg

However, soon after the capture of the capital, the two leaders of the coup quarreled with each other. Sayyid Zia was especially disliked by the people because of his past connections with the

British, despite the fact that he had officially canceled the Anglo-Persian Agreement. He was made the new prime minister but proceeded to use his power ruthlessly, ordering the arrest of many politicians, regardless of their beliefs or allegiances. In the end, Reza Khan believed the former journalist was unable to lead the country. He was also annoyed by his partner's constant meddling with the military. So, he forced Sayyid Zia to resign in May. The latter fled from Iran and remained in exile for a few decades until he eventually returned.

Just like that, Reza Khan, the commander of the Cossack Brigade, had emerged as the sole leader of the coup. Even before Sayyid Zia's resignation, he had already demonstrated that he had a clear vision and goals in mind and that he was a capable commander who was fit to lead. Five days after taking the capital, on February 26th, Reza Khan signed the Russo-Iranian Treaty of Friendship, establishing peaceful relations with the Bolsheviks and forcing their troops to leave Persia. By November 1921, Reza Khan defeated the resistance groups that had appeared throughout the Persian territories, which further contributed to the stabilization of the situation and neutralized the tribal and regional threats that had existed in the country for many years. Then, Reza Khan proceeded to reform the Gendarmerie, replacing the Swiss officers with capable Iranian personnel and uniting the scattered parts of the military from the different provinces of Persia.

Crucially, in 1924, not a year after his appointment as prime minister, Reza Khan was met with a challenge from the governor of Khuzestan, Sheikh Khazal, who had led an Arab revolt against the new government. Khuzestan had long been a rogue province, and Sheikh Khazal refused to pay taxes to the new government in Tehran. He was supported by the British, who supplied his men with arms. Although Reza Khan had been warned by the British to back down from attacking Khuzestan, afraid that an armed conflict would be destructive toward their oilfields in the region, Reza Khan nevertheless advanced on the rebels, managing to suppress the rebellion relatively easily and suffering minor casualties. By reasserting control over the province and demonstrating that his reorganization of the army had indeed been successful, Reza Khan's popularity skyrocketed. The people respected his leadership skills and ability to not back down from a challenge, even if it was against Britain.

While the coup in Tehran was happening, similar developments were unfolding in the Ottoman Empire, where a Turkish nationalist movement had toppled the monarchy and triumphed under the empire's first president, Mustafa Kemal. Most people in Persia were anti-monarchy, as the victory of nationalism and the successes of republicans under Reza Khan had swayed a lot of the population. This opinion was shared by the Majles, which had reconvened and had been running ever since the coup in 1921. It had grown increasingly liberal after its fifth iteration was assembled in 1923. Because of its aspirations to modernize and develop the country's society, the Majles adopted European-style names, dropping the traditional titles that were associated with the old regime (Reza Khan thus became Reza Pahlavi after this change). It also authorized some of the prime minister's initiatives and was generally on good terms with the leader of the coup. Motivated by republicanism's triumph in Turkey and the general public discontent toward Ahmad Shah Qajar, the Majles debated the option of abolishing the monarchy in Persia, a move that would definitely be a radical step toward modernization and fully embrace republican ideals. However, after the more conservative members of the Majles came out to vehemently oppose this idea, the liberal wing backed down.

In the end, an agreement was reached that was probably good for everyone. The Qajar dynasty would be abolished, but the monarchy would be preserved, with Reza Khan being nominated as the new shah. Thus, on February 14th, 1925, while Ahmad Shah Qajar was still on his journey in Europe (which was where he was for most of his time as shah), Reza Pahlavi was proclaimed as the new shah of Persia, putting an end to more than 130 years of Qajar rule in Iran.

Chapter 9: From Reza Shah Pahlavi to the Islamic Revolution

Reza Shah Pahlavi

With the accession of Reza Shah to the Persian throne, we enter into the second stage of modern Iranian history. This period is significant, as it would mark the emergence of Persia as a modern nation-state with an effective constitutional monarchy as its political system. Reza Shah Pahlavi is often considered the founder of modern Iran due to his basic but, at the same time, long-overdue projects that consolidated Persia's position as a sovereign nation-state on the world's political stage. Indeed, the reign of the first Pahlavi monarch saw a drastic improvement from the previous decades under Qajar rule. Reza Shah's rule was characterized by increased levels of domestic stability, economic growth, and sociocultural revival.

As a military commander, Reza Shah Pahlavi's first endeavor was the unification of Persia's armies under one cohesive system. Pahlavi had already made significant developments in this regard even before he had become shah, as he had reorganized both the Cossack Brigade and the formerly Swiss-led Gendarmerie. By 1930, Persia's military would be far more advanced, counting nearly 100,000 men who were properly trained, equipped, and paid. Military compounds around the country were developed to adhere to modern standards. The conscription laws, which had been one of the first legislative reforms of the Majles under Reza Shah Pahlavi, greatly helped the new shah in creating a system that finally ended the turmoil caused by regional and tribal armed groups.

However, Reza Shah's main goal was not to wage foreign wars and expand. Instead, the shah correctly realized that such endeavors would be increasingly difficult after the events of World War I, especially since Persia found itself surrounded by far more powerful global powers. The objective of the army reform was to create a force capable of keeping peace and security—two things that helped to guarantee prosperity and a higher quality of life. Although Reza Shah faced many different regional rebellions on his way to creating a united Persian army based on conscription, all of the resistance was relatively easily defeated thanks to the shah's resilience and excellent leadership.

In addition to reforming the military, Reza Shah Pahlavi implemented changes that touched upon other aspects of life. For example, to catch up with the vastly more modernized regional powers, Persia saw a great increase in domestic industry and infrastructure under Reza Shah's administration. Thousands of miles of new roads and highways were constructed throughout the country, finally eliminating the connectivity issues that had plagued Iran since, well, forever. The crucial Trans-Iranian Railway was completed under his rule in 1938, which connected the country from the Caspian Sea to the Persian Gulf.

In terms of developing administration, new bureaucratic systems were put in place to increase government involvement in decentralized public affairs and to maintain strong control over what was going on in the country. This was followed by the creation of a new education system. The government funded hundreds of new institutions, which greatly increased the literacy rates of Iranian citizens, making them more qualified laborers in different fields of the economy. Economic growth during Reza Shah's reign was perhaps not as excellent as he would have liked, but efforts to monopolize several channels of production certainly led to more centralization of power and the creation of a stronger middle class, which was essential in establishing a full-on transition to a functional capitalistic society.

It is undeniable that Reza Shah Pahlavi had been greatly influenced by his Turkish counterpart, Mustafa Kemal Ataturk, who had certainly set quite an example after his emergence as a stalwart nationalist in Turkey. In fact, the shah visited and got on good terms with the Turkish president. Reza Shah tried to implement the parts of Ataturk's reforms he believed were essential for the development of Iran. Due to his keenness of Persian nationalism, the sociocultural aspect of the country would be greatly highlighted, with the shah encouraging the study of pre-Islamic Persian history, diminishing the roles of non-Persian minority languages in the country, and promoting the idea that Iran was only for ethnic Persians.

Reza Shah also borrowed quite heavily from Ataturk when it came to the increased importance and eventual emancipation of women, who had traditionally been considered rather insignificant in Islamic culture. The shah was adamant about increasing women's rights, allowing them to increasingly join the workplace and receive public education. He even allowed women students to be admitted to the University of Tehran upon its founding in 1934. He also pushed for laws that would free women from wearing the traditional chador, although this was considered far too radical and was met with fierce opposition from the Shi'ite ulama. Although Reza Shah's endeavors regarding women's rights were less successful than that of Ataturk, whose policies pushed for a very egalitarian society, Reza Shah's reign was nevertheless beneficial for women's eventual emancipation and suffrage in Iran in the 1960s.

In his endeavors to promote a sovereign Persian nation-state, Reza Shah Pahlavi ultimately had to confront the question of religion, which had been a central part of Iranian history in one way or another for more than a thousand years. The shah considered Shi'a Islam as the main bond that was shared between the Persian people and acknowledged its importance in state-building and the development of Persian culture and identity. Still, despite the fact that he asserted Shi'ism was one of the pillars of the state ever since his accession, the shah's ultimate goal was to assert the state's dominance over religion. Many liberal intellectuals believed that Islam acted in resistance to the shah's aspirations, considering a foreign religion had caused the underdevelopment of

Persia due to the country's reliance on and embracement of it.

Unlike Turkey, Pahlavi was not able to achieve a complete separation of state and religion, but he certainly managed to strip the ulama from some of the privileges they had held in the country for a long time. Mainly, he reorganized the bureaucracy and the legal system, leading to diminished power for religious officials when it came to non-religious activities, although Sharia law was still respected and used as a model for legal procedures. The opening of many private and state-owned educational institutions and a woman's ability to attend them also lessened the influence of the Shi'ite clergy over such matters. Still, the shah financed the creation of new religious sites. He especially promoted the city of Qom as a center of Shi'a Islam, which pleased the otherwise not-so-content ulama.

Reza Shah Abdicates

All in all, Reza Shah Pahlavi had chosen the correct trajectory to develop the country. Although he faced some resistance from more conservative domestic forces, his quest to form a sovereign Persian nation-state went rather successfully. However, alongside being a reform-minded nationalist who contributed a lot to Iran's much-needed modernization, Reza Shah quickly showed a much darker side. Firstly, Pahlavi was able to accumulate much personal wealth through his policies, victories against the rebellions that rose up against him, and behind-the-scenes dealings. He perhaps even eclipsed the material possessions of the latter Qajar monarchs. Reza Shah came from a poor background with no real wealth to his name, but by the end of his reign, he had come into possession of hundreds of thousands of acres of land in different parts of Iran, as well as a fortune that the monarch is said to have safely kept in foreign banks.

In addition to his dictator-scale personal wealth, Reza Shah's authoritarian, almost totalitarian, tendencies showed in his conduct toward some of the opposing forces during his reign, especially those that criticized the shah's more successful policies and did not share his more radical-leaning nationalist values. Reza Shah's reign saw the oppression and general intolerance toward minority groups and marginalized political communities and societies. For example, after consolidating his power and reorganizing the army, Reza Shah arrested and exiled many of the politicians of the Majles who had opposed either his accession or his proposed reforms.

By the end of his reign, Shah Pahlavi had slowly gotten rid of the figures who had helped him come into power to further reinforce his image as the sole leader of the nationalist movement. He also largely monopolized state control over many different aspects of Persian life, not only the economy but also the press, which was censored and became a tool for spreading nationalist propaganda. The shah especially cracked down on the socialists and communists in the country, often sending armed forces and state police to disperse their meetings. He eventually banned their political parties and general activities.

Reza Shah Pahlavi's demise began in the mid-1930s, not long after he increasingly pursued his nationalist policies to form a common national identity among the Persian people. Of course, as we mentioned above, some of the developments during this period, such as the creation of new educational institutions and the emancipation of women, were clearly progressive steps. However, it was as if Reza Shah soon became obsessed with his quest to pursue nationalism. He tried to symbolize the modernization of Persia under his rule in strange ways. For example, he insisted that the country officially adopt the name "Iran" instead of "Persia" as a means of showcasing the Westernization of the state. He was also increasingly hostile toward foreign nations that sometimes criticized his undemocratic actions.

Eventually, as part of the endeavor to strengthen the sovereign Iranian nation and to further reduce the influence of the great powers in the country's domestic affairs, the shah increasingly engaged in strategic relations with Nazi Germany. In the 1930s, the Third Reich became Iran's largest trading partner. The decision that would clearly display the shah's attitude toward the British would be the cancellation of the oil concession for the Anglo-Persian Oil Company in November 1932. The contract, which had been signed for a period of fifty years, did not expire for another three decades, so it is unsurprising that London took the case to court in the League of Nations. Before the court could come to a decision, Reza Shah agreed to sign another concession in April 1933. It was not a significant improvement over the last one, as it gave Britain access to a reduced number of oilfields for another sixty years.

The newly made German connections would become a target for the British and the Soviets in 1941, two years after the beginning of World War II and soon after German declared war on the Soviet Union. Having the same common enemy again, Britain and the USSR naturally became allies and sought to fight off the fascists wherever they could, including Iran, where they perceived the increased German presence as a threat to the British oilfields. The Allies soon issued an ultimatum, demanding the expulsion of all German citizens and the termination of German enterprises, something the shah declined to do.

In response, the British and the Soviets coordinated a joint surprise offensive on Iran in August 1941 to guarantee that the supply routes would not be taken over by the pro-German forces in the country. Reza Shah Pahlavi, who was under pressure from two sides and outgunned by superior armies, was forced to abdicate, fleeing the country in September.

Soviet tanks in Tabriz after the invasion, 1941.
https://commons.wikimedia.org/wiki/File:Soviet_tankmen_of_the_6th_Armoured_Divisi
on_drive_through_the_streets_of_Tabriz_(2).jpg

Iran in World War II

The Anglo-Soviet invasion of 1941, dubbed Operation Countenance by the two countries, led to another partitioning of Iran into Russian (Soviet) and British spheres of influence. The two powers eventually decided to place the son of Reza Shah,

Mohammad Reza Khan, on the throne of Iran. However, he was inexperienced and did not hold nearly as much power or enjoy as much prestige as his father. The foreign powers proceeded to backtrack on a lot of the developments made under Reza Shah, weakening Iran's military and government and exploiting the country's rich resources for their own benefit.

Still, having Iran on their side was a gamechanger for the Allies, who utilized the Trans-Iranian Railway and the country's improved infrastructure to transport millions of tons of aid from the American Lend-Lease program to the Soviet Union, shipping ammunition, arms, military vehicles, food, oil, and other supplies to Russia through the Caspian Sea. Iran still remained technically neutral in the war and contributed no forces.

Although Mohammad Reza Shah was unable to resist the Allies using his country as a corridor for supplying Moscow, he nevertheless managed to gain a relatively favorable position with the foreign powers due to his cooperation or, rather, lack of resistance. This was confirmed in 1942 and 1943 after Iran signed agreements with the British, the Soviets, and the Americans that bound the Allies to guarantee the safety and sovereignty of Iran throughout the war, as well as to withdraw their personnel from Iran's borders once the war was over. The Allies also pledged financial support to Iran for its contributions to the war effort. This ultimately resulted in America's increased interest in Iran as a potential trade partner for oil and caused Iranian politicians to increasingly invite Americans to take part in the country's political and economic activities.

However, by the end of the war, it would be the Soviets who would try to destabilize the seemingly peaceful situation in Iran. Perhaps concerned that the British and the Americans wanted to undermine their presence in Iran and alarmed at the planned concession of Iranian oilfields to the US in 1944, the Soviets demanded that the Iranian government make oilfield concessions to Moscow in all the northern territories that were occupied by the Soviet troops after the 1941 invasion. The Majles, led by future Prime Minister Muhammad Saed, declined, instead asserting that the discussion of potential concessions to foreign countries was prohibited before the end of the war. The Soviets pressed further, as they had cultivated communist and socialist forces in Iran that had been suppressed by Reza Shah. To create a sense of chaos, they instigated the creation of radical separatist movements and rebellions in Azerbaijan and Kurdistan in late 1945, leading to what is often referred to as the first post-WWII and Cold War crisis.

In January 1946, Iran pleaded its case in front of the newly created United Nations, accusing the Soviet Union of meddling with Iranian national affairs and not respecting its agreement. Both Britain and the US had already withdrawn their forces from southern Iran. They supported the plea and pressured the Soviets to uphold their part of the deal. Finally, in March 1946, Moscow, faced with a potential armed confrontation against its former allies over a relatively unimportant matter (the provinces occupied by the Soviets did not even possess any oil), decided to succumb to the pressure and withdrew its troops from Iran. It was a national victory for the Iranians, who had seemingly gotten rid of foreign powers. Later that year, they proceeded to defeat the Kurdish and Azeri communist separatist movements, with the Soviets not willing to intervene.

The Rise and Fall of Mohammad Mosaddegh

The post-war years turned out to be extremely beneficial for Mohammad Reza Shah, who somehow managed to gain a lot of political traction and a favorable position among the Iranian people. Although he had been relatively inactive during the negotiation procedures with the Soviets and the British, the relative success Iran accomplished led many to believe that it was the shah who was in charge of the diplomatic victories. This view was further reinforced when the shah led his forces against the Azeri and the Kurdish separatists in December 1946, as this move portrayed him as a capable military commander, further increasing his prestige. Such a change in the shah's public image also resulted in increased numbers of royalist conservatives in the Majles, giving Mohammad Reza the ability to pass legislation that imposed the monarch's dominance over the assembly. By late 1949, Mohammad Reza Shah enjoyed quite a bit of popularity in the country, although he did not hold as much authoritarian power as his father.

However, the domination of foreign powers during the war period led to the creation of different parties, which occupied seats in the Majles and pushed for their own visions. There were three main political parties in the Majles that were not particularly supportive of the shah: the socialist-leftist Tudeh Party, which was especially popular among the youth and was well known for its organized street protests; the conservative Fada-iyan-e Islam Party, which was a far-right, anti-secularist organization led by a popular religious figure named Abol-Ghasem Kashani and was known for attracting radical sympathizers; and lastly, the National Front Party, led by Mohammad Mosaddegh, which was a coalition of all the nationalist, anti-royalist factions that fell in between the two extremes.

Mosaddegh was known and respected in the political spectrum for his liberal views and determined vision of the country. He wished to be free of foreign influences and was the first to float the idea of canceling the Anglo-Iranian Oil Company (AIOC). He wanted to nationalize all the oilfields in the country, an idea that was largely supported by all the groups in the Majles.

The National Front would soon gain more and more followers, even forming a sort of an alliance with the conservative Fada-iyan-e. Mosaddegh and Kashani became the two main advocates for pushing the oil nationalization legislature. They were helped by the Tudeh activists, who would regularly protest in the streets, further putting pressure on the shah, who had been accused of being pro-British since he did not want to go through with the dissolution of the AIOC. The shah answered these demonstrations by appointing a former military commander, Ali Razmara, as the new prime minister. Razmara managed to push many pro-royalist laws with the help of the Majles majority.

Still, the National Front demanded that the prime minister consider the idea of nationalizing the country's oil reserves in February 1951. Razmara rejected the proposal. This led to his assassination by a radical member of the Fada-iyan-e the following month, which created a sense of chaos in the country. The chaos resulted in more demonstrations and more firm demands from the National Front to push the nationalization bill, which eventually passed in mid-March, both in the Majles and the Senate, which had also been dominated by royalists.

With the pressure mounting, Mohammad Reza Shah found himself confronted with fierce opposition, and in May, he was forced to agree to the Majles' proposal to appoint Mosaddegh as the prime minister, marking the beginning of a very influential two-year tenure that had immense consequences for modern Iran.

Prime Minister Mosaddegh.
https://commons.wikimedia.org/wiki/File:Mohammad_Mosaddegh_portrait.jpg

After being appointed to office, Mosaddegh immediately went ahead and dissolved the AIOC, replacing it with the National Iranian Oil Company (NIOC), which was seen as another triumph of nationalist Iran over the imperialist foreigners. However, although the idea of the nationalization of oil seemed really beneficial for Iranians on paper, the actual transition proved to be much more difficult in practice. Britain, which had been especially dependent on the income from Iran's oilfields for its ruined post-war economy, had long warned of the catastrophic consequences the country would face if it went ahead with the decision, something that was not taken into consideration by the National Front, whose main motivation had been to undermine the shah's authority. When London argued in The Hague and then at the

UN Security Council that Mosaddegh had violated an official agreement between the two countries and urged the international community to back its position, the Iranian prime minister fiercely defended his country, gaining support from the International Court of Justice and the UN, which ruled that the matter should have been resolved between the two countries separately. This caused a national crisis in Britain, and the country turned to its wartime hero, the one and only Winston Churchill, to save it from international humiliation and resolve the situation in London's favor.

The new conservative British government harshly responded, rendering Mosaddegh's nationalization of oil practically useless. Churchill was reluctant to use the armed forces Britain possessed in the area, so he imposed immense economic pressure on Iran, whose economy was greatly dependent on the export of oil.

After the Iranian takeover, all of the British employees were prohibited from continuing to work for the NIOC and were escorted out of the country by British troops. Since the British had operated the oilfields for many decades and constituted the vast majority of the competent workers of the AIOC, this greatly hurt the NIOC's production, as its workforce was reduced to locals who were inexperienced. Churchill's government also froze all Iranian assets in British banks and imposed a boycott of all Iranian products, following it up with a blockade of the country's exports. When Mosaddegh tried to borrow funds from the US, Washington denied the prime minister's request, something that had been made sure by Churchill.

All in all, the British reaction further reduced Iran's already struggling economy. By the end of 1951, Mosaddegh's influence and prestige in the country were fading. The Iranian prime minister tried to regain support by manipulating the 17th Majles in a way that gave more power to the voter classes that supported his party, but he still failed to get a majority in the assembly. In July, after the shah's denial to appoint Mosaddegh's candidate as the new war minister, he briefly resigned from office before the shah was forced to bring him back just five days later after pressure from violent demonstrations in Iran, which took the lives of over 250 protesters.

However, in the second half of 1952, Mosaddegh made a political comeback, desperately defending his actions and trying to remain in power. Still under the impression that he enjoyed popular support, the prime minister gained enough followers in the Majles to grant himself "emergency powers" for a period of six years. This allowed Mosaddegh to be in control of virtually the whole country by himself, although he was aided by his political allies in the Tudeh and Fada-iyan-e.

Mosaddegh rejected the British proposal of another oil deal. He even broke off diplomatic relations in October and arrested several pro-British Iranian figures. Then, he went ahead and reduced the budget for the royal family, imposing his authority over the shah and forcing Mohammad Reza's politically outspoken sister into exile. By the end of the year, his "emergency powers" were approved to continue for another twelve months by the Majles, leading to more measures that increased the prime minister's authority and pushed his populist policies to increase his support.

However, Mosaddegh tried to increase his own power and increasingly pushed for more left-leaning policies, like the redistribution of lands and heavy taxes on the upper classes, to appease the Tudeh Party, which had supported the prime minister by organizing street demonstrations time and time again. More conservative-leaning political allies started to retract their support. The defunding of the military also caused the armed forces to become loyal to the shah, as they saw him as the true leader of the country. Internal support also dwindled due to the horrible impact the British actions had on the Iranian economy, with inflation rates reaching all-time highs and domestic production plummeting. More and more factions within and outside of the country disliked Mosaddegh's decisions, although some of them had been sympathetic toward his initial aspirations of nationalizing the oilfields.

The Americans had grown wary of the Iranian prime minister. The US was a close ally of Britain and criticized Mosaddegh for a long time. However, what pushed Washington to start thinking about the dangers that might arise from Tehran was the increased influence of the Tudeh socialist left. The US feared that the hostile Soviet Union might interfere and install a leftist, pro-Soviet government in place of Mosaddegh. Thus, in early May 1953, after seeing Mosaddegh overexercise the powers that had been bestowed upon him by himself, the CIA and British MI-6 started planning a joint operation codenamed Operation Ajax to instigate a coup in Iran and overthrow the prime minister. Their plan was to stir up public opinion against Mosaddegh, especially in rural provinces and tribes, by spreading propaganda and paying people to pose as his supporters during the protests to make the prime minister believe he had more public support than he really did. The CIA then communicated the matter to Mohammad Reza Shah, who reluctantly agreed to carry out the plan.

By this time, Mosaddegh had already suspected that domestic forces were brewing a conspiracy against him and tried to crack down on anyone whom he thought would oppose him. The prime minister decided to hold a national referendum to dissolve the Majles in July. The ballots for the referendum were not secret, as there were separate boxes for voting against or for the proposal. The boxes were guarded by forces loyal to Mosaddegh, which helped the CIA portray Mosaddegh as a non-democratic, totalitarian ruler who did not care for his people. Unsurprisingly, with more than 99 percent of the votes in favor of dissolving the Majles, the referendum gave the prime minister even more power. The shah believed that the coup had failed and fled the country. This resulted in Mosaddegh openly campaigning for the monarchy's abolishment, leading to more demonstrations in August. His supporters toppled Reza Shah's statues, which also ironically contributed to the CIA's cause.

In reality, though, most of the protesters were those who had been paid by the CIA to pose as radical leftists. If they had not been there, the actual protest would not have been that big or threatening. Mosaddegh believed the radicals were not only trying to abolish the monarchy but also overthrow him, ordering army contingents loyal to him to suppress the activists. On August 19th, it was clear that the CIA's operation had been successful, as thousands of anti-Mosaddegh protesters took to the streets, storming government buildings and causing unrest. Soon, the protesters, led by prominent local activists like Shaban Jafari, were joined by royalist armed forces led by General Fazlullah Zahedi, who had been in communication with the CIA and was well aware that the coup was underway. Motivated and financed by the foreign intelligence forces, the protesters stormed Mosaddegh's residence and captured him. The shah returned to Tehran on August 22nd and appointed Zahedi as the new prime minister.

People in Tehran celebrate after the successful coup in 1953.
https://commons.wikimedia.org/wiki/File:Operationajax.jpg

The coup of 1953 managed to get rid of one of the most ambitious leaders Iran had ever seen. Mohammad Mosaddegh would spend the rest of his years in exile under house arrest and would die not long after the coup. To this day, he remains a classic example of someone who became corrupted by having too much power. He used the trust of many of the Iranian people in a way that did little to benefit the country, although he had good intentions at the beginning of his political struggle. Although he had been fighting to end the blatant exploitation of his country and its resources by a foreign power, Mosaddegh turned out not to be strong enough to confront the might of the Americans and the British, who proceeded to influence the new prime minister to strike a new deal on oil concessions. Despite the fact that Mosaddegh ultimately fell to his own desire to pursue more power and had clear authoritarian tendencies, the coup of 1953 is still deeply embedded in the minds of the Iranian people as yet another instance when their country became a victim of foreign intervention.

After Mosaddegh: The White Revolution

The new administration under Prime Minister Zahedi had essentially been appointed by the CIA, so it is unsurprising that the Americans and British would mainly benefit from the policies that were implemented immediately after Mosaddegh's demise. Although the rest of the decade would be relatively calmer for Iran and more influential political processes would take place starting in the 1960s, the 1950s still saw some important changes. In 1954, for example, Iran struck a new deal on its oil reserves. In exchange for US investment, compensation to the AIOC, and contractual obligations to foreign companies, the country's oil reserves were once again fully nationalized, with more Iranian employees being retrained to boost production. The US influence was even clear with Iran's willingness to participate in new multilateral treaties, mainly the Baghdad Pact of 1955, also known as CENTO, which saw Tehran enter into a defensive military alliance with Turkey, Pakistan, and Iraq. Two years later, with the creation of a new secret service institution dubbed SAVAK, US-influenced Iran increased its efforts of cracking down on the far-left groups of the Tudeh, further appeasing the United States, which was an advocate for an all-out war on socialism and communism.

By 1960, the weakening of the political opposition in the country resulted in the growing influence of the shah, who managed to eventually consolidate his power to a level comparable to his father. The Majles, which would be dissolved in 1961, was dominated by two conservative parties that were openly favored by the shah. A year later, in 1962, the shah's ministers proposed the Land Reform Act, which made the biggest landowners sell their lands to the government for it to be redistributed by the state. In 1963, Mohammad Reza Shah declared his intention for a complete reform of the Iranian society and economy. He wanted to push for more modernization, industrialization, and urban development and create an economic surplus.

The Shah and People Revolution, also known as the White Revolution, was launched by the shah in January 1963. He had twenty points or goals he wanted to reach, with six being implemented right at the time of the proclamation: the land redistribution reform, which allowed members of the lower classes to buy the seized lands for lower prices and lower interest rates to boost their own wealth; nationalization of all forests of the country; the sale of state-owned factories and production enterprises to promote the creation of new private businesses and industries; the so-called "profit sharing" plan for workers, which allowed them to get additional profits on top of their salaries; the crucial decision to grant women the right to vote; and lastly, the creation of a literacy corps to boost public education throughout the country, especially in non-urban areas. After launching a public referendum, which triumphed with more than five million votes for its support (no more than five thousand votes opposed it), the White Revolution was underway.

Although the ambitious set of reforms was supposed to modernize the country, it was met with fierce opposition. Of course, the proposed changes benefited the country in many aspects. Hundreds of thousands of new families purchased lands at low prices and were lifted out of poverty. The social status of women was greatly ameliorated, and the education reform had positive effects on the rural population, who simply did not have access to schools before. The White Revolution was opposed by different social groups, most prominently the ulama.

The religious elite was the most upset with the shah, with some of their issues stemming from the new rights granted to women, which went against traditional Islam. In addition, the shah's reforms also undermined their power and influence in Iranian society. Many rural communities, for example, had previously been educated by religious figures who brought up the youth with knowledge and respect toward Shi'a Islam. The literacy corps took over educating the children. The land reforms also impacted the ulama, who had been dependent on the income from the *waqf* (plots of land that had been donated to the religious establishment by its followers).

Mohammad Reza Shah Pahlavi handing out documents about the new reforms during the White Revolution.

https://commons.wikimedia.org/wiki/File:Mrplandreform1.jpg

In the first few weeks after the revolution's proclamation, different protests erupted throughout the country. The protests were swiftly dealt with by the shah's forces. Critics of the shah's reforms spoke out all over the country. A certain religious leader and professor in Qom by the name of Ruhollah Khomeini heavily criticized the undermining of the ulama's influence by Mohammad Reza. His comments quickly attracted the attention of the shah's government, and SAVAK proceeded to storm his school and arrest him. Khomeini was later exiled, spending his time in different countries of the Middle East and Europe but never stopping his active involvement in Iranian matters.

In parallel to Mohammad Reza Shah's ambitious program, which envisioned developments in Iran's social, political, and economic spheres, he also increasingly pursued autocratic policies. After 1963, the shah worked tirelessly to portray himself as the successor of the great Persian monarchs, like Cyrus the Great. He portrayed himself as a sort of savior worthy of the people's trust. In 1967, he organized his official crowning ceremony in Tehran, assuming the ancient title of the *shahanshah* to further underline his status. This was followed by his proclamation of 2,500 continuous years of the Persian monarchy, a national event that was lavishly celebrated in 1971 in Persepolis to commemorate the founding of the Achaemenid Empire. This blatant narcissistic propaganda was accompanied by other decisions aimed at increasing his direct power, such as the buildup of the military.

Although Mohammad Reza Shah had gradually grown out of being a literal US puppet, the threat of Soviet influence and invasion was enough for Washington to sell Iran an egregious number of arms to the point that the country accumulated one of the largest armed forces in the world by the mid-1970s. With the increased might of the army and the reduction of Britain's presence in the Middle East, the shah authorized a military intervention during a war in Oman, where Iran fought to suppress the socialists. The increased revenue from oil exports, after the oil price had been redefined after the war between Egypt, Syria, and Israel, came as a great help to the shah. The new price almost sextupled the price of a single oil barrel, making the industry Iran's most profitable endeavor.

By the second half of the 1970s, the problems of the White Revolution started to show, significantly affecting the lives of most of the Iranian people in one way or another and forcing them to develop anti-shah sympathies. The ambitious nature of the modernization reforms simply could not be supported by Iran's infrastructure and resources. For example, despite having large energy resources, most of the country did not have reliable access to electricity, including Tehran, which suffered regular blackouts. The economy also could not handle the influx of cash from the increased oil prices, leading to high levels of inflation and an eventual economic crisis, even if, generally speaking, the average Iranian became richer after the White Revolution. The land reform also seemed to be a failure, with agricultural production declining and more and more peasants abandoning their estates and flocking to urban centers, causing unrest and overpopulation. This, when paired with the increased feelings of xenophobia in the population due to the shah's cooperation with countries that were once considered former enemies, produced a pivotal reaction that once again greatly altered the course of Iranian history.

Chapter 10: The Islamic Republic of Iran

Islamic Revolution

Slowly, the discontent among members of the public grew. By early 1978, it was easy to see the chaos that had been created in the country due to the shah's actions. More and more authoritarian measures, like the suppression of opposition parties and undermining the Majles and the ulama, increasingly caused criticism, not only from Iranians but also from abroad, as the international community recognized the effect Mohammad Reza's reforms had. The situation only needed a spark. Unfortunately for the shah, multiple events would take place starting in early 1978, which would produce yet another wave of mass protests and, eventually, what has come to be known as the Islamic Revolution.

However, every revolution needs a leader, a prominent persona capable of voicing the people's discontent. The Iranians found their leader in Ayatollah Ruhollah Khomeini, who, despite being exiled in 1964 from the country due to his criticism of the shah, had never ceased to point out the terrible nature of Mohammad Reza's reign and the concerns he had of the country's further development. Khomeini's populist remarks were quickly upheld by the conservative Shi'a Iranians and the secular liberals, who had grown tired of the shah's lavish, unproductive, and authoritarian endeavors and wished to see his reign come to an end.

Thus, with the growing discontent and the increased voice of the ulama, which had been undermined for years ever since the Constitutional Revolution at the beginning of the century, the religious institution once again became a prominent force and united the majority of the people. The growing revolution attracted many Iranians, including those who criticized the undemocratic nature of Mohammad Reza Shah's rule, those who held xenophobic stances and did not like foreign influences on Iran, and more conservative Iranians, who saw the ulama as a necessary force to guide Iran out of the crisis.

Ayatollah Ruhollah Khomeini.
https://commons.wikimedia.org/wiki/File:Ruhollah_Khomeini_portrait_1.jpg

In January 1978, the government became aware of a peculiar alliance between different types of protesters and condemned the soon-to-be revolutionary groups with a Tehrani newspaper article, stating they had no morals and shared objectives. The article described Khomeini as nothing more than a foreign spy who wanted to use the Iranian people for his own benefit. This was the first nail in the coffin of Mohammad Reza Shah's rule, as thousands of Khomeini sympathizers took to the streets. Protests erupted in all major public gathering places, like the central bazaars of the big cities. Most of the activists were religious students who shared the same conservative Shi'ite views as Khomeini, although they were joined by smaller, less right-wing groups who had been negatively affected by the shah's reforms and wished to see him perish. They were further incentivized by Khomeini himself, who continued to preach from his exile in Iraq that the country needed religious guidance under a "supreme jurist," a notion that was quickly upheld by his sympathizers.

The government's response to this was what one would expect from an autocratic leader who feels power slipping away from their hands: a harsh police crackdown and violent suppressions of the street protests, which resulted in the deaths of hundreds of people by the end of the revolution. However, the actions of the shah-controlled SAVAK did not put an end to the activists, and the deaths of their compatriots sparked a sense that they had died for a noble cause, as they were considered to be martyrs for a just revolution. This is significant, as Islamic culture emphasizes the role of martyrdom. It is likely this idea fueled the protesters, whose numbers increased with each demonstration.

When the shah did not allow for the peaceful commemoration of the protestors who had died, which had assembled after forty days had passed since the death of the first protesters (in line with Shi'a traditions), the activists were even more outraged. Soon, it became clear that all the groups, regardless of their political views or economic stance, were uniting under the banner of their religion. The Shi'a leaders emerged as the overall leaders of the revolution.

By mid-1978, the protests were continually taking place in big cities, with each one growing in number and violently clashing with state police. Mohammad Reza Shah declared martial law in September, assuming total control of the state (if he hadn't already) as the supreme commander of its forces and radicalizing many more of his opponents. He also requested that Iraq's leader, Saddam Hussein, expel Ayatollah Khomeini from his country in October, agreeing that the religious jurist should take refuge in

Paris.

However, Khomeini's arrival in France had dire consequences for the shah. Mohammad Reza had expected that close communications would cease between Khomeini and the revolutionaries after his departure from neighboring Iraq. Instead, Khomeini was aided by many like-minded Iranian and non-Iranian individuals in France to continue his preaching, and the bond between him and the protesters in Iran only became stronger. By the end of October, as the situation became more and more unbearable, local workers started going on strikes, bringing domestic industries, including oil production, to a halt, which significantly hurt the shah's position. He realized that the inevitable was coming for him, just as it had for an array of dictators before him. By this time, however, it was too late.

By the end of the year, Tehran, Tabriz, Qom, and other major cities were filled with protesters, and other civic activities had almost completely ceased. The police were not able to handle the hundreds of thousands of people who were united for a common cause: to get rid of the shah. In January 1979, one year after the start of the major protests, the shah and his family fled the country, officially stating that they were going on a royal vacation abroad. The revolutionaries knew that victory was close, as the government established during Mohammad Reza's absence was unable to do anything. On February 1ˢᵗ, an estimated one million people gathered in the streets of Tehran, demanding that the government be dissolved and that the shah abdicate. Ayatollah Ruhollah Khomeini arrived in the capital, joining the protesters. By the end of the month, the armed forces realized they were fighting for the losing side and declared their neutrality. The government also gave up. The Islamic Revolution had triumphed.

Post-Revolutionary Iran

Following their triumph and the shah's escape, the revolutionaries slowly started to take over the country, with Khomeini, of course, emerging as their natural leader, despite having no political experience whatsoever. In late March, he organized a national referendum, which voted overwhelmingly in favor of the establishment of an Islamic republic in place of the monarchy.

Although Khomeini had been considered the leader of the movement and most of the activists had been fighting under the banner of Shi'a Islam against the corrupt regime of Mohammad Reza, the proclamation of the Islamic Republic of Iran ultimately resulted in divisions among the more conservative and secularist-liberal revolutionaries. The wedge that had been driven between these two groups of activists was further widened by Khomeini's blatant promotion of anti-Western propaganda, condemnation of democratic principles, and the purge of hundreds of secularist sympathizers.

Soon after the referendum, Khomeini and his supporters reinforced their dominance by creating several governmental institutions that asserted Islam's importance in the country and were used by Khomeini to accumulate more power. Eventually, separate revolutionary movements, based not only on ideological but also ethnic grounds, sparked throughout the country, most importantly in Khuzestan and Kurdistan. They were eventually dealt with by the Islamic government.

Although the revolution had been perceived by many as a means of ending the shah's authoritarian regime, it soon became clear that a relatively oppressive regime had been established by Khomeini, as he used his power to greatly alter the social and political landscape of the country. We have to remember that the revolutionaries took over a country that had been basically paralyzed in every aspect, with almost all economic activities having ceased and governmental institutions fully collapsed. This gave virtually unlimited power to Khomeini and his sympathizers, who were quick to impose an almost totalitarian Islamic rule, patrolling the streets and forcing people to behave and dress in the traditional Shi'ite way.

One of their first decisions was the retraction of many women's rights and freedoms, something that had been a central point of protest for the religious conservative groups. To enforce his authority, Khomeini also created his own police force—the Islamic Revolutionary Guard Corps—which was comprised of volunteers and fanatic devotees to Khomeini's cause.

Protesters during the Islamic Revolution with a banner that reads "We want an Islamic government, led by Imam Khomeini."
https://commons.wikimedia.org/wiki/File:Islamic_Government_(17_Shahrivar).jpg

As the "Supreme Leader" or *rahbar*, Khomeini assumed a special position, one beyond the scope of the republican government and the Constitution, giving him almost a free hand in the country's affairs. This allowed him to continue his crackdown on everything that symbolized Western influence on Iran, which eventually culminated with demonstrations at the US Embassy in Tehran in November 1979. The protesters demanded that Mohammad Reza Shah be expedited by the Americans, as the exiled shah had been undergoing cancer treatment in the US at that time. Perhaps fearing that Mohammad Reza might be planning another coup with the CIA to come back into power just as he had in 1953, the protesters stormed the embassy building, taking sixty-six US citizens as hostages, something which has come to be known as the Iran hostage crisis.

If Iran-US relations had not already been affected by the conservative, anti-Western takeover of the Islamic Revolution, the hostage crisis strained the relationship between the two to its breaking point, forcing Washington to adopt a wary view of Tehran, which has not faded since. After about a year of political maneuvering and negotiations, harsh sanctions from the Jimmy Carter administration, and pressure from the international community (which completely killed the already dwindling Iranian economy), the hostages were released in January 1981.

Two armed protesters outside of the US Embassy.
https://commons.wikimedia.org/wiki/File:Enghlab_Iran.jpg

Aside from the hostage crisis, the suppression of minority and opposition groups, the adoption of what many have called totalitarian measures, and the enforcement of a more traditional way of Islamic life, Khomeini's post-revolutionary Iran also saw the country get dragged into a war with its neighbor, Iraq. The official justification behind the Iraqi invasion in September 1980 was the border disputes the two countries had had for several decades. In reality, though, Saddam Hussein sought to take over the westernmost Iranian province of Khuzestan, an oil-rich region that also housed the largest Arab population in the country. Hussein saw the unstable situation that had been created in Iran due to the harsh measures Khomeini had put in place, so he believed that it was a good time to wage war, especially since Iran had lost its close ties with foreign powers that could intervene in the conflict on their side.

Hussein hoped for a quick and decisive victory, believing that Khomeini had no time to respond adequately to the invasion since he was busy consolidating his power in Tehran. Additionally, the Iranian military had been greatly disorganized because of the Islamic Revolution. And immediately after the start of the war, Iraqi forces made significant headway toward their objectives and occupied important parts of southwestern and western Iran.

However, despite Hussein's best hopes, the war turned out to be exactly what Khomeini and the revolutionaries needed to set aside their differences and unite against a common enemy. Led by Supreme Leader Khomeini, the people rallied behind the Islamic government, with the newly created Revolutionary Guard Corps leading the way. The corps was transferred from the cities to the front lines and essentially replaced most of Iran's armed forces. War is a good tool for exploiting your enemy's domestic weaknesses, but it is also an excuse for internal conflicts to stop in order to confront a bigger external challenge, which was what happened with the Iranian people.

After a few months of fierce fighting, the Iranian forces recaptured the lost territories and even pushed into eastern Iraq by the summer of 1982. The two sides relentlessly engaged in combat, targeting not only military compounds but also civilian houses, urban centers, and oil refineries, trying to weaken each other as much as possible. Khomeini and the Islamic government utilized the war to further consolidate their grasp over the country, emerging as leaders against a foreign Sunni invader. The international community could do nothing but watch as the two Middle Eastern countries effectively destroyed each other.

After the Iranian counteroffensive of 1982, the war stalled for six years. Although the fighting never truly stopped, neither side decided to fully commit all of its strength. Khomeini had managed to hold his ground, much to Hussein's surprise. Khomeini ironically used much of the American equipment and weapons to fight off the Iraqis. As for the United States, Washington mobilized some of its forces in the Gulf states, as the war had been a strain on oil exports in the region.

One crucial development was the accidental shooting of Iran Air Flight 665, a domestic passenger flight, in July 1988 by a US cruiser, which had incorrectly assumed the plane was a hostile jet. The incident cost the lives of about three hundred people and soon became another instance of cancerous foreign interference, at least in the eyes of the Iranian people.

As for the war itself, the two sides agreed to a UN-mediated ceasefire by the end of the summer of 1988, with neither country achieving anything significant, as they both returned to their prewar borders. Although the war was technically not a victory, it allowed Khomeini to quell and throw off much of the domestic resistance that had been sparked in response to his authoritarian measures.

All in all, the Islamic Revolution was a culmination of a series of power struggles between the domestic forces in Iran throughout the 20th century. However, the era of Ayatollah Ruhollah Khomeini, the Supreme Leader and one of the most popular Iranian public figures in the history of the country, did not perhaps achieve the results that had been promised before the revolution took place. As the years went by and as Khomeini implemented more and more radical measures to ensure his total power, it became apparent that Iran still could not become as prosperous as it could be. Although the absolute monarchy of Muhammad Reza Pahlavi was gone, it had been replaced by an equally autocratic regime. The quality of life for the Iranian people did not really improve, which many soon realized.

Ruhollah Khomeini, the revolutionary imam who had established the Islamic Republic of Iran and brought the country back to its traditional Shi'ite ways, died in June 1989, but the regime he had built would persist.

Contemporary Iran

We now enter into the final era of Iran, which largely started after the death of Ruhollah Khomeini and his replacement as Supreme Leader, Ali Khamenei, who had previously served as the country's president. Khamenei was chosen by Khomeini before he passed away and still continues to serve as the Supreme Leader as of this writing. Although Khamenei can do very little to eclipse his predecessor in terms of achievements, his tenure has seen the strengthening of Iran's position as a powerful international and regional actor, as well as the development of a political system that is still dominated by religious authority.

As of today, Iran finds itself in a difficult situation, as the rest of the world has become more liberal, secular, and democratic than ever. In fact, the political processes in Iran since the death of Khomeini have been dominated by the clash between the conservative majority, which supports the religious foundations of the country, and a more liberal minority, which pushes toward more modernization and stabilization of foreign relations.

Supreme Leader Ali Khamenei
Official website of Ali Khamenei, CC BY 4.0
<https://creativecommons.org/licenses/by/4.0>, via Wikimedia Commons
https://commons.wikimedia.org/wiki/File:Supreme_leader_Ali_Khamenei_meeting_with_the_air_force_commanders_and_personnel_(5).jpg

After the "promotion" of Khamenei to Supreme Leader from president, Ali-Akbar Hashemi Rafsanjani became the new president of the country for two consecutive four-year terms, ending his tenure in 1997. Deemed by many as an example of "pragmatic conservatism," Rafsanjani's tenure was characterized by his push for the country's economic revival, as the nation had suffered a lot. He mainly sought to do this by ending the state's control over different nationalized industries and encouraging greater public involvement in the economy to grow private wealth.

Although Rafsanjani was technically a conservative (he opposed the West in many ways, such as US involvement in the Persian Gulf War), he was not favored by the conservative religious groups, as they believed his policies contributed to the loss of the firm grip they had held over the country.

However, some of the processes that took place in the 1990s were not really brought about by Rafsanjani and the government; technological developments were introduced to the country during this period, which eventually led to the furthering of political culture that was keener on better relationships with the West. In this regard, the main advocates for more Westernization were young adults who were too young to remember the Pahlavi regime or the Islamic Revolution and simply wanted to live in a prosperous country that enjoyed the same benefits as other Western societies. During this period, world awareness of the undemocratic, authoritarian measures and human rights violations of post-revolutionary Iran increased as well, leading to many international actors demanding the creation of a freer society, which simply wasn't possible as long as the Shi'ite ulama maintained their firm control over the country.

The increased drive for change manifested itself in the 1997 presidential elections. Mohammad Khatami, a more liberal reformist, emerged victorious, something that came as an unpleasant surprise for the conservative forces at the head of the country. Winning with over two-thirds of the votes, Khatami had promised social changes to his voters that would positively alter some of the restrictions that had been put in place. He mainly wished to reduce state censorship and pushed to reduce the religious influence on state affairs, although he was greatly opposed by the conservative government in this endeavor.

Khatami was by no means a radical leftist who pushed for reforms that opposed the religious establishment. Instead, he was a moderate who tried to balance his policies so that they appeased the majority of the country. Still, Supreme Leader Khamenei interfered when it came to the actual implementation of changes. This became even clearer when the reformists swept the local elections of 1999, winning the majority of seats in local governments. The police, which was controlled by Khamenei, cracked down on the president's anti-conservative sympathizers, who mainly consisted of the youth. Student-led protests were suppressed around the country. Even after being reelected to office in 2001, Khamenei could not push his agenda through the conservative parliament, and the elections of 2005 rendered his efforts almost completely useless.

In 2005, the power dynamic once again changed in Iran, as the conservative Mahmud Ahmadinejad emerged victorious in the presidential election, famously kissing the hand of Supreme Leader Khamenei in 2006 after being sworn in. Ahmadinejad, who had the full support of Khamenei, further consolidated the state's control over the lives of the Iranian people, implementing harsh censorship measures. His first tenure also coincided with the growth of Iran's regional power after the US intervention in Iraq had led to the overthrow of the totalitarian Saddam Hussein, a long-standing rival to Tehran.

However, Ahmadinejad's time in office was strained by high rates of inflation, which had been caused by another series of economic sanctions by the international community, which had suspected Iran of developing its own nuclear weapons program. The allegations claimed that Tehran had refuted the commitments it had made to the International Atomic Energy Agency, citing evidence of Tehran's increased interest in nuclear research and the opening of nuclear power plants and uranium mines and refineries. The embargo many countries placed on Iran caused economic difficulties that proved difficult for Ahmadinejad to surmount, affecting his position in the country and eventually resulting in the election of Hassan Rouhani as the new president in 2013.

Conclusion

Few countries can claim to have as exciting and intriguing of a history as Iran. Located in western Asia, the region around the Zagros Mountains, sandwiched between the Caspian Sea to the north and the Persian Gulf to the south, Iran has been home to different civilizations for thousands of years. From prehistoric times all the way to the creation of the Islamic Republic of Iran in its modern form, Iran's history is full of memorable moments and developments that shaped the country and its people. Dominated by constant warfare, the struggle for freedom and survival, and the will to maintain their rich and important culture, the Iranian people persevered.

What makes Iran's case so different from other countries with rich histories is the fact that the civilizations that inhabited the region were all very relevant during their respective eras, even back in ancient times. It comes as no surprise that the founding and subsequent domination of Achaemenid Persia is considered to be one of the golden ages in Iranian history, as it was, realistically, the first time that an advanced Persian empire was able to dominate the region stretching from Anatolia to modern-day India. It even controlled territories in the Levant and Egypt. From Cyrus the Great to Darius the Great to Persia's conquest by Alexander to its Hellenization under the Seleucids to the emergence of the Parthians and later the Sassanids, the roughly one thousand years up until the beginning of the medieval ages were filled with exciting social and political occurrences. A multitude of diverse cultures and religions thrived and helped make ancient Persia one of the most compelling civilizations in world history.

Since the Early Middle Ages, with the Arab conquest and the subsequent introduction of Islam, we stumble upon a new age in Iranian history, one that is dominated by relative instability and chaos. Iran's people had to adapt their largely tribal, ritualistic, and heavily tradition-based lifestyle to a new, Islamic way of life, which forever entered their psyche. Still, despite foreign domination and the relative weakness of local states, Iran still managed to maintain its cultural and social roots, even after the Mongols and Timurids took over. This period produced one of the most stunning developments to Iranian heritage, as it gave birth to the first instances of a unique mix of Islamic and pre-Islamic architecture, literature, traditions, art, and many other aspects of life.

Iran's slow process of globalization and more involvement in foreign affairs arguably began with the emergence of the Safavid dynasty and the reestablishment of an Iranian monarchy after centuries of enduring the Mongol yoke. During the Safavid era, Iran embraced Shi'a Islam, something that would become a fundamental part of the country's identity by the collapse of Safavid Persia in the 18th century. This influential but ultimately unstable dynasty ruled lands far beyond modern Iranian borders but eventually crumbled. The Safavids would eventually be replaced by the Qajars, who would be confronted with perhaps the most difficult time for monarchies in the early modern world: the pivotal 19th century. Europe saw a gradual shift to liberalism and nationalism, and Persia tried unsuccessfully to keep up. Plagued with an array of problems, the majority of Qajar rulers rarely had time to indulge in activities that would lead to modernization, at least according to European standards, especially with the increased influence of the Shi'ite ulama, which became one of the strongest forces in the country during this period.

As the European nations expanded their global power, exploiting their superiority, the Qajar monarchs came increasingly under the scrutiny of the Persians, who realized that the state could have been doing more to change things for the better. The fall of the Qajars in the 20th century started the final period in Iran's history, a period of constant struggle for modernization. Over the past 120 years, the Iranian people have seen multiple governments come and go, all promising to be operating for their best interests but ultimately failing in one way or another. In fact, the Constitutional Revolution and the first half of the Pahlavi monarchy saw great improvements in almost all aspects of life. It was as if the country was up and running again and on track to realizing its huge potential. However, the more prosperous years slowly turned into regimes that were increasingly autocratic, leading to the loss of the people's trust. In the late 1970s, Iran underwent its final major change and was reorganized as an Islamic republic. The Islamic Republic of Iran still exists today, and it will be very interesting to see what will happen in the future, especially with the current protests that are taking place. Only time will tell whether or not the country can function adequately in the age of modernity and technology.

The history of Iran isn't just about its many wars or rulers. Instead, what has caught the eye of many historians is the transformation of its people throughout the different eras. They adapted to changes and established one of the most thriving and diverse cultures in the world.

Here's another book by Enthralling History that you might like

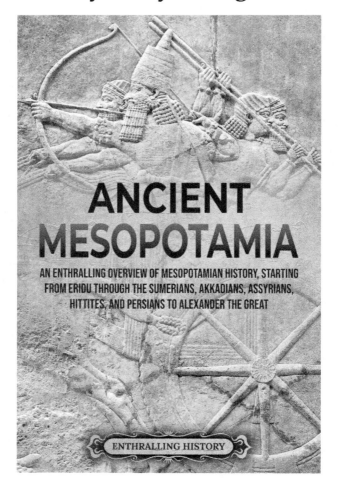

Free limited time bonus

Stop for a moment. We have a free bonus set up for you. The problem is this: we forget 90% of everything that we read after 7 days. Crazy fact, right? Here's the solution: we've created a printable, 1-page pdf summary for this book that you're reading now. All you have to do to get your free pdf summary is to go to the following website:

https://livetolearn.lpages.co/enthrallinghistory/

Once you do, it will be intuitive. Enjoy, and thank you!

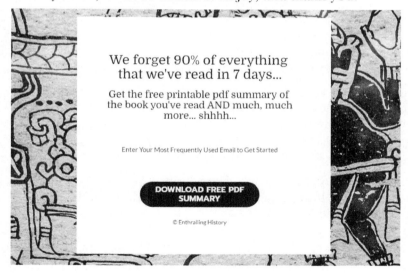

We forget 90% of everything that we've read in 7 days...

Get the free printable pdf summary of the book you've read AND much, much more... shhhh...

Enter Your Most Frequently Used Email to Get Started

DOWNLOAD FREE PDF SUMMARY

© Enthralling History

Bibliography

"Achaemenid Judicial and Legal Systems." *Encyclopaedia Iranica.* Vol. XV, Fasc. 2 (2012): 174-177.

Anderson, Steven D., and Rodger C. Young. "The Remembrance of Daniel's Darius the Mede in Berossus and Harpocration." *Bibliotheca Sacra* 173 (July-September 2016): 315-23.

Arrian. *Alexander the Great: The Anabasis and the Indica.* Translated by Martin Hammond. Oxford: Oxford University Press, 2013.

"Artaxerxes III." *Encyclopaedia Iranica.* Vol. II, Fasc. 6 (2011): 658-59.

Austin, M. M. "Greek Tyrants and the Persians, 546-479 B. C." *The Classical Quarterly* 40, no. 2 (1990): 289-306. Accessed September 6, 2021. http://www.jstor.org/stable/639090.

Badian, E. "Darius III." *Harvard Studies in Classical Philology* 100 (2000): 241-67. https://doi.org/10.2307/3185218.

Bahadori, Ali and Negin Miri. "The So-called Achaemenid Capitals and the Problem of Royal Court Residence." *Iran,* (2021) DOI: 10.1080/05786967.2021.1960881.

Beaulieu, Paul-Alain. "Nabonidus the Mad King: A Reconsideration of His Steles from Harran and Babylon." In *Representations of Political Power,* edited by Marlies Heinz and Marian H. Feldman, 137-167. Winona Lake: Eisenbrauns, 2007.

Beaulieu, Paul-Alain. *Reign of Nabonidus, King of Babylon (556-539 BC).* New Haven: Yale University Press, 1989.

Bennett, Bob, and Mike Roberts. *The Wars of Alexander's Successors, 323-281 BC (Commanders and Campaigns Book 1).* South Yorkshire: Pen & Sword Military, 2013.

Bennett, Bob, and Mike Roberts. *The Wars of Alexander's Successors 323 - 281 BC. Volume 2: Battles and Tactics*. South Yorkshire: Pen & Sword Military, 2009.

Bertman, Stephen. *Handbook to Life in Ancient Mesopotamia*. Oxford: Oxford University Press, 2005.

Brosius, Maria. *A History of Ancient Persia: The Achaemenid Empire*. Hoboken, NJ: Wiley Blackwell, 2020.

Carter, R., and Graham Philip, eds. *Beyond the Ubaid: Transformation and Integration in the Late Prehistoric Societies of the Middle East*. Chicago: The Oriental Institute, University of Chicago, 2010.

Charles, Michael B. "Achaemenid Elite Cavalry: From Xerxes to Darius III." *The Classical Quarterly* 65, no. 1 (2015): 14–34. http://www.jstor.org/stable/43905638.

Chavalas, M. W., ed. *The Ancient Near East: Historical Sources in Translation*. Malden, MA: Blackwell Publishing, 2006.

Clark, Peter. *Zoroastrianism: An Introduction to an Ancient Faith (Beliefs & Practices)*. East Sussex: Sussex Academic Press, 1998.

Cyrus Cylinder. Translated by Irving Finkel. The British Museum. https://www.britishmuseum.org/collection/object/W_1880-0617-1941.

Darius I. *The Behistun Inscription*. Livius. https://www.livius.org/articles/place/behistun/behistun-3/.

Da Riva, Rocío. "The Figure of Nabopolassar in Late Achaemenid and Hellenistic Historiographic Tradition: BM 34793 and CUA 90." *Journal of Near Eastern Studies* 76, no.1. https://www.journals.uchicago.edu/doi/full/10.1086/690464.

"Dāta." *Encyclopaedia Iranica*. Vol. VII, Fasc. 1 (2011): 114-115. https://www.iranicaonline.org/articles/data.

De Graef, Katrien. "Dual Power in Susa: Chronicle of a Transitional Period from Ur III via Šimaški to the Sukkalmaḫs." *Bulletin of the School of Oriental and African Studies, University of London* 75, no. 3 (2012): 525–46. http://www.jstor.org/stable/41811207.

Enthralling History. *Ancient Mesopotamia: An Enthralling Overview of Mesopotamian History,*

Starting from Eridu through the Sumerians, Akkadian Empire, Assyrians, Hittites, and Persians to Alexander the Great. Coppell, Texas: Joelan AB, 2022.

Ershad, Alijani. "Thousands in Iran use King's Anniversary to Protest against Ruling Regime." *France 24: The Observers*. April 11, 2016. https://observers.france24.com/en/20161103-iran-cyrus-king-regime-protest.

Grayson, A. K. *Assyrian Rulers of the Early First Millennium BC II (858-745 BC)* (Royal Inscriptions of Mesopotamia. Assyrian Periods. Volume 3), Toronto: University of Toronto Press, 1996.

Herodotus. *Capture of Babylon.* Livius.

Herodotus, *The Histories.* Translated by George Rawlinson. New York: Dutton & Co, 1862. http://classics.mit.edu/Herodotus/history.html.

Josephus, Flavius. *Antiquities of the Jews.* Translated by William Whiston. Project Gutenberg. https://www.gutenberg.org/files/2848/2848-h/2848-h.htm

Kent, Roland. *Old Persian: Grammar, Texts, Lexicon.* New Haven: American Oriental Society, 1950.

Kerrigan, Michael. *The Ancients in Their Own Words.* London: Amber Books, 2019.

Kuhrt, Amélie. *The Persian Empire: A Corpus of Sources from the Achaemenid Period.* London: Routledge, 2007.

Lorenzi, Rossella. "Vanished Persian Army Said Found in Desert." *NBC News: Science News,* November 9, 2009. https://www.nbcnews.com/id/wbna33791672.

Mark, Joshua J. "Behistun Inscription." *World History Encyclopedia.* https://www.worldhistory.org/Behistun_Inscription/.

Mark, Joshua J. "The Battle of Pelusium: A Victory Decided by Cats." *World History Encyclopedia.* https://www.worldhistory.org/article/43/the-battle-of-pelusium-a-victory-decided-by-cats/.

Melamed, Karmel. "Cyrus Accords' Old Seeds of Peace: Iran & Israel's Forgotten Friendship." *The Times of Israel.* April 4, 2021. https://blogs.timesofisrael.com/cyrus-accords-old-seeds-of-peace-iran-israels-forgotten-friendship/.

Mildenberg, Leo. "Artaxerxes III Ochus (358 – 338 B.C.). A Note on the Maligned King." *Zeitschrift Des Deutschen Palästina-Vereins (1953-)* 115, no. 2 (1999): 201-27. http://www.jstor.org/stable/27931620.

Nemet-Nejat, Karen Rhea. *Daily Life in Ancient Mesopotamia.* Westport, Connecticut: Greenwood Press, 1998.

Photius' Excerpt of Ctesias' Persica. Livius. https://www.livius.org/sources/content/ctesias-overview-of-the-works/photius-excerpt-of-ctesias-persica/#34.

Plutarch, *The Parallel Lives: The Life of Artaxerxes.* The Loeb Classical Library edition.

https://penelope.uchicago.edu/Thayer/E/Roman/Texts/Plutarch/Lives/Ar taxerxes*.html.

Pollock, Susan. *Ancient Mesopotamia*. Cambridge: Cambridge University Press, 1999.

Polyaenus. *Stratagems: Book Seven*. Translated by R. Shepherd (1793). http://www.attalus.org/translate/polyaenus7.html

Postgate, Nicholas. *Early Mesopotamia: Society and Economy at the Dawn of History*. Oxfordshire: Routledge, 1994.

Prayer of Nabonidus (4Q242). Livius. https://www.livius.org/sources/content/dss/4q242-prayer-of-nabonidus/

Reade, J. E. "Kassites and Assyrians in Iran." *Iran* 16 (1978): 137–43. https://www.jstor.org/stable/4299653?origin=crossref

Sackrider, Scott. "The History of Astronomy in Ancient Mesopotamia." *The NEKAAL Observer* 234. https://nekaal.org/observer/ar/ObserverArticle234.pdf

Shenkar, Michael. "Temple Architecture in the Iranian World before the Macedonian Conquest." *Iran & the Caucasus* 11, no. 2 (2007): 169–94. http://www.jstor.org/stable/25597331.

Siculus, Diodorus. *Library of History*. Volume II. Loeb Classical Library Edition. https://penelope.uchicago.edu/Thayer/E/Roman/Texts/Diodorus_Siculus/16C*.html

Stol, Marten. "Women in Mesopotamia." *Journal of the Economic and Social History of the Orient* 38, no. 2 (1995): 123–44. http://www.jstor.org/stable/3632512.

Teall, Emily K. "Medicine and Doctoring in Ancient Mesopotamia." *Grand Valley Journal of History* 3:1 (2014), Article 2. https://scholarworks.gvsu.edu/gvjh/vol3/iss1/2

The Chronicle Concerning the Reign of Nabonidus (ABC 7). Livius, 2020. https://www.livius.org/sources/content/mesopotamian-chronicles-content/abc-7-nabonidus-chronicle/

The Tanakh: Full Text. Jewish Virtual Library: A Project of AICE. 1997. https://www.jewishvirtuallibrary.org/the-tanakh-full-text

Thucydides, *The War of the Peloponnesians, and the Athenians*. Translated by Jeremy Mynott. Cambridge: Cambridge University Press, 2013.

Van De Mieroop, Marc. *A History of the Ancient Near East ca. 3000 - 323 BC*. Hoboken: Blackwell Publishing, 2006.

Verse Account of Nabonidus. Translated by A. Leo Oppenheim. Livius. https://www.livius.org/sources/content/anet/verse-account-of-nabonidus/

Waters, Matt. *Ancient Persia: A Concise History of the Achaemenid Empire, 550-330 BCE.* New York: Cambridge University Press, 2014.

Weiershäuser, Frauke, and Jamie Novotny. *The Royal Inscriptions of Amēl-Marduk (561–560 BC), Neriglissar (559–556 BC), and Nabonidus (555–539 BC), Kings of Babylon* (PDF). Winona Lake: Eisenbrauns, 2020.

Worthington, Ian. *By the Spear: Philip II, Alexander the Great, and the Rise and Fall of the Macedonian Empire (Ancient Warfare and Civilization).* Oxford: Oxford University Press, 2016.

Xenophon. *Cyropaedia: The Education of Cyrus.* Translated by Henry Graham Dakyns. Project Gutenberg eBook. https://www.gutenberg.org/files/2085/2085-h/2085-h.htm

Xenophon. *The Landmark Xenophon's Hellenika.* Translated by John Marincola. New York: Anchor, 2010.

Zarghamee, Reza. *Discovering Cyrus: The Persian Conqueror Astride the Ancient World.* Washington, DC: Mage Publishers, 2018.

Abrahamian, E. (1974). "Oriental Despotism: The Case of Qajar Iran." International Journal of Middle East Studies, 5(1), 3–31. http://www.jstor.org/stable/162341.

Abrahamian, E. (1979). "The Causes of the Constitutional Revolution in Iran." International Journal of Middle East Studies, 10(3), 381–414. http://www.jstor.org/stable/162146.

Arjomand, S. A. (1985). "The Causes and Significance of the Iranian Revolution." State, Culture, and Society, 1(3), 41–66. http://www.jstor.org/stable/20006816.

Arjomand, S. A. (1986). "Iran's Islamic Revolution in Comparative Perspective." World Politics, 38(3), 383–414. https://doi.org/10.2307/2010199.

Babayan, K. (1994). "The Safavid Synthesis: From Qizilbash Islam to Imamite" Shi'ism. Iranian Studies, 27(1/4), 135–161. http://www.jstor.org/stable/4310890.

Bhagat, G. BHAGAT, G. (1987). "Khomeini: Leader of Islamic Revolution in Iran." The Indian Journal of Political Science, 48(1), 31–41. http://www.jstor.org/stable/41855864.

Britannica, T. Editors of Encyclopedia (2021, April 29). "Iran summary." Encyclopedia Britannica. https://www.britannica.com/summary/Iran.

Brosius, M. (2013). *Greek Sources on Achaemenid Iran.*

Daniel, E. L. (2012). *The History of Iran (Second, Ser. The Greenwood Histories of the Modern Nations)*. Greenwood. Retrieved November 1, 2022.

Faghfoory, M. H. (1987). "The Ulama-State Relations in Iran: 1921-1941." International Journal of Middle East Studies, 19(4), 413-432. http://www.jstor.org/stable/163209

Ghods, M. R. (1991). "Iranian Nationalism and Reza Shah." Middle Eastern Studies, 27(1), 35-45. http://www.jstor.org/stable/4283413.

Hunt, C. (2005). *The History of Iraq (Ser. The Greenwood Histories of the Modern Nations)*. Greenwood Press. Retrieved November 5, 2022.

Keddie, N. R. (1983). "Iranian Revolutions in Comparative Perspective." The American Historical Review, 88(3), 579-598. https://doi.org/10.2307/1864588.

KEDDIE, N. R. (2000). "Women in Iran since 1979." Social Research, 67(2), 405-438. http://www.jstor.org/stable/40971478.

Morony, M. G. (1976). "The Effects of the Muslim Conquest on the Persian Population of Iraq." Iran, 14, 41-59. https://doi.org/10.2307/4300543.

Paul, J. (1998). "Early Islamic History of Iran: From the Arab Conquest to the Mongol Invasion." Iranian Studies, 31(3/4), 463-471. http://www.jstor.org/stable/4311181.

Perry, J. R. (1971). "The Last Ṣafavids, 1722-1773." Iran, 9, 59-69. https://doi.org/10.2307/4300438.

Rabi, U., & Ter-Oganov, N. (2012). "The Military of Qajar Iran: The Features of an Irregular Army from the Eighteenth to the Early Twentieth Century." Iranian Studies, 45(3), 333-354. http://www.jstor.org/stable/41445213.

Sykes, P. (2022). *History of Persia*. Routledge.